MICHAEL FOOT: A PORTRAIT

Michael Foot: a portrait

Simon Hoggart and David Leigh

HODDER AND STOUGHTON
LONDON SYDNEY AUCKLAND TORONTO

British Library Cataloguing in Publication Data
Hoggart, Simon
　Michael Foot.
　1. Foot, Michael
　2. Statesmen – Great Britain – Biography
　I. Title　　II. Leigh, David
　941.085′092′4　　　　DA591.F/

　ISBN 0-340-27040-3
　ISBN 0-340-27600-2 Pbk

Hodder and Stoughton Editorial Office: 47 Bedford Square, London WC15 3DP

ACKNOWLEDGMENTS

Although this is not an 'authorised' biography, Michael Foot spent much time patiently answering our questions. Among the many people who willingly helped us were Ian Aitken, Albert Booth, Barbara Castle, James Callaghan, Jill Craigie, Dick Clements, Una Couze, Sir John Cripps, Lord Davies of Leek, the late Peggy Duff, Robert Edwards, Ron Evans, Lord Foot, Lady Foot, Paul Foot, Sarah Foot, Anthony Gillett, Nicholas Gillett, Lord Greenwood, Bill Harry, Thomas Hopkins, Lady Hornby, Clive Jenkins, Neil Kinnock, Baroness Lee, Ron Lemin, Ian Mikardo, James Molyneaux, Sheila Noble, Stan Orme, Lord Reilly, Lord Strauss, Reg Scott, David Steel, A. J. P. Taylor, George Malcolm Thomson, Liz Thomas, Ion Trewin, Eric Varley, Michael White and Sir Harold Wilson.

Special thanks are due to Ian Aitken, who kindly read the manuscript, though of course the errors and the opinions are all our own. Peter Preston, the editor of the *Guardian*, was very helpful in permitting us time off our duties there to complete the book, and last of all Peter and Susan Hillmore put us up and put up with us in the tranquillity of their beautiful house in the Cotswolds.

ILLUSTRATIONS

ACKNOWLEDGMENTS

1   Family photograph
2   BBC Hulton Picture Library
3   Jill Craigie
4   Ron Lemin
5   Pictorial Press
6   John Cura
7   Press Association
8   Central Press Photos
9   Popperfoto
10   *Tribune*
11   Keystone
12   The Beaverbrook Foundation/A.J.P. Taylor

CONTENTS

CARTOONS IN TEXT

FAMILY TREE

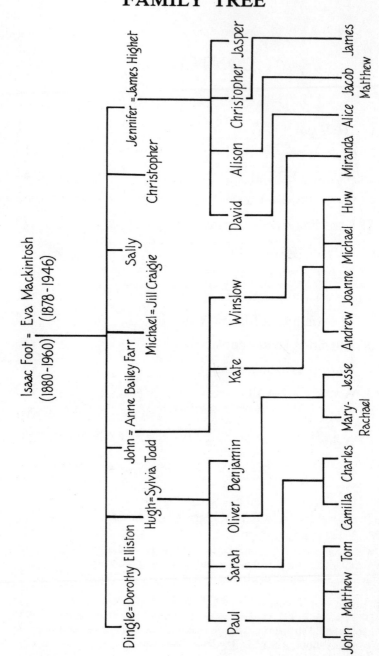

1

"HE'S GOT IT..."

Denis Healey, the former Chancellor of the Exchequer, sat waiting in his office with a small group of friends and colleagues on the afternoon of November 10th, 1980. He was the right-wing candidate for the leadership of the Labour party, and for more than four years it had been assumed by all those in the know — MPs, union leaders, the press — that he would almost automatically assume the job when James Callaghan resigned. A messenger knocked on the door and brought in a short note. Healey read it, smiled, if somewhat stiffly, and said, "He's got it." He then left to go to the meeting of MPs where the result was to be announced, and walked into the committee room grinning broadly, looking pleased and relaxed. Joel Barnett, the Manchester MP who had been Healey's deputy at the Treasury in the 1974-79 Labour government, rushed up to Ian Mikardo, the Commons' amateur bookmaker, and insisted on putting five pounds on a Healey victory. It was the easiest fiver Mikardo ever earned.

The man who had "got it" was Michael Foot, a left-wing socialist who had been in the thick of radical Labour politics for forty-six years. Foot went into the meeting looking drawn and anxious, almost, one of his supporters said, as if he had suffered some awful shock. Several of them assumed that he had lost, though a few who knew him better guessed that this would be his reaction to success. Healey would look cheerful precisely because he had lost; Foot would look depressed as he faced the problems of victory. The party chairman, Fred Willey, read out the result: Foot had won by 139 votes to 129. The MPs broke out into their bizarre Westminster form of cheering, a muted "yer, yer, yer" which centuries ago meant "hear hear", and is today combined with a gentle pattering on desk tops. One of Foot's leading campaigners, the Welsh MP,

Neil Kinnock, felt this response was inadequate: his substantial fist crashed down on the table and he let out a blood-curdling Indian war whoop. At the age of sixty-seven, the Labour party's favourite figurehead, the angry old man of the left, the man who carried the Ark of its socialist covenant, had finally become its leader.

Foot made a short speech, and quoted Aneurin Bevan, the left-wing politician who founded the National Health Service and who for more than twenty years had been his hero, mentor, patron and occasional exasperated opponent. Bevan had said: "Never underestimate the passion for unity in the party, and never forget that it is the decent instinct of people who want to do something." Foot gave a press conference, still with that air of shocked surprise, and at one point, forgetting the microphones were switched on, turned to his wife and said, "It's not so easy, is it?" Then he went to the nearby St. Ermin's Hotel, where the Trade Unionists for a Labour Victory, essentially the senior union moneybags of the Labour party, were holding a dinner. When he walked in they gave him a standing ovation. It was a poignant moment; the St. Ermin's had been the plotting ground for the old, right-wing trade union leaders of the 'Fifties who had worked on their plans to destroy Bevan and Foot, his follower.

Back at the Commons he had a celebratory drink with the people who had helped in his election. Someone asked him to tape a few remarks which might, with luck, ring down through history. He got as far as saying, "Comrades, this is a historic and unique occasion," when the exuberant Kinnock interrupted, shouting, "Yes, we bloody won!" Then they headed for the Gay Hussar in Soho, a popular restaurant with politicians, especially left-wing politicians, for decades. Peter Shore, the former Environment Secretary joined them, though it was Foot's decision to stand which cost him his own chance of the leadership. They sang the Italian republican song "Avanti Populo" and after the meal, inevitably, the "Red Flag". Yet it remained a slightly muted occasion. People were pleased, but perhaps too tired to be ecstatic. There was no sense, Kinnock observed, of a New Dawn of Socialism. A photographer from the *New Standard* arrived and asked to take a picture, but Foot was insistent that he didn't. He was afraid that the paper would depict the meal as a drunken celebration in an expensive Soho restaurant — no bad thing for a victory celebration. "Well-lubricated" might be a kinder word: the drinking was moderate. It was another ironic reminder of Foot's past, for this was the paper which (as the *Evening Standard*) he had edited, lured there by Lord Beaverbrook, one of the first men of power and influence to spot the young Foot's gifts.

Rarely can a man have been bludgeoned into success by his friends with such ruthless efficiency. Foot's extraordinary personal diffidence, his unwillingness to push himself forward, comes as a surprise to people who only know the often savage power of his oratory, and the manic glare which can come into his eyes when he faces a vast and adoring crowd. But to reach out to grab power is alien to his character; he constantly needs the reassurance of his friends. Ever since Labour had lost the general election of May 1979, he had ducked the subject of whether he ought to run as the next leader of the party. He had actively tried to make sure that he was never even faced with the problem of deciding. There were, after all, books he wanted to write.

After that election it was assumed that Callaghan would retire as leader within the following year or so. He was already sixty-seven and had been Prime Minister in a minority government for three years, a government whose principal achievement seemed to have been to cling to office and so keep out Mrs. Thatcher's Conservatives. He was disheartened by the wrangling within the party, and had come to detest the meetings of the National Executive Committee, which increasingly dominated his life. The NEC, nominally the governing body of the Labour party between annual conferences, was controlled by the left wing, which used it as a convenient forum to maintain a continuous attack on the comparatively right-wing leadership and the existing constitutional structure of the party. Callaghan said glumly that he thought the party's job was to attack the new Conservative government in a united fashion; the left believe, with some justice, that the period immediately after an election defeat is exactly the time for the party to resolve its own internal arguments. Callaghan, who had gone into the election certain of defeat, came out depressed and anxious to resign. He twice consulted Foot, whose loyalty throughout the three years had been unshakeable, and each time Foot urged him not to retire. The party, he said, needed him more than ever before.

But Callaghan had had enough. In October 1980 he chaired the usual Wednesday meeting of the Shadow Cabinet and told them of his decision. As soon as he had spoken he rose to go, but Foot took him by the elbow and held him back to allow a short speech of thanks. "There is nothing but friendship around this table for you," he said. At that time Foot had no serious intention of attempting to replace him.

In 1976, when Harold Wilson had resigned, it had taken a fairly hefty effort by his friends to persuade Foot to offer himself for the leadership, and it is probably true to say that their task of egging him on was made simpler because he stood not the slightest chance of winning. In the middle of that campaign, an old friend had asked him if he truly wanted to become Prime Minister. Foot paused for quite some time before slowly saying "yes". There were six candidates, and Foot lasted longer than any of the other challengers. On the first ballot he had even managed to win ninety votes, six more than Callaghan. It was a remarkable tribute to his personal popularity.

In 1980, Kinnock was a leading figure in the small group which began to ponder a campaign to stop Healey, universally assumed to be the next party leader. It is important to remember that this was why the campaign began, and though Foot later insisted that he would never stand merely to block somebody else, his original backers saw him filling precisely that role. They had come to the conclusion that Foot, who trailed a great cloud of personal respect and popularity around the party, was the only possible candidate who stood a realistic chance of beating Healey. Kinnock first raised the issue with him at the beginning of 1980, and Foot reacted as he normally does when somebody raises an embarrassing topic. He gave Kinnock a baffled glance ("He is the Clausewitz of the quizzical look," Kinnock says) and barked, "Yes, well, yes, we can talk about that", which is Foot's way of saying "we can ignore that for as long as possible".

Kinnock, with left-wing MPs Peter Snape from West

Bromwich, and Jim Marshall from Leicester, began to talk to their colleagues and to do the first sums. At the party conference that October, Kinnock gave Foot the figures they had worked out. He had found 112 people who would definitely vote for him, and a further 14 who would probably do so. Another nine were in genuine doubt, some so puzzled that they were actually talking about abstention. The three figures added up to 135, precisely the number that the winning candidate would need. Kinnock told Foot that the figures did not indicate that he would win, but that he stood a very reasonable chance, and a much better chance than anyone else against Healey.

Yet, when Callaghan announced his resignation, Foot was still extremely dubious. He was worried about his age. While he felt perfectly fit at sixty-seven, he thought MPs would have anxieties about his health and stamina. He would probably have reached seventy by the next general election, and he was unwilling to stand in the way of a younger man, particularly Peter Shore, who was his own favourite candidate. What, he thought, if he merely prevented Shore from winning, without succeeding himself? Stanley Orme, a former Cabinet minister and one of Foot's closest political friends, asked Shore and John Silkin, the former Agriculture Minister, to Foot's room for a discussion on tactics. Orme said that there was room for only one candidate of the left. Silkin, either through a kind of misguided bravado or else from genuine ignorance, announced that he could win and would run whatever anyone else decided. Foot said that he thought Shore stood the best chance of beating Healey. Shore, more cautiously than Silkin, agreed. He was banking on Foot's wholehearted support, knowing he stood only a slight chance without it. Foot let the press know that, while he had not finally decided, he thought it most improbable that he would run, and next morning the papers hardly bothered to discuss his chances.

The moves to draft Foot cranked slowly into action. The next afternoon, on Thursday, three prominent union leaders — Moss Evans of the Transport and General Workers' Union, David Basnett of the General and Municipal Workers, and Clive Jenkins of the Association of Scientific, Technical and Managerial Staffs — had a meeting with John Nott, the Trade

Secretary, to discuss import controls. Afterwards Basnett suggested to the other two that they might have a drink with him at his union's small London office near Euston station. Casually chatting over a bottle of wine, the three men found they all agreed that Foot would be the best new leader. The problem remained of how to persuade him to stand. Jenkins, who knew him slightly better than the others, offered to contact him. They had to get to work before the weekend. Both Jenkins and Kinnock, quite separately, realised what Foot needed to persuade him. They rang everybody they could think of: trade unionists, constituency parties, friends and colleagues of Foot from his earliest days in the Labour party. They had the same message for all: if they wanted Michael to stand, they should phone him or telegraph him immediately. Letters, calls and telegrams began to arrive at the Foots' comfortable house in Pilgrim's Lane, near Hampstead Heath, at first in a trickle and then in a flood. Mikardo, who had worked with Foot in various left-wing groups since 1945, phoned him on the Friday morning and told him that he would be "off his rocker" if he didn't stand. Foot was still not persuaded. He told Stan Orme that night that he was doubtful about his ability to lead the party to a general election victory, and in any case he, too, thought that Healey was bound to coast home.

That weekend he left for Ireland and on Sunday spoke in the pulpit of St. Patrick's Cathedral, Dublin, commemorating the death of one of his many literary heroes, Dean Swift, in 1745. He gave away nothing about his own plans, but said that the best recommendation he could make was that everyone standing for political office anywhere should take an examination in Gulliver's Travels, a work of which Foot knows large parts by heart.

In the evening, after his return to Hampstead, a large and disparate group of people descended on Pilgrim's Lane, including Jenkins, Moss Evans, Mikardo, Jo Richardson, who had been Mikardo's secretary and is now MP for Barking, Arthur Scargill, and several of their wives. Mrs. Mikardo brought along the first course, and Foot's wife, Jill, prepared the rest. Jenkins took a case of good wine. "I am totally opposed to the idea that the Social Democrats should have all the best claret," he said later. It was an informal occasion; Jenkins, for example, lay on the floor, though this was due to a shortage of chairs rather than an excess of claret. Foot said several times that he did not want to be a blocking candidate, and they assured him that he was wanted for his own qualities. Nearly all the people who left the quiet, book-lined villa that chilly night felt convinced that he had made up his mind to stand. So did Stan Orme, who spoke to him on the phone before he went to bed.

He announced the decison to his fellow Labour MPs the following morning. It was a shattering blow to Peter Shore, but Shore is a decent man and there was never any danger that he would act vindictively in the hope of destroying Foot's later chances. Foot's campaigning team got to work straight away with scant help from their figurehead. "Right up to the last few days, Michael gave the impression that he couldn't care less. He was a bloody awful campaigner," one of them says. At first the task was mainly one of counting, endlessly going over the lists of supporters and possibles, checking and re-checking promises and half-promises.

Most MPs become spies at election time, trained to divine voting intentions in the slightest hint. They could learn from chats about the weather. One of them said: "If I go up to a chap and say, 'How are you, brother?' and he says, 'I'm with you all the way, lad', then he's probably — not certainly — going to vote for Michael. But if he says, 'Looks like rain, doesn't it?' then he's against us and doesn't want to talk about it."

The Foot people were particularly proud of one device they used for smoking out MPs thought, perhaps, to be somewhat lacking in candour. One of their supporters, a new MP whose allegiance was not generally known, was despatched to speak to these characters in *faux naif* terms, explaining that he had been unable to make up his mind, begging their advice and counsel, the fruits of their experience, and so forth. Whichever way the MP steered him was assumed to be his real opinion.

Some asked to see Foot himself, and he would always agree. Sometimes the doubtful MP was genuinely anxious about a point of policy, sometimes he wanted simply to feel a mild glow of self-importance. The majority, however, had already made up their minds; perhaps between a quarter and a fifth were still doubtful.

Foot did himself more good than he might have expected by obliging the *Guardian* with an article, a sparkling 1,000 word rallying cry against Mrs. Thatcher and the Tory government. It was printed around a distinctly sniffy little letter from Healey, declining to write a similar article on the grounds that his views were already well known. Almost all Labour MPs see the *Guardian* each day, and Kinnock noted that five people mentioned the piece to him as he walked to his office that morning.

Healey, who had also more or less stopped appearing on television, found his gloss tarnished even further by the debate on unemployment, which took place on October 29th. The Shadow Chancellor's speech was adequate if a little dull, and it lacked the untrammelled aggression for which his parliamentary disquisitions have usually been noted. Some MPs suspected that he was nervous. Foot, however, wound up the debate for the Opposition in dazzling form. Parliamentary humour always transcribes badly into the real world; it depends on a sense of occasion and a feel for the mood of the House as much as wit. Jokes which look flat and dull on the newspaper page have seemed hilarious beyond measure in the fevered atmosphere of a debate at nine fifteen the previous evening. Foot had a word of sharp abuse for most members of the Cabinet: Sir Ian Gilmour, the Lord Privy Seal, was a "philosopher Tory — like 'military intelligence', a contradiction in terms"; Mr. St. John-Stevas, who had recently made a veiled attack on his own government, had come out in his true colours: "and we can all imagine what a gaudy performance that would be". Labour, he said, would shortly begin a nationwide campaign against unemployment, similar to Gladstone's Midlothian campaign. Gladstone, he recalled, had been sixty-eight at the time and had gone on to form three more administrations. "So there is hope for all my honourable friends," he said, and then, with a wave towards Healey, "including this one." Even Healey grinned at that. The jokes are simple enough, but they delighted their listeners, and reminded them of Foot's remarkable oratorical power. Morale is important to an Opposition, and any front-bencher who offers them the prospect of cutting and sustained verbal assaults on the government will earn their warm support.

The voting figures for the first round, announced on November 4th, were, though not all MPs realised so at the time, the end of Healey's chances. He had a clear lead, but had taken only 112 votes. Foot had eighty-three, Silkin thirty-eight and Shore only thirty-two. Shore was now bottom, but had the slight consolation of knowing that the result of the poll depended now largely on him and his supporters. As his and Silkin's votes together were fewer than Foot's, they were both eliminated.

The Foot camp knew they could rely on nearly all of Silkin's thirty-eight votes, most of which came from left-wingers. But Shore's support was different. He had much left-wing backing because of his implacable opposition to British membership of the Common Market. He also supported the "alternative strategy" in the Callaghan Cabinet, pressing for an end to the monetarist policy of cuts and deflation. But he by no means subscribed to the whole left-wing ticket and on some issues was even rather chauvinistic. His vote might as easily be switched to Healey as to Foot.

So although Shore came out quickly and publicly in favour of Foot, some of his supporters were less keen. A few were furious at Foot wrecking their man's chances. Others wanted a promise that Shore would be made Shadow Chancellor. Some of the MPs in Foot's team implored him to agree, pointing out that it might win a handful of crucial votes. Foot hedged, as he always does when asked to do something which does not please him. "Well, yes, Peter has been absolutely splendid," he would say. So, they argued, why not promise him the job? "No, he hasn't made an approach, he's been absolutely splendid, a wonderful chap, he's a good fellow, you know."

He droned on in this manner as his campaign team saw the votes disappearing in front of their eyes. Foot was probably wise, however. Shore was the obvious Shadow Chancellor, which he later became; by pleasing one person with a promise, a candidate can easily displease others who might have hoped for the same job.

Meanwhile, Labour MPs were learning from their constituency parties that Foot was overwhelmingly the most popular candidate among the groups of activists in almost every seat. Some saw him as a caretaker, keeping the job warm for Tony Benn. Others saw him leading the party into the next general election. Few of them cared that Healey was clearly much more popular with the public as a whole.

Healey supporters now say that they lost because the parliamentary party wanted a quiet political life, and that many voted for Foot against their own natural inclinations. The Foot camp claims that at most two or three people backed Foot purely in the hope that his victory would appease the left and keep the ramshackle party together. In other words, both sides claim what suits their own view of the election. Among those who voted for Foot in the decisive ballot was Sir Harold Wilson, who held the view that Foot would be more likely to unify the party. But Sir Harold had voted for Healey on the first ballot, because he wanted him to win a healthy score. James Callaghan voted for Healey both times.

On the eve of the final ballot, most Foot supporters — with the inevitable exception of Foot himself — were confident. That night Foot's nephew, the journalist Paul Foot, with his wife, called at his uncle's house, where they found Foot muttering that it would be "close, very close". Jill Foot knew better. She told Paul that it was "wrapped up". People would be surprised at the size of Michael's majority. Stan Orme had worked out the figures, taken some last-minute soundings, and concluded that Foot would win by 130 votes to 138. He was wrong by one vote on each side.

It was a victory for the left, certainly. It was a victory for the man who for decades had been presented by the press as a wild, long-haired Marxist extremist, and who had now, suddenly and unexpectedly, emerged as the possible next Prime Minister. But it was also a victory for a mild, popular, highly cultured man, whose roots in British radicalism go back into the nineteenth century.

It was no longer good enough to call Foot names. Now both the party and the country as a whole wanted to know where he was going and where he had come from. It had been a long and remarkable journey.

2

CHOSEN PEOPLE: THE FOOT FAMILY

Michael Foot's father, Isaac, was a celebrated political Don Quixote. He never became a great statesman, but turned instead into a West Country character: as an MP he would salute the statue of Oliver Cromwell whenever he walked through Westminster; as Lord Mayor of Plymouth he would make his chauffeur learn Gray's *Elegy* off by heart; he would also startle female guests in the small hours by absent-mindedly rooting through the stacks of first editions which lined their bedroom walls in his house in east Cornwall. He was born a Liberal, and an old-fashioned nonconformist Liberal — drink was banned in the house, there were family prayers in the morning, and he thought Free Trade an issue worth quitting the government for in 1932. He was famous for Tory-baiting, for his sense of fun, for preaching, memorising, loving books as much as the words contained within them, and fathering a tribe of political sons. It is Michael Foot's mother whose portrait has a place of honour on his Hampstead study mantelpiece (along with Nye Bevan's), but he adored his father, admired the happy inner balance of his life, and spent much of his political career hero-worshipping one powerful father-figure after another. Loyalty and admiration come naturally to him. So do bookishness, speech-making and an all-pervasive radicalism. Socialism came from elsewhere, and his feminism, after a childhood which suppressed the women of the family, came a great deal later.

"Fight the good fight and keep the faith." That message was dinned into the Foot children by their father. Michael recalls:

Books were weapons, the most beloved and sharpest. And there, spread out before us, were enemies enough for a lifetime: historical figures and their modern counterparts

11

melted into one; protectionists, papists, apologists for Lord North and the Chamberlain family; Spanish tyrants and Stuart kings; Simonites and appeasers; men of Munich and of Suez; sons of Belial or Beelzebub, normally disguised as West Country Tories, an exceptionally reprehensible branch of the species.

The Foots marched up the slopes of the British middle-class, from obscure artisans to Cabinet ministers in three generations. Their grandfather, also called Isaac, started as a carpenter and undertaker, and made the first family money. His son was thus able to enter a profession — he became a solicitor — and had the precious time to take up literature. His sons in turn had public school educations, went to Oxbridge and won entry into a political elite. But throughout that rapid rise they all clung hard to the idea that they belonged to another England, a biblical, moralistic, self-taught, Methodist England. They loathed the England of Toryism and privilege and, much as they approved of gaining salvation through earning one's own living, none of them had any time either for the meritocratic kind of Toryism which apparently involved locking oneself into the lavatories at Balliol and emerging with a plum in one's mouth. It was important to be a success in this world. It was also important to be morally good.

The Foots were, and remain, puritans. Michael Foot calls himself a "lapsed" puritan. The children of puritan households can sometimes lead dreadful later lives, driven by a harsh and unimaginative little god in their heads which destroys their warmest and most creative impulses. Foot has escaped that fate, but he understands the problem. When Kingsley Martin, the editor of the *New Statesman*, died in 1969, Foot wrote about him and his father, another nonconformist. The Reverend Basil Martin was a fine old dissenting preacher, he said, who even tried to persuade his fellow Congregationalist ministers to form a trade union. He "gradually lost his faith but devised to take its place pretty well the complete humanist creed which has served most of the English left ever since". Edmund Gosse's *Father and Son*, on the other hand, presented "an indictment of the narrow prison walls in which the puritan tradition incarcerated generations of unhappy children. Kingsley Martin's book,

Father Figures, showed how another strand in that tradition set them free and, for good measure, sold them a weekly Bible to guide their footsteps along the broad and winding path."

Foot was not talking just about the Reverend Basil Martin; he was describing his own family. And he was probably not just talking about the "weekly Bible" of the *New Statesman*, but about his own weekly Bible, on and off, for some thirty years — its rival, the left-wing weekly *Tribune*, sometime editor Michael Foot.

The founders of this dynasty were Foot's grandfather, and his wife, Eliza Ryder. Isaac was a Methodist, and pictures of him in later life show a beaky, waistcoated, prosperous and confident man, with a fringe of beard and no moustache, his hand resting on his wife's lace-covered shoulder. It was Eliza by all accounts, with her high-necked dresses, who was the strong, matriarchal figure, bearing seven children and keeping the household organised, while Isaac prayed and advanced his business career. They had met through the Methodist movement; Isaac had been struck by her lovely singing voice in the Plymouth chapel choir.

The first Foot anecdote — and West Country people love to embroider stories about those they remember — has Isaac the elder making his way down the village street in Horrabridge in the 1870s, hunched from sawing, hammering and planing, looking a little like the Italian organ-grinders bent over their hurdy-gurdies, familiar in Victorian England. "Hey there, Ikey," called out one of a gang of drunken tin-miners, "where's your monkey?" Isaac, so the story goes, presented him with his back and shouted, "Jump up!" His political descendants have also loved dealing with hecklers.

Isaac amassed the sum of five pounds and moved in from the south-west edge of Dartmoor to the city of Plymouth, eventually becoming a successful small builder. He believed in the power of prayer to make men transcend their surroundings, and he built his workshop in the teeming slums of Notte Street. "Every house and indeed almost every room seemed full of people," the younger Isaac recalled, and the juvenile gang warfare in the streets impressed him more than anything else in the great city.

During one of these battles I have seen the High Street army sweep Notte Street clear from the bottom to the top. The victors would then encamp in triumph, sometimes around an impoverished fire fed with weapons taken from the enemy. Meanwhile the defeated Notte Streeters took refuge in their homes, nursing their wounds. That was literally true, for sometimes there was actual bloodshed. On these bigger occasions no policeman came in sight. Nothing but a body of police could have coped with that formidable situation.

Isaac the elder built a mission hall in Notte Street, stepping from joist to joist across the uncompleted first floor with the three-year-old Isaac clutched, terrified, in his arms. The workmen, by now his employees, cheered when he reached the other side. Industrious and abstemious, he was working his way out of the surrounding poverty and noisy anarchy of the streets.

He sent little Isaac to Plymouth Public School, paying twopence a week, and then on to the Hoe Grammar School. Out of hours he and his schoolfriends would play on the Hoe, under Francis Drake's statue, or down on the quays, "long hours sitting on the sun-warmed slabs of the Sutton wharf with our legs dangling over the side, fishing for crabs with a long piece of string and bait carefully selected from the great bins which the fishermen left". In later life, young Isaac became passionately sentimental about his home town, and the heroic men of action who had walked the same streets as him: "Along Notte Street must have walked Humphrey Gilbert, Sir John Hawkins, Sir Francis Drake, Martin Frobisher, Sir Walter Ralegh, Admiral Robert Blake, and in later years Captain Cook and Admiral Nelson," he reminisced on the radio in 1951, in his rich Devon burr.

School was not an unqualified success. "The classes were very large and sometimes eighty or a hundred of us would be committed to the charge of some unfortunate single teacher. I remember very little of what I was taught but I suppose I learned something." The sabbatarian chapel home taught him more: singing, sermonising and poetry. His father would sing "To be a farmer's boy" at the piano, when not preaching the sermon. Isaac was sent to Band of Hope meetings and solemnly signed the pledge at the age of nine. His teetotalism was strongly reinforced when, as an adolescent, he saw in the street a carpenter friend of his, fighting drunk, hit his own protesting mother across the face.

At the Band of Hope someone recited Macaulay:

> Lars Porsena of Clusium,
> By the Nine Gods he swore,
> That the great house of Tarquin,
> Should suffer wrong no more . . .

From that moment he was fascinated, even obsessed, by declamatory literature. "I walked home that night on air," he said. "A fire was kindled within me which has never ceased to burn." Macaulay was more potent than any wine for him, Michael Foot now says. The two Isaacs eventually donated twenty-five pounds each if Michael himself abjured alcohol until the age of twenty-one. He collected the money, got drunk with his brother in Paris, and has remained on good terms with both poetry and liquor since. Drink has always been a puzzle for nonconformist socialists as well as for Liberals: when Michael Foot entered West Country Labour politics, he found he had to keep up a teetotal front with the lay preachers who had migrated to the Plymouth Labour party.

The accusation "he was drunk" has special puritan over-tones in the Labour party, which is one reason why much later Foot became agitated by the factional question of who had been the greater drinker: his opponent Hugh Gaitskell or his hero Nye Bevan.

Young Isaac was an active child, so with four other sons and two daughters, Eliza Foot had her work cut out. "Her discipline was severe," the middle-aged Isaac was to tell a Methodist conference, "but in her later years she became all gentleness, all fragrance and all grace. Barrie said, 'The God to whom little boys say their prayers has a face very like their mothers.' I expect most of us here have found that to be true."

He left school at fourteen, in 1894, and was despatched to the starched white-collar world to work as a boy-clerk at the Admiralty in London. It took him an hour to walk to work, time that Isaac filled by declaiming Macaulay aloud as he plodded across the most deserted parts of Kensington Gardens and Hyde Park in the early morning. Writers excited him more than anything in his entire life. Milton, Shelley, Keats, Coleridge he read in W. T. Stead's little yellow Penny Poets; Cromwell's letters and speeches he read in an abridged version. The boy became a familiar figure in the second-hand book-shops of the Charing Cross Road, clutching the remains of his fourteen-shillings-a-week pay packet. It was the start of a long haunting of the Charing Cross Road, and as he grew into old age, his visits became even more frequent, manic, and eventually quite furtive. His son Michael used to shop there too, a bibliophile poring over the long and dusty shelves like his father. Once Isaac was given five sovereigns by his father to put into a savings account, but he spent it all on books.

He sat the civil service exams, but his heart was still in Plymouth. By this time the elder Isaac was sufficiently well-to-do to article him to a Plymouth solicitor for five years, and, incidentally, to build a large family house in a somewhat florid style in the city. It had wrought-iron balconies, a courtyard, and a long glass conservatory which projected from the front door to the street.

Eva Mackintosh, a doctor's daughter, half-Scottish, half-Cornish, was, characteristically, caring for a man when Isaac, now twenty-one, first saw her, looking after "Gruffy" Dingle, her grandfather, in the small Cornish market town of Callington. They met on a Wesley Guild excursion to Cambridge, Eva being chapel. Only the fox-hunting classes and hangers-on were church, in the West Country of that time. She was two years his senior. Isaac proposed the day after they first met, and Eva's prudence held him off for no more than six weeks of importunate domestic visiting, resplendent in high hat and frock coat. He had a dazzling smile which lit up the fortunate recipient.

"Callington 11.5 train," he wrote in his diary, ecstatic but punctilious. "Called at office before leaving. Rode to Herbert's for music. Splendid ride down by coach. Mr. Dingle met me. Dinner: rode to Kit Hill and walked. Eva said 'Yes'. Glorious time on hilltop. Tea: walk to Frogwell. Spoke to Mr. D. Result favourable. This day a red letter day in my history. 'Praise God from whom all blessings flow.'"

There was a three-year engagement during which he qualified as a solicitor, and after the wedding a honeymoon in Switzerland. Eva believed women should be self-effacing and supportive to their men and went canvassing with Isaac when he took up politics. She bought the soft chintzes and early Victorian Cornish paintings to furnish their houses. She gave birth to seven children and took firm charge of their discipline, just as her mother-in-law, Eliza Foot, had before her. She tried to keep her children to Methodism, although she succeeded with only one of them, Hugh. She made sure that Isaac appeared on time, collected the things he had forgotten, and tried to keep him properly dressed — like her daughter-in-law Jill with Michael. She reproved her husband when he neglected the Liberal party for his books: "Come along now, the world is waiting to be saved."

"Others might be sick or tired or temperamental," Hugh recorded. "It never entered her head or ours that she could be any such thing. Human failings were for us, not for her. Never complaining, never short-tempered, she made us all laugh at ourselves and at each other. My picture of her is as she sang in a high clear voice, seldom quite in tune, in our family pew in the chapel at Callington or slipped away to take her Sunday school class, or at her place at our crowded dining table with tears in her eyes as she helplessly laughed at the nonsense we talked. And at night, when she at last abandoned her efforts to get us to go to bed, she would give us all a brisk nod at the door of the library with a final comprehensive loving rebuke. She set us all an example of devotion and gaiety."

The men of the family — leaving aside Isaac's later obsession with second-hand books — could do no wrong. Life must have been more difficult for the daughters, Jennifer and Sally. They did not go to Oxbridge, and did not have any of the five study rooms set aside in the house for the boys. While Isaac and the boys argued, read the papers or combed great works for quotations, the girls fell in with their mother's tasks: they picked up the boys' pyjamas, helped to do the cooking, and were as much a part of the domestic service as the cook and the housemaid. They would not have been human if they had not felt some resentment against the situation. Isaac was in favour of votes for women, but within a world where women stayed at home.

"My mother ruled every roost where she and my father ever alighted," Foot later wrote, but immediately undermined his own claim: "She knew something of women's rights, but still had little enough time to enjoy them, having to rear seven children, five of them males, each with his streak of armour-plated male aggressiveness which she condemned in theory and unwittingly encouraged in practice."

Isaac's law practice in Plymouth prospered. About 1903 he went into partnership with a stolid conveyancer, Edgar Bowden, and his own father probably made the early days easier by putting some property work their way. The firm of Foot and Bowden matured into a small, successful family business, then grew into the second-largest firm in Plymouth. Now it employs fifteen highly specialised partners.

Isaac, the lay preacher, did much of his orating in magistrates' courts, although he had little interest in prosecutions. He was thirty-four when the First World War began but because of a weak chest he was exempted from military service, and found a great deal of work defending conscientious objectors at tribunals. Sometimes he was handling as many as fifteen of these cases a day. To be a conscientious objector was a serious affair. Loathed by a jingoistic public, they were thrown into prison, and sometimes shipped out to France by the Army. Isaac took much criticism for supporting the "conchies" but they also made him wealthy. At its peak, the practice of Foot and Bowden was probably earning him £5,000 a year, a huge sum in those days of low income tax, yet barely enough to send all his five sons to boarding school and on to Oxford or Cambridge.

Isaac hurled himself into every activity he tackled. When he went to watch Plymouth Argyle play football, he cheered and shouted until he was hoarse. Music was part of the life of almost every Methodist household; on Sundays Isaac could always be heard at the grand piano (presented to him by Totnes Liberals in 1910), loudly thumping the keyboard and singing:

> Oh Beulah Land, sweet Beulah Land,
> As on thy highest mount I stand,

I look away across the sea
Where mansions are prepared for me
And view the shining glory shore,
My heaven, my home, for evermore.

His Irish setter, Roddy, would join in, baying enthusiastically.

Later Isaac became enthralled by Bach. He would get up at dawn, put a favourite record on his old gramophone, turn up the volume to maximum and retire to his upstairs bedroom to listen as he read. The rest of the family grew accustomed to being blasted out of their beds in this fashion. (Michael Foot must have remembered the trick, terrifying to strangers, as he did the same thing to Lord Beaverbrook at the height of the Second World War.) In his seventies, Isaac was capable of driving to London from Cornwall, shouting "take that man's number" as he narrowly avoided terrible collisions, heading straight for the Festival Hall without any break for food, and sitting there most of the night with a score on his knees, transported by the *St. John Passion*.

Isaac did not merely read books. He devoured them, gutted them for quotations to write out in his hundreds of "commonplace books", underlined, marked and commented on them in the margins, memorised them in reams, and gave dramatic recitations, acting out scenes in front of his family. He would appear as Macbeth: "Is this a dagger that I see before me?" or as Jean Valjean escaping through the sewers of Paris, or in the murder scene from A. E. W. Mason's *House of the Arrow*. He learned whole plays of Shakespeare and all of *Paradise Lost* by heart. He taught himself French and Greek. From his earliest days as a boy clerk, he had trained himself to wake up earlier and earlier to give himself more time for reading; in the end he could carve out four or five hours a day in which he disappeared into his beloved books. He was a self-educated radical democrat, bounding up the steps of the Winter Palace of literature, and seizing the inheritance of the common man. There was nothing, for him, that could stand between a man and his God, a man and his Bible, a man and his country's literary heritage and a man and the government of his own country. His radicalism stopped short at the ideas which could be found in the literature of the preceding three centuries; it did not include the full liberation of women, or the overthrow of private property. He was a Roundhead, but not a Leveller.

He became what Michael Foot — who inherited the addiction — called a "bibliophilial drunkard", building up a library of more than 60,000 volumes. The house had two pungent smells: Eva's furniture polish and old books. The joists groaned with the weight of these volumes, shelf upon shelf of Bunyan, Hardy, Carlyle, Milton, Marvell, Cromwell, Abraham Lincoln, Wordsworth, Conrad, Macaulay, and, most of all, the great declaimer Edmund Burke. When Isaac preached on the text "In my father's house are many mansions" in the Wesleyan chapel, the tiny Michael Foot could only think of rows of shelves: "I would picture in my mind whole lofts and barns and outhouses crowded with histories and autobiographies and collected works."

Foot's father's house was filled with rooms devoted to single subjects or even single authors. A Bibles room had 450 Greek testaments alone, and a French Revolution Room 2,000 volumes if one included those about Napoleon. There was a room given over to detective novels and a room filled with modern poetry. There were books in piles lining the stairs, so that visitors had to pick their way gingerly to their rooms, and more books arrived by every post. An ordinary bibliophile might be pleased to have one first edition of *Paradise Lost*; Isaac had two. When Eva finally put her foot down, Isaac resorted, like an alcoholic hiding his gin bottles, to deceit. Eva would open the door of a wardrobe and find several suitcases full of second-hand volumes from the Charing Cross Road. He went to the United States and came back with eleven crates full of books. In his old age, his second wife was sometimes in tears as her husband tried to smuggle more books in through the back door. When the children left home, Eva must have felt some regret, but Isaac would gleefully devote another room to Dr. Johnson or to Milton. He would ask his guests jocularly: "Where would you like to sleep tonight — with Lucrezia Borgia, Dorothy Wordsworth or Josephine Beauharnais?"

Isaac was a fine literary preacher. He naturally knew the Bible off by heart, but he carefully composed and wrote out his sermons, which were then typed by one of his daughters before being tried out on the assembled family. Once one of the girls had mistaken the phrase "public conveyance", which he had included, and he asked weightily, "How often do you see someone reading their Bible in a public convenience?" The children screamed with laughter, and it became a family joke for years afterwards, the kind of private memory which helps to bind a family together. They became one of those large families which can be slightly exasperating to the outsider, full of hidden codes, jokes, skeletons in the cupboard, ferociously rude to each other, but utterly loyal in the face of the outside world. Having Isaac for a father was just one of the things which convinced the Foots that they were a remarkable and special clan.

Michael learnt his first oratory from listening to his father preach. "Hope," Isaac would whisper, and the little Cornish chapel would become utterly still. "The gospel of hope"; he had the congregation in his hand. Within a few sentences the language would become stirring and resonant.

> Hope, and the paramount duty that heaven lays
> For its own honour, on man's suffering heart.

"Outside, the world seemed sharply brighter than when we went in."

Naturally, Isaac went into politics. What better outlet could there be for his theatrical temperament, his Victorian public spirit and his conviction that all the greatest Englishmen were crusaders?

Over the years old election posters filled the house. In 1910 he fought Totnes, getting nothing from it except the grand piano, and in the same year he ran in Bodmin and lost by forty-one votes. All his electoral fights were in tough Tory West Country seats, which may explain why he lost most of them. After the First World War he lost in Plymouth to Lady Astor, which started off an odd friendship. Nancy Astor, the wife of Waldorf Astor, a rich American who acquired a peerage, the *Observer* and a gigantic mansion at Cliveden, was a curious woman — superficial, rude, erratic and probably frigid. This did not prevent her from becoming the first woman to take a seat in the Commons, charming her starstruck Devon constituents and generally behaving, as A. J. P. Taylor has put it, like a Chinese firecracker, discharging sparks in all directions. Isaac genuinely liked her; they had an affection for Plymouth in common, and were both violent teetotallers. Isaac was susceptible to pretty women, though far too upright even to flirt; Nancy Astor liked nothing better than to be admired from a distance. Throughout the campaigning years of the 'Twenties and 'Thirties, the Foot household would bawl out:

> Who's that knocking at the door?
> Who's that knocking at the door?
> If it's Astor and his wife,
> We'll stab 'em with a knife,
> And they won't be Tories any more.

This jovial jingle was discreetly forgotten when Isaac and Lady Astor became friends. She discovered him poring over his commonplace book of Milton quotations on the train as they travelled together to London. She borrowed it, and while Isaac made increasingly frantic efforts over the next few weeks to get it back, she secretly had it printed into fifty leather-bound gilded copies inscribed, "Arranged by Isaac Foot and presented to him by Nancy Astor." After that she could do no wrong, at least until the final days of the appeasing Cliveden set.

Isaac won a sensational by-election at Bodmin in 1922, standing as a Liberal Wee Free Asquithian against the Lloyd George coalition, and its candidate, Sir Frederick Poole.

> Foot's a man and Poole's a mouse,
> Foot's a man for Parliament House.

He held Bodmin in 1923, was defeated in 1924, and returned in 1929. Electioneering must have been almost continuous when Michael was a boy. At open-air meetings in 1910, women would shout, "Vote for Pole-Carew!" and Isaac would yell back, "Cock-a-doodle-doo!" Hecklers would shout questions, and Isaac would reply, "My dear man, I can answer your questions, but I can't give you the brains to understand." They would shout, "Are you Jewish, Isaac?" and he would riposte,

"No, but I intend to be one of the chosen people!" Now and again a rotten tomato would catch him on the back of his neck, or a chagrined Tory spit in his wife's face. Tory agents would watch him play to his audiences as if they were his congregations, and would growl, "There's Isaac Foot holding another of his bloody little prayer meetings." The young Michael watched and learned, seeing "A full hour, maybe, of rollicking humour and invective, fifteen minutes of passionate argument, and a peroration to take the roof off." Isaac adored slugging it out, man to man, with his opponents. When a neighbouring candidate asked his advice about a Conservative ploy, he shouted into the telephone another remark that went straight into the Foot family mythology: "Tell them it is a lie. Tell them it is a damned lie. Tell them it is no less of a damned lie because it is uttered by a Tory gentleman of title."

The brewers disliked him because they thought he was bad for trade. When they proposed a campaign in which sportsmen would advertise pubs, Isaac distributed a pamphlet he called "Blood Money". "Why not give us poster pictures of the chauffeur or the bus driver at the wheel saying, 'I drive on beer'?" he demanded. He attacked Sir Edgar Sanderson, director of the Brewers' Society, with venom and the holy writ: "Your scheme is concerned with *profit*. Here is a passage on profit: 'But who shall cause one of these little ones . . . to stumble, it is profitable for him that a great millstone should be hanged about his neck and that he should sink in the depth of the sea.'"

In 1925 he headed a Liberal expedition to Lloyd George's lair at Churt, where the weekend was spent in trying to work out a compact to end the personal quarrels which had split the party. The Asquithians thought Lloyd George a great traitor: the party was in fact dying in front of Isaac's eyes, though he did not realise it until the terrible shock of the 1945 election. Lloyd George bade farewell to his guests on the Monday morning, saying cheerfully, "Let our slogan be Measures, not Men." Isaac, who told this story against himself, was unable to resist showing off, and remarked, "Edmund Burke had something to say about that. I think you'll find it on page 500 or thereabouts of that beautiful Beaconsfield edition of Burke I saw on your shelves." With luck, Lloyd George never did look it up; Isaac went home and discovered that what it actually said was: "The cant of Not Men But Measures: a sort of charm by which many people get loose from every honourable engagement." This anecdote did not prevent the younger Foot from taking over "Measures, not Men" as one of his own slogans, and holding to it; he would have forgiven Hugh Gaitskell what he saw as foul crimes against Nye Bevan if Gaitskell had ever swung round on policy.

Eva brought up the children the while, at first in the family villa in Lipson Terrace, Plymouth, then, during the First World War, on the edge of Bodmin Moor in a small Georgian house at St. Cleer, and finally in Pencrebar, the white Victorian manor house just outside her own home town of Callington. Pencrebar had been built in 1849 by the Horndon family, the local squires, and it had twenty bedrooms and six and a half acres of lawns and shrubberies, all set in the rich Cornish woods and hills. For thirty-three years it was the Castle Foot, famous to all West-Country Liberals as the home of "Our Isaac", and a campaign headquarters for the whole family at innumerable elections. On its lawns, Isaac held a succession of Liberal garden parties, for the party never entirely lost its base in the West Country. In the 'Fifties, when the party struck bottom nationally, two of the guests were young candidates who were going to use the West Country as a springboard for a great revival: Peter Bessell, who later won Isaac's old constituency of Bodmin, and Jeremy Thorpe. The world of get-rich-quick schemes and public-school homosexuality could hardly have been more distant from Isaac's own. His son must have winced years later at Thorpe's Old Bailey trial and acquittal on a charge of conspiracy to murder; for Bessell testified that the pair had a kind of code for referring to Cornwall, where they had planned some shady scheme: "Let me give you an Isaac Foot answer . . ."

Michael, born in 1913, was the fourth son. First came Dingle, named after his grandmother's family, then Hugh and John. Two daughters followed, Sally and Jennifer, and finally the youngest son, Christopher.

"My mother was the centre of all our lives," said Hugh, "working and planning for us all the time, uncompromising in her strict adherence to Methodist and Liberal principles, always long-suffering and compassionate." She certainly put long hours into her chores. By six a.m. she was dressed and heading upstairs with a pot of tea for the cook and parlour-maid, who shared a bedroom. "She was like a second mother to me," the parlourmaid Ruth Stephens recalls. By six thirty, the servants were downstairs making fires and cooking break-fast. They struck the gong at eight a.m. sharp and the boys were expected to arrive immediately in the kitchen. When breakfast had been cleared away, servants, children and wife gathered in the dining room while Isaac conducted morning prayers. Eva saw him off to his office in Plymouth from the dining-room window. In their previous house in St. Cleer his routine was slightly different; when Eva didn't drive him to the station in the donkey cart, he would stride three miles across the moor and down the lanes to the train at Liskeard, declaiming sonnets. He had a hundred off by heart; in the hour's walk he could declaim exactly thirty.

But by this time he had a car, which he drove extremely erratically. He tooted the horn and shouted out of the window most mornings as he left, and Eva would send the parlourmaid running down the drive with whatever he had forgotten. Then she laundered most of the clothes, made the household jam and marmalade, baked the bread, or did whatever other task needed to be done. The boys all went to boarding schools and Eva laboriously sewed nametapes on their vests, shirts, trousers, socks, jumpers, cricket flannels, football shorts, caps, raincoats and ties. In the afternoon she took a short rest in bed. When the children had become less demanding, she sat on the local magistrates' bench on Wednesday afternoons, and Isaac took advantage of her absences to smuggle more books into the house.

The daughters of the family had to help with all this labour. But when the boys were home, then Isaac would return from his deed-boxes and the magistrates' court to play huge games of cricket in the field at the back, or he would read out loud *Les Misérables*, translating as he went, under the big lamp in the crowded main room. He paid Hugh a shilling an hour to teach him schoolboy Greek, so that he could read the New Testament in the original. The boys bickered and jockeyed with each other, snorting with derision when Hugh was discovered copying out great chunks of his father's common-place books to pad out supposedly erudite school essays. They went for long walks and runs, but fishing, which Isaac thought barbarous, was discouraged. He was one of life's champions of the underdog, and not, like some politicians, chiefly in the animal kingdom; he fought for compensation for tin-miners injured in an accident at the Lizard in 1915; he backed the Indian nationalists in the 1920s, championed the needs of the "distressed areas" in the 1930s, and at the age of seventy-nine was still making speeches and printing pamphlets in Cornwall on behalf of black Africans arrested in Nyasaland because of their politics.

Michael would run down Liskeard Road, up the stiff bracken-covered hill to the top of Cadsonbury Tor, the Iron Age fort above the River Lynher, and back again, timing himself. Or the brothers would stride seven miles to Clapper Bridge, or up to the moorland crest of Kit Hill, the old meeting-place of the medieval tinners' parliament. Twice Michael set out from Pencrebar and walked the entire length of the Cornish coast, once in a fraternal expedition, once on his own.

It was an overwhelming family, demanding, competitive, success-orientated, at least for the boys. The two daughters are not mentioned when people talk of the "famous Foots", and Jennifer, the younger girl, was the most self-effacing of all. She was intelligent and well-read, and although she went to Grenoble and learned fluent French, she and her sister were not expected to upset the natural order of things and equip themselves for public life. In the late 1930s she went to Palestine, where her brother Hugh was working as a colonial administrator. She met James Highet, a dashing young man who was working for an oil company, and married him. She spent the war in India, and returned with two young children to take over Pencrebar. Eva had died in 1946, and Isaac needed to be looked after.

Her niece Sarah (Hugh's daughter) remembers her as a kind of goddess of the kitchen, "where the huge scrubbed pine table stood and the stove warmed the large pans of milk for cream . . . I could sit there for hours and feel the contentment and warmth that Aunt Jennifer seemed to instil into the room". Jennifer filled the gap left by Eva "with her warm smile, gentle ways and fine features; with her sturdy frame and her deep chuckle of a laugh; with her obvious concern and compassion for all the family's problems . . . she bore everyone's woes and complaints as if they were her own".

After Isaac remarried in 1951, Jennifer and her family took over a small farm on the South Devon coast not far from Sidmouth, where she lives and works quietly with her husband near to her four children and three grandchildren.

Sally showed more obvious signs of frustration. Some of the family think she was the most articulate, literate and witty of all the Foots. As the years passed, she channelled her passions into horses. Her conversational style became sharp, deflating, even cynical. She taught riding at a number of public schools, and became friendly with Louis MacNeice, the poet. After the war and her mother's death, she brought horses into the Pencrebar stables, and ran a riding school on the sanded tennis court. As she cantered down the Devon lanes she, too, would declaim poetry aloud. After Isaac remarried, she withdrew to a caravan on the banks of the River Lynher, a short distance from the house, surrounded by her beloved ponies and her dogs.

One day she was drowned in the river. It might have been an accident, she might have become dizzy through the drugs she was taking, or it might have been suicide. The family think it was probably an accident, for the river was in flood that day. John Foot gave evidence at the inquest, and said that his sister had led a life entirely of her own seeking, a nomad sort of life.

Christopher, the youngest, is the other and saddest cul-de-sac in the Foot lineage. He has an uncontainable degenerative illness, Huntingdon's Chorea, marked by characteristic convulsive movements and a progressive collapse of functions until the sufferer is reduced to an inert state. Christopher joined the family law firm in the early 1930s, and managed to continue there until shortly after the war. From then on, the story is one of increasingly distressing experiences for the rest of the family until, at the beginning of the 1970s, he was placed in an institution.

The other four brothers were the achievers. One knight, two

lords and a party leader. Three presidents of the Oxford Union and one president of the Cambridge Union. One Cabinet minister, two other ministers, a governor-general and a QC. One Liberal, two more-or-less Lib-Lab, one a left-wing socialist.

Dingle was the eldest and, like many eldest sons, the most respectable and even sedate. He had a tubercular right arm, and it hung stiffly by his side for the rest of his life. He became a barrister, but cross-examining on the Western circuit was not his métier. He was good, however, at the preparation of complex and arcane briefs for presentation to the appellate committee of the Privy Council, and defending civil liberties in the courts of Commonwealth countries. He had a huge black and Asian clientele, and when a Conservative government returned Chief Enaharo to face political trial by his rivals in Nigeria, Dingle undertook his defence, though the Nigerian government refused to let him in.

He began life as a Liberal, and there his heart remained, though he later followed Michael into the Labour party. He fought his first election in 1929 and in 1931 won the selection for a Dundee constituency full of desperately poor and unemployed families. In Parliament he joined his father, and remained there through the 1935 election and the "national" government, then through the war. He took a junior minister-ial post in the Churchill coalition of 1940. He was driven by a learned, academic radicalism, and a sense of humour so dry that it wasn't always distinguishable from the pomposity his nieces used to giggle about. Once they gave him a joke drinking glass with a tiny hole bored in the side, and they could never work out whether he was surreptitiously wiping his chin and gallantly falling in with the joke, or was simply too stuffy to ask what was going on.

He married Dorothy Elliston, known jokingly to some of the family as "Dingle's Tory Wife" because of her social style. She was Church of England, reputed to possess a diamond tiara, and organised his political entertaining.

Dingle lost Dundee in 1945, another victim of the Liberal massacre. It looked as if his "Vote for Dingle Foot" posters would join the other family relics in the attic including the posters saying "Vote for Isaac" and "Vote for John", which the children used to make into paper boats and float down the river. In 1955, after long consideration, Dingle joined the Labour party and won the nomination for Ipswich, which he represented in Parliament from 1957. The first Wilson government brought him the post of Solicitor-General, the junior law officer's job, with its traditional knighthood. He resigned quietly and discreetly towards the end of that administration because he did not want to be associated with what he saw as a sell-out of black Rhodesians. In 1970 he was among the Labour MPs to lose their seats, largely because his election address consisted entirely of a list of points on which he disagreed with the Labour manifesto — not least their illiberal attitude to immigration. He died choking on a sandwich in the Far East, while attending to another of his Commonwealth briefs.

Hugh Mackintosh Foot, Lord Caradon, known as "Mac" throughout the family, was anxious and even envious of his elder brother. He adopted an ostentatiously different style, demanding to go to a different public school from Dingle and to Cambridge, not Oxford. He went in for rowing, the most politically backward of all Cambridge activities. "It was a brutish life we led. We met early in the morning for a training run. We rowed every afternoon. We dined together in Hall at night. Female society was entirely excluded and despised. The language was startlingly foul. When we were not in training, vast quantities of beer were consumed."

This was something of a pose. He actually remained dutifully teetotal until he was twenty-one, and helped the other members of the Boat Club to stagger to bed after dinner. Whatever his attempts to distinguish himself separately from his clever elder brother, and the two smart young brothers coming up behind him, he was constitutionally incapable of the racism and easy snobbery which sometimes went with the life of a Cambridge hearty.

"When we were living on the edge of Bodmin Moor and I was about ten years old, I used to escape to the gypsy encampments. There in their tents I learnt how to make clothes pegs and broom handles. Sitting with the gypsy children around the fire, I felt their contempt for the settled life of people who live in the comfort and complacent security of houses. And I remember the feeling of intense moral indignation when my mother objected to my bringing my small gypsy friends home to tea. This struck me as gross discrimination, an intolerable social injustice."

Hugh did have a smattering of the family's absorption in politics and public speaking. He could be seen travelling round Devon in a van with Selwyn Lloyd — then a Liberal — haranguing very small crowds on behalf of the Liberal Land Campaign. He got his father to address the Union in 1929, and mused: "To interest, arouse and hold an audience. To persuade, convince people and move them to agreement, concern or indignation. To stir them from their lethargy or complacency. These things can be done by writing and speaking."

He finally ignored politics and the law, and went off to Palestine on behalf of the Foreign Office. Isaac, meanwhile, paid off his college debts. In Palestine, where bloodshed between Arabs, Jews and the British was worsening daily, he had the difficult job of colonial administrator. Soon after he arrived he met Sylvia Tod in Haifa, courted her in an enormous open Buick which he had bought, and married her in 1936. They had four children, and the eldest son, Paul, ran true to the Foot form. He too became President of the Oxford Union. ("A wonderful thing," said Hugh, "to hear one's father speaking in the voice of one's son.") Paul began as a Liberal, rapidly moved left, and became a leading light of the Socialist Workers' party. He fought hopeless parliamentary elections, and spoiled whatever reputation he had as a flint-hearted Marxist by refusing to heckle his uncle Michael at a by-election in Stetchford. This was absolutely true to the Foot tradition: Michael would never speak for Labour in his father's old Liberal seat of Bodmin, and his brother John, while a Liberal himself, urged those in the Plymouth Devonport constituency to vote for the Labour candidate, Michael Foot, in 1945. Paul is a radical and a bibliophile; his own flat off the Finchley Road in North London is lined floor to ceiling with books. Like Michael, to whom he is close, he is an aggressive journalist, who in the early 1980s was writing a prize-winning column in the *Daily Mirror* exposing various big business and Conservative scandals.

Hugh himself became one of the architects of decolonisation, as Chief Secretary of Nigeria, as Captain-General (a title his father, an admirer of the Duke of Marlborough, must have relished) of Jamaica and as Governor of Cyprus. There he steered his way through the EOKA rebellion, the prospect of civil war, and the island's eventual independence from Britain. His optimism about the course of the Macmillan government ended only in 1962, when he resigned as chief spokesman at the United Nations in protest against the treatment of black aspirations in Southern Rhodesia. This in turn helped to win a post as chief British spokesman at the UN under the Wilson government and the title Lord Caradon.

When the situation in Cyprus was at its most perilous, Isaac sent his son biblical quotations to fortify him, and Hugh quoted lavishly from his father's heroes in his own memoirs. Of his resignation, he quoted Abraham Lincoln: "I must have some consciousness of being somewhere near the right; I must have some standard of principle fixed within myself." The right-wing at home thought him a dangerous soft lefty. His family teased him but stuck loyally by him. Michael wrote in the *Evening Standard*:

> Sir Hugh was never considered the brightest of the brood. Ideas he took ready-made, usually straight from his father's commonplace book . . . he acquired strange tastes and pastimes which the rest of us wouldn't be seen dead at — such as rowing, playing polo, dressing up in Goering-like uniforms and enjoying it, and occasionally, even, at a pinch, putting some trust in the word of Tory prime ministers . . . unsuspected by his suspicious brothers, Sir Hugh had grasped the main point about our convulsive Commonwealth. One man is as good as another. Each has an equal right to control his own destinies. How would they learn responsibility? Give it to them; it's the only way. As for colour, who cares? No one but the stupidest snob.

The third brother, John, was less boisterous, less well noticed. He was, like Dingle, brilliant at Oxford and naturally became President of the Union. That is what the Foots did. He was a radical left-winger in the Liberal party, but he has stayed there. He fought Basingstoke for the party in a by-election in

1934, just after he had come down from Oxford, and he fought it again in the 1935 general election. He married a charming and forthright American, Anne Bailey Farr, and they became only the third of the seven Foot offspring to have children themselves — a boy and a girl.

Dingle had gone to the Bar and Hugh into the Colonial Service, but the family practice was waiting for someone to take it on. Isaac was now in his fifties, and the only other partner was Edgar Bowden, who died in 1954. After that the practice expanded considerably. John trained as a solicitor, and moved into the old-fashioned premises in Lockyer Street, just below Plymouth Hoe. Hugh had broken away and persuaded his father to send him to a different public school, Leighton Park, near Reading, the "snob Quaker public school" as A. J. P. Taylor later called it. John did not get a scholarship there, but followed Dingle to the minor public school at Bembridge on the Isle of Wight, set up by an acquaintance of Isaac's, who was a Liberal politician and a keen educationalist — and also a flagrant homosexual, according to the pupils there at the time. The school was limited academically, and Dingle had been sent there to give him a small arena in which he could compete, even with his stiff right arm. Naturally neither Dingle nor John ever told their parents about the headmaster's proclivities for which, the consensus was, it was a miracle he was never prosecuted. The experience seems to have done neither of them any harm.

John was a witty public speaker, and an even wittier private one. Like the rest of the family, he was appalled by Munich and spoke out against it so vigorously that when he applied to join the RASC as a driver at the outbreak of war, his appointment was held up for several weeks while he was investigated by MI5. Only on his colonel's intercession was he allowed to join up; in those days passionate anti-fascism was still thought dangerous.

After the war, John rejoined the firm and helped to rebuild it. The original premises had been bombed to smithereens, along with much of the rest of Plymouth. He fought for the Liberals in the 1945 election, this time in Bodmin. He lost. So did Dingle in Dundee and Isaac in Tavistock.

John stayed on in Bodmin and fought it again, but the

Liberal party was on a downhill slide, and he never won. But his efforts against racial prejudice led to him becoming the head of the United Kingdom Immigration Advisory Service. After the 1945 election, when Dingle decided to cross to the Labour party, he tried to persuade John to join him. It seemed the only way to achieve any sort of political influence in the foreseeable future. Isaac would probably have tolerated them changing camp; Liberalism had already broken in 1945, with one wave going left and the other right. A defection to the Tories would have been insupportable.

Dingle and John held conclaves. Would Dingle be selected for a Labour seat? It did not seem likely. And while it was one thing to pursue one's own political ambitions, it seemed to John quite another to damage the sacred cause of Liberalism by a mass defection. Dingle went and John stayed. Eventually Jeremy Thorpe made him a Liberal peer.

"If you contract out and interest yourself in peripheral things, you can achieve something," John says. As Lord Foot, he travels regularly to London from the family's solid villa outside Plymouth, at Crapstone, a village not far from Horrabridge, whence his grandfather came, and prods the cause of penal reform or nudges the cause of conservation. He inherited much from Isaac Foot. His father's skill with his hands, for example, left him able to construct a complete puppet theatre for his nieces and nephews, and to build an impressive dry-stone wall around his house. But it is hard to avoid the impression that Isaac's creed of the happy warrior, the swashbuckling Liberal, played a sensitive and deeply talented man slightly false, if only by tying him down to the Liberal party. Michael, the fourth son, set out on a road which, if not entirely his own, was some way distant from that of his father and his brothers.

3

A YOUNG LIBERAL

Isaac Foot liked metaphors drawn from stone. One phrase became the family motto: "Pit and Rock", and all the members of the family, even Michael's undergraduate nephew Paul, would sign off letters with it. It came from the book of Isaiah: "Look unto the Rock whence ye are hewn and to the hole of the pit whence ye are digged."

Isaac's home was not as strict and puritanical as that of his own parents and brothers. The children were allowed, for example, to play games on Sundays. Michael, however, faced two difficulties. He was the youngest of the four brothers, and was often overborne by the clamorous egos around him. He described later how: "There were plenty of others to keep me in my place. I often revolted against these 'overlords', and this must have something to do with my being a socialist." Much more painfully, as he grew up he developed eczema, an ugly and infuriating skin ailment which covered his face and hands with itchy scales and marks. He also suffered from asthma, which often left him gasping for breath. Both lasted until middle age, which meant that he spent much of his life feeling ugly, uncomfortable, shy and suddenly liable to acute physical distress. Some people thought that these two afflictions might be the cause of his savage speeches and writings, yet they never made him anything other than polite and diffident in private. And he was never an invalid; he played rugby at school, ran up and down hills attempting to improve his personal best, and went for massive solitary hikes. At his prep school he was centre-forward in the school soccer team and was remembered for scoring the record number of goals in a term.

Another theory is that the asthma and the eczema, like his socialism, were actually products of inner psychological stress. This is simply not true. The two diseases are connected, and while stress can make the symptoms worse, the asthma and the eczema were genetic. All the Foot children had eczema except Hugh and John. Dingle, the eldest, much to his mother's alarm, was born with it. In the 1920s, in an effort to get the children cured by doctors in Harley Street, Isaac moved the whole family to Norwood in South London, where they remained, having regular treatment, for eighteen months.

Foot's early schooldays were spartan. The boys were sent to Forres preparatory school, near Swanage, which was Church of England. It was a regime of dawn reveilles, chapel morning and night, cold baths. They were known collectively as "The Feet" and Michael belonged to the Cubs.

His public school had a much greater impact on him; belonging to the Cubs was a routine matter at Forres, but the Boy Scouts were an issue of some moral sensitivity at Leighton Park. It was not an ordinary public school — except insofar as it was expensive — and it shaped the attitudes which can still be seen in Foot, the party leader. Leighton Park was a Quaker school, founded in an attempt to persuade wealthy Quakers not to send their children to Eton, where they would be corrupted by the Officers' Training Corps. Most education in the 1920s was tinged with jingoism: there would be frequent visits from the Navy League, and fourteen-year-olds were given rifles with which to blaze away at targets painted as Germans. At Leighton Park, however, they formed a League of Nations branch and flew the League of Nations flag. An anguished debate over the Boy Scouts took place on the question of whether it was compatible with Quaker ethics to fly the Union Jack. It was eventually decided to fly it alongside the League of Nations flag. The boys at Leighton Park, with their intense internationalist, pacifist ethos, knew that they were different from other public-school boys. Rugby fixtures were a constant problem, especially those against the tough nautical school at Pangbourne. Matches were suspended during the time Foot was there, after a brutish forward had kicked one of his classmates in the back; they were resumed only to end in disorder when the Pangbourne crowd insisted on chanting at Leighton Park's Chinese forward: "Chinky, Chinky, Chinaman!"

Leighton Park was based in several large converted suburban homes on the outskirts of Reading. There were no girls: the Gillett family, who owned a bank, had offered to donate money to build accommodation for some, but the offer was refused. There were "meetings" on Sunday mornings and "programme meetings" on Sunday evenings, with outside preachers brought in to address the boys. As Nicholas Gillett, one of Foot's classmates, puts it: "The kernel of the Quaker outlook is that inside everybody is something so important that it goes beyond race, for example. It makes it impossible to treat political opponents, prisoners or mental patients as animals, as something less than human." Foot's passion for disarmament was nourished at Leighton Park. So, perhaps less obviously, was the manner in which he looked for the divine spark in everybody — even in reprehensible newspaper proprietors such as Lord Beaverbook, or the quite outrageous Randolph Churchill. Foot's niceness to other people, and his inability to conduct vendettas in private, whatever he says in public, have been put down to simple good nature, weakness or even frivolity. But it is just as likely that the moral basis for this behaviour was laid down at Leighton Park.

The school had barely a hundred boys. In the height of the Depression, when once-rich Quakers were having to remove their sons, Hugh demanded to go there so as to get away from Dingle, with whom he already furiously competed. The school was near enough to Isaac's own ethical code for him to agree. The Foots and the Gilletts, the backbone of the temperance movement in Somerset, were even distantly related. In fact some of the pupils were by no means the offspring of idealistic and progressive families; some had simply failed to get into better-known public schools, and were often the thick-headed sons of right-wing stockbrokers.

The dormitory bell woke them at seven a.m. Rugby and cricket were compulsory in the afternoons, long hours of study in the evenings. One hour a day was set aside for compulsory "hobbies" — Foot disappeared into the library. There was no drinking or smoking of course, and no trips to the cinema. Exhibitions were arranged on improving subjects, such as the inequity of tariff walls.

Foot may have been asthmatic, myopic and covered in eczema, but was also tough, angular and energetic. His classmates gave him the pointless nickname "Navvy" Foot because he had big feet and walked with them splayed out. He made the first cricket X1 as a somewhat idiosyncratic bowler (he later played cricket for the *Tribune* team), went for enormous walks and rose so far as to become vice-captain of the rugby team, which happened to be short of players. He was a wing-forward. This is a testament to his enthusiasm rather than to his sporting prowess.

He arrived full of Isaac's notions. His father believed that reading and learning were not enough, and meant nothing without political action. "Public life is a situation of power and energy," Isaac would declaim to his sons as he stood in front of the fireplace. "He trespasses against his duty who sleeps upon his watch." Michael was enraptured by the idea of fire and commitment, and would chant, "The land, the land, the land on which we stand; God gave the land to the people." He had already begun a career as a public speaker. In 1926 his father had brought him to speak to a Liberal garden party at Pencrebar, and while the text of his speech is lost, one member of the audience remembers the thirteen-year-old's style: "There was a lot of flaying of arms and shouting."

He drew many of his ideas and heroes from Trevelyan's *History of England* — John Bright, the great parliamentary orator who was a distant ancestor of Nicholas Gillett, Garibaldi, the ardent nationalist, Charles James Fox and, of course, Cromwell. By the time he reached the sixth form, he was lending his classmates his father's books, with the striking passages marked not just with underlining but with an elaborately drawn hand with pointing finger and cuff. His best friend Gillett was a socialist whose mother had joined the Labour party as early as 1906 because of its attitude on votes for women. But Michael still thought of himself as a Liberal and tried to convert his friends. He saw politics in terms of romantic heroes, and told Gillett: "If you find an issue, find the person who represents it." He shone at the sixth-form discussion classes. The headmaster, Edgar Castle, who had learned progressive educational ideas at Bedales School, would take news items, generally drawn from that Liberal and nonconformist paper, the *Manchester Guardian*, and ask the boys: "What is at stake? What is the framework in which we ought to see this?" Foot, so often the silent younger brother at home, would rise to the challenge. He would talk and talk. He talked away in the Debating Society too, and there he received his first political setback. In the J. B. Hodgkin Speech Competition, an occasion of much importance at Leighton Park, he gave an oration on "Liberalism" and came only second. He was better as an actor, playing the title role in Barrie's *The Admirable Crichton*, fascinating the audience with the rich brogue, copied from his father, which he also used as the Sergeant of Police in *The Pirates of Penzance*.

The boys were expected to show an unselfish interest in the working classes. Gillett and Foot organised a youth club in the Scout Hut for the youngsters from the nearby council estates. He was taken to visit miners' homes in South Wales. In the holidays, when not walking in North Cornwall with the Gillett family, he led a supervised expedition taking the youth club to a summer camp at Hayling Island.

Naturally he specialised in the two great family subjects, English and History, and he shone academically, particularly by the less than dazzling standards of Leighton Park. The key to Oxford and Cambridge was not a clutch of A Levels in 1930, but the ability to pay the fees. John, who went up in 1927, was costing his father £270 a year, and there were three younger children still at school. Instead of putting in for Balliol with its massive prestige, Michael applied to Wadham, where he thought it might be easier to gain a scholarship.

He got it through an extraordinary stroke of luck, or perhaps a demonstration of the intimacy of the elite to which he belonged, a world where the children of politicians, even radical politicians, slipped in easily and moved about confidently. Isaac was a Liberal MP for the second time, during Ramsay MacDonald's ill-fated minority government. In 1930 already two and a half million people were out of work, Wall Street had crashed, pits and shipyards were standing idle. Isaac however was embroiled in the more distant problem of the Indian Empire. Gandhi, the "naked fakir", had embarked on his campaign of passive resistance and civil disobedience, and a long search had begun by liberals of all parties to find some means of reconciling the Indians to British rule. Independence was not yet on the agenda.

William Wedgwood Benn, father of Tony Benn, had been appointed Secretary of State for India by MacDonald, and he proposed two round-table conferences of which Isaac was a member. The conferences were at first boycotted by the Congress Party since the government was too weak to offer the one concession they wanted: full self-governing status. Isaac was exceedingly pro-Indian, and Michael's own sympathy with the country began around this time. Gandhi was released from jail to come to Britain and was fêted by the left. In 1931 200 people gave a vegetarian dinner for his sixty-second birthday; Bertrand Russell, Kingsley Martin, Hewlett Johnson the "Red Dean", James Maxton of the ILP and Clement Attlee all joined in the meal of fruit and nuts.

Michael, now eighteen, took the train from Plymouth to London the day before his scholarship exams at Oxford, and went with his father for dinner in the cavernous gloom of the National Liberal Club near Whitehall. Isaac expounded in his jerky and animated manner exactly what the round-table conference proposed to recommend on the Untouchables, and on the British proposals for an Indian federation. Next day Michael travelled to Oxford and inspected the Wadham exam paper. One question read: "What should be recommended by the round-table Conference on India?" Foot calmly copied out what might have been his greatest newspaper scoop. When Lord David Cecil gave him his oral examination, Foot demonstrated his knowledge of the great historians, Macaulay, Carlyle and the rest, who had been almost a part of his family. He was in.

While he waited to become an undergraduate, MacDonald's government, hemmed in by the Liberals, needing to placate the bankers, and devoid of any knowledge of expansionist economics, fell with a crash which still reverberated in the Labour party fifty years later, when Foot had come to lead it. Writing with hindsight, Foot saw that MacDonald's betrayal had not been a sudden and dastardly act. The seeds of the government's decision to cut the dole, balance the Budget, cling to the Gold Standard and split the party in two, had been planted at the beginning of the government. It was the wild and romantic "extremists" of the left who had been right, he was to decide, and the MacDonald supporters, anxious to demonstrate that they were somehow "fit to govern" who had been in the wrong. Maxton and the ILP, who had been championing measures which sounded like economic lunacy, were in fact preaching early Keynesianism. So was the government's own Economic Advisory Council, on which Keynes was actually serving. So was Oswald Mosley, a convert to the Labour party. Mosley launched a plan for cutting unemployment by expanding credit, boosting demand by increasing social services and pensions, and starting industrial planning and import controls. One of the young MPs who backed Mosley was an ex-coal miner from the Welsh valleys, battling rhetorically against the Means Tests in his first Parliament. This was Aneurin Bevan, who was even then learning the two great lessons which he later passed on to his most fervent disciple, Michael Foot.

The first was to stay at all costs inside the Labour party, and fight its conventional attitudes. After the MacDonald debacle, Bevan told Jennie Lee of the ILP, the fiery young Scottish socialist whom he later married, and who was on the brink of leaving the Labour party: "I will tell you what the epitaph on you Scottish dissenters will be: pure but impotent . . . you will not influence the course of politics by as much as a hairs-breadth. Why don't you get into a nunnery and be done with it? . . . I tell you it is the Labour party or nothing. I know all its faults, all its dangers. But it is the party we have taught millions of working people to look to and regard as their own. We can't undo what they have done. And I am by no means convinced that something cannot be made of it yet."

The second lesson was that oratory was a democratic weapon. Bevan had already won a reputation for the power and the stridency of his speeches, skills learned wandering alone in the desolate hills above his home town of Tredegar, where thirty years later Foot himself was to become the MP. Bevan's personal assaults were notorious. Of Chamberlain, the defender of the Poor Law: "The worst thing I can say about democracy is that it has tolerated the Rt. Hon. Gentleman for four and a half years"; and on Lloyd George: "We are asking you for once to be decent to the miners — not to pay lip service, not so say that you are very sorry for them, not to say that you are very sorry that these accidents occur, not to say that you are very sorry for the low level of wages and for the conditions of famine which have existed in the mining districts since the war, and then to use all your parliamentary skill, all your rhetoric, in an act of pure demagogy, to expose the mining community of this country to another few years of misery . . ."

What Foot admired in Bevan was his commitment to fighting rhetoric like this, to the "passion play" of politics, as Bevan called it. Democracy could be made to work by exciting people, by thrilling them with the great issues, just as Isaac's sermons had thrilled the chapel congregation at Callington. "Democracy," he declared, "will never show much interest in a statistical abstract or a mutual admiration society . . . policies must be identified with persons, the persons reponsible."

In 1931, MacDonald's government collapsed, to be replaced by a National government headed by him. When the confusions of the 'Thirties began, Foot was still a Liberal. In the general election of 1931, the Liberals were divided three ways: the followers of Sir John Simon supported the National government, a handful of Lloyd George's followers stayed out, and the backers of Sir Herbert Samuel, who included Isaac Foot, joined the National government but took a firm stand in favour of Free Trade. The Labour party, fighting against MacDonald and his "National" supporters, was almost wiped out, standing against candidates who were part of the pact between MacDonald and the Conservatives. The total Labour vote fell from thirty-seven per cent to thirty per cent, but its number of seats dropped from 288 to a rump of fifty-two. The National government took 554 seats in the new House.

Young Dingle joined his father, having been elected for Dundee. He was appalled by what he found in his new constituency. "I used to go to the party offices — they were opposite a graveyard with seats in it. And the seats were always full with people doing nothing at all. They were permanently unemployed." Isaac was made Parliamentary Secretary in the Department of Mines. The Liberals opposed nationalisation of the coal industry, but Isaac's own warm sympathies had won him the nickname "The Member for the Depressed Areas". He devoted his ministerial lunchtimes to declamatory walks across St. James's Park to the Reform Club, to eat with the self-satisfied figure of Sir John Simon. His passion at the time was for Shelley's *Adonais*: "By dividing the poem into two, I could comfortably begin and complete the reading of fifty-five stanzas."

On going up to Oxford in 1931, Michael, though loyal still to his father's old party, found that most of his friends were socialists. One was Paul Reilly, son of the prominent left-wing architect Sir Charles Reilly, who ran the Liverpool School of Architecture. Both were reading PPE and, having a common interest in Indian nationalism, they belonged to the "Lotus Club", consisting of twenty-five Indians and twenty-five Britons; Foot also supported Krishna Menon's India League. One of their friends, Bhosu Karaka, became the first Indian president of the Union. Reilly became a distinguished design specialist, and was later ennobled; he wrote a warm congratulatory note to Foot in 1980.

Another Union friend and Labour Club luminary was Anthony Greenwood, who, according to his friends, spent most of his Oxford years chasing (and catching) girls. Reilly, with whom he shared digs, did too, with less success, but Michael, shy, dishevelled, with his eczema and his self-effacing manner, hardly chased them at all. Greenwood's father, Arthur, was a prominent Labour personality who had been Minister of Health under MacDonald, a convivial, self-taught, working-class intellectual. Tony Greenwood remained an affectionate friend of Foot, and together they fought several campaigns inside the Labour party, right into the 'Sixties.

But Foot's closest friend, a man who shared his pacifist ideals and then helped to push him finally into socialism, was John Cripps. Cripps was a strikingly intelligent youth: he left Oxford with a first-class degree, became a Quaker, edited the magazine *The Countryman* for twenty-four years, eventually headed the Countryside Commission and was knighted. His father, Sir Stafford Cripps, had been Solicitor-General under MacDonald and just managed to hold his Bristol seat for Labour in the disastrous 1931 election. Sir Stafford's father, as Lord Parmoor, had also been a Labour Cabinet minister, and his aunt was Beatrice Webb.

The family almost adopted Foot. John Cripps, who had left Winchester and hurled himself into street-corner electioneering for his father near the Bristol docks, threw himself with equal vigour into Oxford politics. He met Foot through the Union, and though his new friend was a Liberal, took him along to Labour Club meetings.

Even then, the Union had more of a whiff of Zuleika Dobson than of revolution. Foot spoke on the same side as Angus Maude, later a Tory Cabinet minister, at an Eights Week dinner in May 1933. Foot, who was Treasurer, and his fellow Union officials, decked out in white ties and evening dress, entertained their sisters and girlfriends with a menu of "Darne de Saumon Condorcet, Cotelettes d'Agneau Parisienne, Poulet de Printemps Roti au Cresson, Coupe Emma Calve and Scotch Woodcock". Distinguished speakers included the journalist Hannen Swaffer and Father Ronald Knox. The motion Foot and Maude were supporting was: "This House flatly declines to view anything with concern, alarm or apprehension."

This stylised undergraduate insouciance concealed the pace at which the university was heading leftwards. Hitler had come to power three months before that debate, and anti-fascism and unemployment were two of the most urgent topics which undergraduates debated in their long late-night coffee sessions. In Tony Greenwood's rooms a group of his friends founded the Communist October Club, named after the month of the Bolshevik Revolution. Foot and many others visited its meetings for a while, and it became the largest society in Oxford before the proctors closed it down. Foot attended the crowded Thursday morning lectures given by G. D. H. Cole, the architect of Guild Socialism, who also ran a high-toned and not especially lively Marxist study group.

This was the period when heavy underground recruitment to the Russian cause was going on among undergradutes. At Cambridge, Kim Philby, Anthony Blunt, Alan Nunn May, Donald Maclean and Guy Burgess were the nucleus of the notorious spy ring which penetrated the very centre of British intelligence. Burgess, full of charm and Etonian sparkle, made frequent reconnaissances to Oxford. He and Goronwy Rees, then a young fellow of All Souls, were both dinner guests of Maurice Bowra, a fellow of Foot's own college, Wadham, and with whom Foot was acquainted.

In the swirl of disaffection among the children of the British intellectual establishment, many became Communists, either covertly or overtly. There were striking parallels between the lives of Foot and Donald Maclean, one of the most notorious of all the Communist moles, and it is intriguing to see why the young Foot came down so fast and so firmly on the side of parliamentary democracy.

Maclean's father, like Isaac Foot, was a puritanical non-conformist solicitor, whose life was centred around God and the Liberal party. He belonged to the same Asquithian faction as Isaac and both became ministers in the 1931 MacDonald government, Maclean at Education, Foot at Mines. While they sat as sober-suited bureaucrats, dignified apostles of Free Trade and teetotalism, their sons were at Oxford and Cambridge denouncing the iniquities of the government both men served. They and their new friends thought the National government a mark of national moral collapse. Young Donald Maclean, who had been repressed in his youth by an over-weening and strict father, found himself contemptuous of old Sir Donald's political outlook. When he questioned it, he was met with a blast of stern self-righteousness. Isaac Foot, on the other hand, kept his sense of humour and was always willing to tolerate deviant creeds among his own children. So, while Donald Maclean was beginning his life as a clandestine traitor, Michael Foot was cheerfully joining the open and democratic party which he saw as the true inheritor of his father's Liberal philosophy. Foot did not read a word of Marx until his mid-twenties.

Not all undergraduates devoted themselves to politics. One man who was to become simultaneously a bitter Tory opponent and an admiring co-campaigner of Foot was sitting locked behind the double doors of his room in Trinity College, Cambridge. Enoch Powell rose before dawn every day, sat alone in front of his Greek literature, and went to bed at nine thirty prompt. He made no friends, even when he became a fellow.

Hugh Gaitskell, who was to become the longest-standing political enemy of Foot's career, was a young economics lecturer at the time, one of the circle clustered around G. D. H. Cole in the SSIP, the Society for Socialist Information and Propaganda. In Labour terms, Gaitskell was left-wing in those days, and in 1932 he was saying, "The Labour party must go straight out for socialism when it is returned to power." Gaitskell was in Vienna in 1934 when the Dollfuss fascist regime crushed the socialist party by setting up machine-guns and artillery in the streets, and opening fire on the workers' strongholds, such as they were, reducing the buildings to rubble and then hanging those party leaders who managed to escape. Gaitskell, who ran considerable risks as he smuggled in funds and smuggled out fleeing socialists, learned two lessons: an intense suspicion of revolutionary rhetoric, and a contempt for the tiny Communist party, which had spent its efforts in attacking the beleaguered socialists, and which was dogmatic, underhand and altogether worsened the situation. By coincidence Kim Philby was in Vienna at the same time, but he learned a different lesson; the bloody defeat of the socialists demonstrated that Stalin's contempt for them had always been right.

Back at Oxford, Foot was still a pacifist, his Quaker education perhaps reinforced by the attitudes of the new Labour leadership. George Lansbury, who led the rump Labour party in Parliament, was a seventy-five-year-old teetotaller. In 1933 he was asked what he would do if he became dictator: "I would close every recruiting station, disband the Army, dismantle the Navy and the Air Force. I would abolish the whole dreadful equipment of war, and say to the world, 'Do your worst.' I believe it would do its best. England would not become a third-class power as some people think. She would become the greatest, the strongest and the safest country in the world . . ."

In that same year, Foot and his fellow students at the Union passed, by a large majority, a motion that became notorious. It read: "This House would in no circumstances fight for King and Country." In 1934 Foot wrote that the resolution had

outraged diehard opinion throughout the country. But . . . it was the outward sign of a genuine pacifist movement that has been steadily growing in the University . . . a counter-demonstration was organised on Armistice Day as a protest against the military nature of the official remembrance service taking place at the War Memorial . . . It cannot be doubted that the student generation is supremely interested in the subject of peace, and that, in the main, its feeling is one of revolt against accepted ideas.

That winter, Foot mounted an all-party anti-Nazi demonstration at which Harry Pollitt, the boilermaker who led the British Communist party, was to speak. Foot also invited Bertrand Russell; one of his friends had just given him a copy of Russell's book *The Conquest of Happiness*, and it had impressed him greatly.

To Foot it was the "Liberal glow of the eighteenth-century enlightenment, which he translated into twentieth-century terms more intrepidly than anyone else."Russell did turn up at the University some time later, and the students were impressed to see that, as his book had promised, he did indeed look remarkably cheerful. He refused to come to the anti-Nazi meeting though, for reasons which showed him less naive than the young Foot. Russell wrote to him: "I can't speak with Pollitt. I was at an anti-fascist meeting in London when, after Ellen Wilkinson had shown implements of torture used by the Nazis, Pollitt made a speech saying 'we' would do all the same things to 'them' when 'our' turn came. One was forced to consider that if he had his way, he would be just as bad as they are."

Meanwhile, Isaac had ditched his own political career wih a stand on ancient Liberal principles. The 1932 Ottawa agreements ended Free Trade, so that he and the other Samuelites created yet another Liberal split by resigning from the government en masse, leaving behind a small gaggle of vengeful time-servers headed by Sir John Simon, Walter Runciman, and Leslie Hore-Belisha, the member for Plymouth Devonport. For the time being, Isaac could look after himself. He declaimed in London, "Free Trade did not fall in open battle. This Caesar did not fall in the long campaigns of Gaul and Spain, this Caesar did not go down on the stricken fields of Thapsus and Pharsalia. This Caesar fell by the stroke of the dagger of Casca Chamberlain and the sword-thrust of Cassius Simon and Brutus Runciman . . ."

Foot was finding the first of his many new political heroes — one who was already the visiting hero of the Oxford Labour

Club — the charming, immaculate and fiercely Marxist William Mellor, sometime editor of the *Daily Herald*. Mellor was a great friend of Tony Greenwood's father Arthur, he had enormous style and panache, and, unlike the retiring young Foot, knew precisely what he thought about most things. "He was a most attractive personality," Greenwood recalls. "Everything he did was done with the most tremendous air. He was a very clear thinker on a Marxist basis, and very kind. He dressed beautifully, and was frightfully good on food and drink. Michael was drawn to him." Foot thought of him as "the granite-like conscience of the Socialist League", granite being a substance of which the Foot family heartily approved. Another person attracted to Mellor was an abrasive redhead called Barbara Betts, though she had graduated before Foot began to attend the Labour Club, and they did not meet until both were living in London, when Foot himself was promptly smitten by her.

Inevitably Foot's political attitudes were being shaped and changed by the socialist friends who surrounded him. Cripps, Greenwood, Reilly and Foot spent their time talking, joking, punting, giving bottle parties — though Foot could still not drink — persuading young women to teach them the waltz, and doing a fair amount of hard work. (Foot and Dingle were both taught to dance at an academy run by Barbara Woodhouse, later to become famous as a TV dog-trainer.)

Foot was racked by his asthma. He gave up sharing digs with Cripps near a building site because he thought that the dust made the illness worse, and he moved uphill to Headington where the air was cleaner. His health seemed to improve a little. He even tried smoking herb cigarettes. There were none of the muscle relaxants which later eased life for asthma sufferers and the exhausting attacks continued. His eczema persisted too. He was one of those people whose clothes never seem to quite fit them. None of this prevented him from becoming a beautifully talented public speaker at the Union. He had pace, wit, rhythm and drive. He could be passionate and funny at the same time, and scarcely bothered to refer to notes. He had listened to enough sermons to have learned all the tricks. "I remember so well his marvellous pauses," Reilly says. "We all held our breath wondering 'what's coming next?'

And he had a withering wit." The student paper *Isis* found him "the most brilliant post-war figure in Oxford politics", not realising that the period they were living in was no longer post-was but pre-war.

In the vacations, Foot began to go to the village of Filkins in Gloucestershire, where the Cripps family lived in their seigneurial home of "Goodfellows". The Beaverbrook Press came to call Cripps the "Red Squire", and the family's style of life was not exactly close to the poverty-stricken unemployed for whom they worked so hard. Sir Stafford and his wife Isobel were thought by the neighbours to be class traitors, and their sons no longer played on the "Goodfellows" tennis court. But Foot and the younger Cripps played there, making sure that they did not beat Sir Stafford. At Filkins Foot met other Labour leaders — Lansbury the pacifist, Bevin the leader of the giant Transport Workers Union, Herbert Morrison and the terse, colourless Attlee. He spent holidays in the Isles of Scilly with Sir Stafford and the rest of the family; they were joined occasionally by Geoffrey Wilson, a Quaker who later headed Oxfam and the Race Relations Board. They stayed at Tregarthen's Hotel on St. Mary's, and Sir Stafford, who was a keen sailor and birdwatcher, would rent a boat. Cripps made no direct effort to convert the young Foot, except by example: he was vigorous, boyish, unselfconsciously certain that he knew all the political answers. Foot was impressed by so magnetic a figure, a man who could draw to him people such as Mellor and Bevan, a man who did not seem ineffectual, like Labour's feeble right-wing, or irrelevant, as the Liberals were coming to appear. Cripps's views were urgent, radical, boldly expressed. He was the leading figure in the Socialist League, which grew in 1932 out of Cole's old ginger group and the ILP politicians who wished to stay inside the Labour party. The League was not supposed to be a sect, but a legitimate organisation within the Labour party, fighting to convert it to a tough left-wing programme instead of the limp gradualism left behind by Ramsay MacDonald. Its popular appeal was non-existent, and at its height its membership did not rise above 3,000. It was regarded sullenly by Transport House as a disruptive body of middle-class intellectuals. It preached workers' control instead of Morrisonian nationalised corporations; co-operation with the Soviet Union and a General Strike against war, instead of reliance on the League of Nations, and above all it advocated what Mellor called "the will to Power".

This was not the Stafford Cripps who became famous in the 1945-51 Labour government as a Chancellor of the Exchequer of stern fiscal rectitude. In the 'Thirties he was regarded, as Hugh Dalton put it, as "a dangerous political lunatic". And his pre-war political career was certainly erratic, even reckless. Foot himself, putting the best face he could on the early Cripps, had to concede later that he was "a political innocent".

Cripps did not enter politics until he was forty-one, in 1930, by which time he was, partly through privilege and partly through talent and hard work, a rich man. His father, Alfred Cripps, was a successful lawyer and Tory MP, who then became a Labour Cabinet minister. Stafford was sent to Winchester, specialised in science, and threw up an Oxford scholarship at New College to work as a research assistant to Sir William Ramsay at University College, London. Finding this unsatisfying, he followed his father to the Bar, where he came to specialise in scientific and patent law, became the youngest KC in the country after only eight years' practice and earned an enormous income as a skilled cross-examiner of technical experts.

He was religious, idealistic and ascetic. When Morrison first tried to persuade him to become a Labour politician, he retorted, "I don't want to enter politics. I am more interested in the Church." He gave much of his money away, employed the workless labourers of Filkins to build cottages, extensions to "Goodfellows", a community centre with hot baths, a surgery, swimming pool and bowling green. He donated to refugees from the Nazis and to Spanish Republicans. He gave huge sums to the Socialist League and the paper it was eventually to found — a temporary campaigning sheet which finally broke away from its puppet-master Cripps to lead a bawling life of its own, but continued under its name of *Tribune*.

His generosity did not save him from Beaverbrook's inimitably mischievous attacks in the *Daily Express*:

The apostle of Socialism in our Time enforced with

machine guns lives in an old farm-house converted into a large country mansion of 30 or 40 rooms. In front of it, screening it from the common gaze, a row of weeping willows, a trout stream, a golf course, tennis courts, gardens of flowers, gardens of luxury fruit of the table, ornamental water, even yew hedges — all tended by three gardeners. Such is "Goodfellows", home of the Red Squire.

Foot himself, in one of his last appearances as a young Liberal, struck a slightly priggish note about the Red Squire's rashness. While Foot and his fellows were refusing to fight for King and Country, Cripps, Cole and the others on the left infuriated Walter Citrine, general secretary of the TUC, and the rest of the official leadership, by advocating what looked to the public like a kind of dictatorship. Since the 1931 crisis had shown that capitalists would always sabotage socialist legislation, Labour had to declare an unequivocally socialist policy to the electorate, ask the King to consent to the abolition of the House of Lords, pass an Emergency Powers Act, and proceed to nationalise the banks. Cripps made a further speech about the need "to overcome opposition from Buckingham Palace". This brought even more anathemas from Fleet Street on his head than a similar remark would do today.

Foot was commissioned by Aylmer Vallance, editor of the *News Chronicle*, to write one of four lengthy articles on the politics of the young generation (which appeared to consist exclusively of Oxford undergraduates). Foot's contribution, which appeared on April 4th, 1934, was accompanied by an unflattering picture of a myopic youth with round spectacles, wavy hair, ears which stuck out and wearing a striped shirt. It was superimposed on a bust of Gladstone, and the article was headed "Why I Am A Liberal".

Outlining some rather hazy proposals, Foot went on, in the only criticism he could summon up of the Labour party:

> All this can be done without the extension of the statutory limit of five years [of the life of a Parliament] and the suppression of criticism, measures which seem to commend themselves to Mr. G. D. H. Cole and the intelligentsia of the socialist movement. Like a famous lawyer of the eighteenth

century, they seem willing to sacrifice a part — if necessary the whole — of the Constitution in order to preserve the remainder.

Foot criticised Rothermere and Churchill, and complained of fascist sympathies among the Tories. He requested a programme of reconstruction for Britain similar to Roosevelt's New Deal in the US. He wrote: "I am a Liberal because I believe it is Liberalism in its more radical moods which has established the social and democratic institutions which this country already enjoys." Liberalism, he thought, offered the best hope of full-hearted support for a resurrected League of Nations and the prospect of fruitful alliances with the US and the Soviet Union: "I am a Liberal, first of all, because of the unfaltering resistance which liberalism is pledged to offer to those twin dangers of fascism and war."

In his 1962 biography of Bevan, Foot attacked the contemporary "mean falsifications" about Cripps in the 'Thirties. He pointed out that people (including, on the evidence, himself in 1934) did not give the proper weight to his "faculty to stir great masses by his burning sincerity combined with an even more evident capacity to subdue other assemblies by sheer intellectual power . . . no one did more in those dismal years after 1931, to revive the fighting spirit of Labour." Cripps's call for Emergency Powers, he said, was a formidable case which had never been answered, and Labour's sweeping victory in 1945 — when it did not have to face capitalist reprisals — was in "entirely unforeseen and exceptional circumstances". He quoted R. H. Tawney, who wrote, also in 1934, that "onions can be eaten leaf by leaf, but you cannot skin a tiger paw by paw". He had made amends for criticising Sir Stafford at the time. Within eighteen months he himself had joined the Labour left, and had become the co-author of a book with Sir Stafford Cripps.

4

SIR STAFFORD'S DISCIPLE

Foot came down from Oxford with a second-class degree, as good as his three brothers. Friends such as Greenwood were clearly committed to a life in party politics, but no one can remember Foot considering the idea. There seemed little point in wanting to become a Liberal MP when the Liberals were plainly disintegrating, even if Dingle had by now been an MP for three years, and John was fighting his by-election at Basingstoke. He had no wish to go into the family firm like John, nor to become a barrister like Dingle. Nicholas Gillett, his old friend from Leighton Park, knowing how bookish Foot was, asked why he didn't become a don. "No," Foot replied, "I want the real world." He thought vaguely about becoming a journalist.

His first by-line had appeared over his *News Chronicle* article "Why I Am A Liberal". Since at that stage he did not really know the answer, it was not surprising that it should be a tame piece of work, despite Aylmer Vallance's efforts to bill it well: "THE NEW GENERATION SPEAKS . . . Four young men, representative of their generation, just emerging from the universities to reveal their political creeds . . . the outlook of youth is always the one exciting thing in the world."

Foot's whistling in the political dark did have one consequence. Krishna Menon asked Foot and the three other contributors — a Tory acquaintance from the Union, Keith Steel-Maitland, Frank Hardie the socialist, and Dick Freeman from the Communist October Club — to produce a full-scale book to be called *Young Oxford and War*. Foot wrote a 12,000-word essay about pacifism, powerfully thought out and showing his Quaker influences. The book is now one of the four he has part written which he does not list in *Who's Who*; the others are *The Struggle For Peace*, which he devilled for

52

Stafford Cripps in 1936, a pamphlet supporting the Labour government in 1948 co-written with a Tribune MP, Donald Bruce, entitled *Who Are The Patriots?*, and an uncritical pre-election picture biography of Harold Wilson written in 1964.

Young Oxford and War is an intriguing corrective for anyone who doubts the origins and sincerity of Foot's opposition to all arms races, and his support for unilateral disarmament. This came long before the invention of nuclear weapons. Trying to analyse the varieties of pacifism, Foot avoided blaming war on capitalism, as many of his future Marxist comrades were doing. Theoretically, he wrote, capitalism was an international force, and it was nationalism that caused wars. Communism did nothing to curb nationalist feelings.

Socialism only becomes an international ideal when the world state is achieved, production and consumption is planned from a world centre. Otherwise it looks inward, rather than outward, and sets up a national economy which every true protectionist should envy. Russia is a powerful national state and has indulged in nationalist policies with the rest of the world.

He objected to the idea of the violent overthrow of capitalism:

A class war, like a world war, would involve the call upon the individual to mutilate and destroy those with whom he has no personal quarrel . . . it would play into the hands of potential Fascists. The possession of the Air Force by the upper-classes would provide them with a more powerful weapon than they have ever had hitherto. No socialist would doubt that they would scruple to use it.

The revulsion against modern weapons was as great in 1934 as it was in 1957 after the H-bomb tests. People could not forget Stanley Baldwin's warning, in 1932, of the horrors of modern war: "The bomber will always get through. It is well also for the man in the street to realise that there is no power on earth that can protect him from being bombed."

Taking some passing swipes at the Church of England and

the Officers' Training Corps in public schools, quoting Burke and Bertrand Russell on the way, Foot declared that the outright pacifist Quaker position was the right one. Pacifism, he said, worked. "Gandhi in India is accomplishing by pacifist means what he could scarcely hope to achieve by force of arms." Optimistically he claimed that the contemporary resistance to Hitler by the evangelical church was preventing him from setting up a totalitarian state. "Clearly pacifism implies unilateral disarmament," he went on, quoting the Quaker statement, "The only true safety is the safety of all, and unless your weapon of defence achieves this work, or works towards this, it is a source of antagonism and therefore of increased peril." He concluded: "The policy of unilateral disarmament has won little support outside the most extreme pacifist circles. Yet . . . unilateral disarmament offers the only way of escape once the policy of collateral disarmament has failed."

Besides his first book, 1934 offered Foot other excitements. He had reached the age of twenty-one without having touched a drop of liquor, or smoked a cigarette (apart from the herbal ones he used for his asthma). He could now travel the world and spend the £50 prize for abstemiousness from his family on the autumn debating trip organised for him and John Cripps through the Oxford Union. But, before that, Foot decided to find out what he had been missing. He went to Paris with his older brother John for a celebratory binge. John introduced him to drink and he liked it, though it was not until the Beaverbrook days, when he had reached his mid-twenties, that he discovered how magically a little off-duty carousing could make his shyness disappear.

From Paris he headed east, to see his other older brother Hugh, in Palestine. Five years before, Hugh had arrived with some vague ideas of adventure. He spent the next nine years constantly embroiled in riots. The coarsely healthy members of his rowing club frequently went into the colonial service in the 'Thirties: the other undergraduates called it "the Blues governing the blacks". Hugh rapidly learned that what was going on was a far cry from his mother and father's stout nonconformist principles about privilege and injustice. The British had sold the same pup twice in Palestine during the

First World War, promising independence to the Arab inhabitants and, with the 1917 Balfour Declaration, a "Jewish National Home" as well. The Palestine Mandate was a long, drawn-out and ignoble failure.

Hugh's first posting came as the indigenous Arabs were rising in rebellion against what they saw as a Jewish take-over. He was by then in charge of the district of Samaria, a little Solomon ruling over 300 Arab villages and a handful of Jewish settlements. When Michael arrived at Trieste to embark for Nablus, Hitler's persecution had turned the trickle of Jewish immigrants into a terrified tide. Foot was overwhelmed by their plight and by their fervour as, the only Gentile on board, he steamed across the Mediterranean for four days. (He found one man to play chess with, and lost every time.) When he arrived and met Hugh he saw the other side of the coin. The Arabs bitterly resented the newcomers, and went on strike, demonstrated, spread rumours that armed resistance was about to begin. It was a sobering experience, and Foot's first acquaintance with the depths of international hatreds.

He left Hugh before Palestine went up in flames and headed for Beirut, where he bought a fourth-class ticket for a boat to Athens. He wanted to see the Acropolis: "The boat was crawling with beetles," he says. "I spent the whole journey trying to avoid them by lying on the deck." He took his first plane trip, north to Salonika, then a boat to Turkey and from there a train to Budapest. It was a modern version of the Grand Tour. Meanwhile, his friend Cripps had gone to Russia with his great-uncle, Sidney Webb, for a round of briefings with Soviet officials, who were quietly amused at his naïveté.

Foot had been reading throughout his travels, mainly socialist books by Arnold Bennett, George Bernard Shaw, and H. G. Wells. The most exciting of the lot was Wells's *Tono Bungay*. "I had devoured *Kipps* and *Mr. Polly* and *Marriage* and all the rest," he says, "and when it came to *Tono Bungay* I rationed the reading to twenty pages a day so that paradise should not come to an end too abruptly."

Cripps and Foot rejoined forces in England and boarded the *Aquitania* to cross the Atlantic for their debating tour. These tours were hectic affairs, bucketing on trains from one college to another, from New England to Virginia, delivering a speech and collapsing into the bunk in another college dormitory. Though this trip helped kill any crude anti-Americanism of which some socialists were then guilty, these jamborees made no great impact on the graduates — they were the quintessential "if this is Thursday, it must be Boston" experiences. The American collegians were extremely solemn. They marshalled card-indexed "arguments" one after another, being awarded points for doing so. The Oxford visitors always shocked their audience with their flippancy. Foot and Cripps were also shocking in another respect: as representatives of the notorious King and Country generation, a motion they had to re-debate dozens of times, they were regarded with appalled excitement. Their other standard motion was even more daringly iconoclastic: "Free Trade Unions are essential in a civilised society."

Foot returned home to find a job. Unemployed graduates at the height of the Depression were ten a penny and there was no systematic way for someone such as Foot to get into journalism. A few years earlier, for example, Tom Driberg, then one of the two members of Oxford's Communist Party (A. J. P. Taylor was briefly the other), was working as a dish-washer in a Soho cafe until Edith Sitwell persuaded Beverley Baxter, managing editor of Beaverbrook's *Daily Express*, to give him a job. Driberg had just become "William Hickey", writing a gossip column full of sharp social criticism and florid neologisms such as "Cinemagnate". Foot's influential contacts were not the Sitwells but the Cripps family, and Sir Stafford wanted to help him. The job he found him might almost have been calculated to push Foot into outright socialism. Sir Stafford's brother, Leonard, was a director of Alfred Holt's merchant shipping company, the Blue Funnel line, which traded with South Africa and the Far East out of Liverpool, a port filled with Irish immigrants, many of them unemployed. This did not perturb Leonard, who believed in the mysterious glories of the market forces around him. "He was an ultra-capitalist," says John Cripps, "a characteristic Liverpool ship-owner who was an outrageous, fanatical, Cobdenite free-trader." Leonard agreed to take his brother's young friend on as a personal assistant in Liverpool.

His father's preoccupation with free trade looked strange when Foot took the train to Merseyside and discovered, as

Dingle had done in Dundee, the rawness of life on the dole. He was outraged by what he saw in Liverpool and he hated working for Leonard Cripps. Forty-six years later, moments after he had been elected Leader of the Labour party, he immediately announced that he would lead a huge demonstration against unemployment in Liverpool. "I first joined the Labour party in Liverpool," he told his first press conference as leader, "because of what I saw of the poverty, the unemployment, and the endless infamies committed on the inhabitants of the back-streets of that city." He swiftly joined the Liverpool Labour party, and would spend his Saturday nights at their meetings. This was the Liverpool of Bessie Braddock and Sydney Silverman, a political world quite unlike anything he had known in the West Country. The Tories of Liverpool were almost all Protestants, and the Labour councillors were nearly all Catholics of Irish descent, with a fringe of atheists. Foot helped to set up a distressed areas group which met in London, and through that committee met Ellen Wilkinson, who was to organise the Jarrow March from her constituency, and Jennie Lee, the ILP member for North Lanark. That autumn Jennie agreed to marry Nye Bevan, after her long and passionate affair with Frank Wise, chairman of the Socialist League, ended with his sudden death in 1933. Brilliant, magnetic, belligerent, never at a loss for words, exuberant about his visits to the Beaverbrook dinner table, full of bitter yet brilliantly coloured memories of his youth in the Welsh coalfields, Bevan was almost hypnotically attractive, though even Jennie Lee wondered at first if he were not too clever by half: 'Ni is quick-silver," she wrote after Wise's heart attack. "He is as unreliable as Frank is reliable. He is moody, self-indulgent, but in a curious way he is a brother to me. Our mining background, our outlooks, hopes and despairs are most similar."

Later she told Foot, "Going around with Ni [the way she always spelled it] in those days when we still hardly knew one another was at times like surf riding on Niagara Falls. You had to be agile, or you would be drowned in the tireless sparkling movement and ebullience."

Foot himself plunged his head under the foam with hero-worshipping ardour. Bevan, then aged thirty-seven, was conducting a weary line-by-line parliamentary war against the National government's Insurance Bill. The dole queues by this time were a fixture in the British landscape. Bevan objected to the proposed "Unemployment Assistance Board", because the hated household means test was to remain. This meant that if a sister got a job, then her brother in the same house had his benefit cut. Sons were expected to keep their unemployed fathers. Bevan lectured the stony faces in front of him on the government benches: "Around the meagre tables of the poor, hells of acrimony arise," he said. "The only way for a man to protest will be to throw a brick through the window . . . you want to suffocate the poor man's cries in a maze of bureaucracy." Typically, Bevan also found himself at odds with trade union bureaucracy, which became irritated as Bevan attacked the clauses in the Bill they approved, confining the right of appeal to union members. This trick was devised to cut out the Communist-dominated Unemployed Workers' Movement, for which Bevan had a soft spot, as the big official unions were failing to champion the hunger-marchers and the jobless.

One night, after a long debate on the Bill, Foot met Bevan for the first time. Bevan was angry with the newspapers for what he thought was inadequate reporting of the committee stages of the Bill in which he was so immersed. As he railed on, Foot shyly tried to make a case for his own journalistic heroes — Swift, Cobbett, the socialist popular educator Robert Blatchford, and his newest discovery, Hazlitt. Bevan swept aside these sacred names as irrelevancies, berating (in Foot's words), "the vulgar cacophony preferred by the popular press". Soon Bevan had become the greatest hero Foot had ever had. "Thereafter I knew him as well as almost anybody else for the rest of his life. He was never a hero-worshipper; but I was."

There was a reason why Foot had suddenly taken to reading Hazlitt. He had just broken the news to Isaac and Eva that their fourth son had become a defector. Isaac, who had seen it coming, said firmly, "If you're going to be a socialist, then you had better read Hazlitt." It was good advice; Foot found a profound influence in the radical essayist and his sinewy English prose. It gave him an approach to radicalism which would outlast any study of Marx. Hazlitt had the approval of his father, he was an excellent prose craftsman and a romantically idealistic social reformer who was also anxious to be a hard-headed realist. For Foot this combination of qualities was unsurpassed. In his late sixties he is still, even increasingly, obsessed by Hazlitt. Writing in 1980, he said that for the left to give a convincing answer to the powerful right-wing intellect of Burke,

> a tougher fibre was needed, a creed of human freedom more firmly founded on the rock . . . He accepted to the full the reformers' doctrine that "men do not become what by nature they are meant to be, but what society makes them". And society could be transformed; the French Revolution looked like romance in action. But the deed would not be done by utopians who would never soil their hands, nor by an arid appeal to reason alone, nor by the economists and utilitarians who inherited the tattered mantle of the revolutionaries . . . he was an idealist who knew that present enemies must be fought here and now, tooth and nail, on their own ground; . . . he took his politics around with him like a giant mastiff, and love me, love my dog, was his motto.

Looking back, Foot still clings passionately to those attitudes he was discovering as a young man. The Hazlitt quotation to which he gives absolute pride of place makes a good motto for the way Foot would like to have lived his own life since becoming a socialist in 1934: "Happy are they who live in the dream of their own existence, and see all things in the light of their own minds; who walk by faith and hope; to whom the guiding star of their youth still shines from afar, and into whom the spirit of the world has not entered. They have not been 'hurt by the archers', nor has the iron entered their souls. The world has no hand on them."

Foot's mother, Eva, was more upset by her son becoming a socialist. She confessed to the Truro Women's Liberal Association in March 1935 that one of her sons had joined the Labour party. "I think he is grievously mistaken," she said, "but I believe he is entirely honest and sincere."

While Foot had been in Liverpool, an ambitious Tory of twenty-seven called Peter Howard was poking fun at the

Liberals in Beaverbrook's *Sunday Express*. Howard wrote the Crossbencher column and delighted in affronting the sensitivities of MPs. He attacked Isaac Foot in a mock parliamentary school report: "Nancy Astor has struck up a friendship with Isaac Foot (Foot Major). She will be sad when Isaac leaves. And I fear he will not be with us next term. They use all their influence in school against drinking, smoking and betting. Their influence is not great." By the autumn of 1935, Howard was needling again:

> We stand a fine chance of losing both the Liberal Foots. Dingle is sure to go and Isaac stands a first-rate chance of defeat. Isaac Foot, the member for Bodmin, is fifty-five years old, grey-haired and severe. He is the leading pussy-foot [Prohibitionist] of Westminster. His thirty-year-old son Dingle, the member for Dundee, is like his father in appearance and manner. Dry as dust the pair of them. Without the Feet, I think the next Parliament should be able to move forward a great deal faster.

Ironically Isaac's own son Michael was to join Beaverbrook and later collaborate with the noxious Howard himself on one of the most notorious pamphlets of the war. But Isaac was never one to bear a grudge, and in the 'Forties used to make jovial remarks about Beaverbrook and "the House of Rimmon".

The general election of 1935 was held in the shadow of the Italy–Abyssinia dispute. Lansbury the pacifist was driven from office before the election, finding sanctions against Italy impossible to live with, and Bevin marked his resignation with a famous conference speech in which he accused the wretched ex-leader of "taking your conscience round from body to body, asking to be told what you ought to do with it". Cripps denounced sanctions as a capitalist plot, and resigned from the NEC, arguing that "our enemy is here". Amid the intellectual confusion on the left, Baldwin simply stole Labour's new clothes by announcing that the government stood foursquare behind the League of Nations and its threat of sanctions against Italy. Labour had little to offer to atone for the fiasco of 1931.

For Isaac Foot, the issues were more immediate. In Bodmin, the Tory brewers poured in money and motor-cars to help unseat the hated "pussyfoot". Most treacherous of all, Simon, Runciman and Hore-Belisha, the three National government time-servers, signed an appeal asking all true Liberals to vote against Isaac Foot; "scurvy treatment", his son called it. Isaac lost the seat.

Foot had been in Liverpool for a year. As soon as the election was announced he caught a train to London and went to Transport House. Were there any seats he could fight, even at such short notice? It happened that there had been a split with the candidate at one hopeless seat, Monmouth. The Reverend Daniel Hughes had withdrawn and the local party in Newport had no cash and little organisation. Major J. A. Herbert, the Tory, was sitting on a 9,000 majority which he had won at a by-election the previous year. (He eventually became Governor of Bengal.) Monmouth had never been Labour or even Liberal since the last century. Tom Powell, the Labour agent, was trying to put on a brave face to the local paper: "We are determined to fight, and will have a candidate in the field."

Foot's arrival cheered him up considerably. He was, Powell told the world, only twenty-two, the son of a well-known Liberal MP, the youngest president of the Oxford Union on record, and "one of the coming men in the Labour party".

In 1935 Foot was still one of those people whom he would describe contemptuously later in his 1940 pamphlet *Guilty Men* as "permeated with severe drenchings of pacifism". He supported economic sanctions against Mussolini, but only just. And rearmament by the brutish Tories he regarded with great suspicion. "The two fundamental problems of the country are peace and poverty," he told his adoption meeting at Newport. "I am a socialist because only socialism can deal adequately with those problems." Looking at the history of capitalism, he told his supporters, one saw the slums it had built and the effect it had on the poor. The community, he said, "must control the means of production".

But even more important than the iniquities of capitalism was the question of peace. Baldwin was looking for a mandate to rearm: "The National government is not really concerned with maintaining the system of law, but builds up national armaments because they believe it can bring security.

"I am firmly not in favour of military sanctions against Italy or any other country. It will lead to a first-class war. I am in favour of economic sanctions, provided they do not lead to war." The only way to tackle fascism was "by maintaining a strong, vigilant and powerful Labour party". This was perhaps arguable, but his peroration was unquestionable. "The National government serves the interests of the big landlords, industrialists, financiers, bankers and brewers. It means continual suffering and possibly war for the working people of this country."

Foot spent the campaign at a series of fairly disorganised meetings around the constituency, banging the drum for the miners, and for the unemployed, against Baldwin's duplicity in calling the election. Sir Stafford Cripps came to speak for him, and Foot won his audiences, though the hastily organised campaign meetings seemed to keep going wrong. An enthusiastic audience turned up at nine p.m. to hear him in Chepstow, but he failed to arrive until half past ten, when virtually everyone had gone home. On the eve-of-poll he managed to address a crowd of several hundred in the Newport produce market. But by the time he had finished it was again ten thirty, and too late to reach the second meeting at Monmouth.

The Conservatives barely bothered to argue about politics or policies. They engaged in a few routine ploys. Major Herbert announced that he would refuse to speak on the Sabbath or on Armistice Day, so demonstrating his patriotic and religious sentiments. The Tory national agent, Major I. C. Vincent, pointed out that Foot was just a young whipper-snapper: "What can a person of such youthful years know about things that matter? What does he know of agriculture, or the crisis of 1918!" Mr. Horace T. Bailey of "The Willows" wrote to the local paper to describe Foot as a "carpet-bagger", "an enterprising young man desirous of getting into Parliament and securing the necessary training for the purpose". Major Herbert held his seat, and so did Stanley Baldwin, who became Prime Minister, although the number of Labour seats rose to 158. It was 1966 before Labour was to win Monmouth.

Isaac Foot, out of Parliament, never returned. Only Dingle

represented the family in the House, and there was not to be
another general election for ten years. Isaac hired halls in
Plymouth, where the traitor Hore-Belisha sat for Devonport,
and in the constituencies of the infamous Simon and
Runciman, and denounced the trio to their electors. In
Devonport Guildhall he smote Hore-Belisha with a curse
drawn from a surprising literary favourite, Lord Alfred
Douglas:

> And when all men shall sing his praise to me,
> I'll not gainsay. But I shall know his soul
> Lies in the bosom of Iscariot.

Michael did not return to Liverpool. Sir Stafford was talking vaguely about starting a full-scale socialist newspaper,
which Foot might join, so he installed himself in London, flung
himself into the soap-box life of the Socialist League, and
persuaded Kingsley Martin, editor of the *New Statesman*, to
give him a temporary job where he could pick up journalistic
experience. Every Thursday night he spent with Allen Hutt of
the *Daily Worker*, an expert in typography. Martin, for all his
intellectual waywardness, had the great journalistic gift of
being able to catch the contemporary wind in his sails and
plunge forward with its gusts. Foot watched him on press days
at Great Turnstile, "staving off Armageddon one week, noting
the collapse of the Heavens the next". He called him a
"political yellow-press man". Foot admired his headline sense
of news and his "week-by-week exploration of the moral and
intellectual conflicts confronting the active left-wing section of
the British people, who hated war and fascism, without knowing which they hated the more or how best to stop either."

One of Martin's bigger mistakes was that he did not discern
Foot's future as a journalist. "I tried him out on the clear
understanding that he would like the experience and we should
not keep him unless he was brilliantly successful," Martin told
a colleague. "He's a good fellow, and not a bad journalist —
but not A-plus." Foot left and was succeeded by Richard
Crossman. Deprived of even the £250 a year Martin paid,
Foot entered the only period of his life when he was actually
poor.

It was also the period of his first love. The shy, buttoned-up asthmatic, his hands and face so scaly with eczema that one landlady hastily told him she had no vacancies, nevertheless had qualities which made him appealing to women, especially slightly older women. He was gentle, genuine, romantic, devoted, enthusiastic and unpretentious, an admirer of women rather than a lady-killer. The Socialist League brought him into the orbit of the devastating redhead who had left Oxford the year before him, the clever, abrasive, endlessly talkative Barbara Betts from Bradford, another of Cripps's disciples. She was eventually to marry the journalist Ted Castle, and as Barbara Castle became one of Foot's longest-lasting post-war colleagues on the left. In the "Guildford Street days", as their friends later thought of them, Foot and Barbara Betts would share cheap meals together — dinner at Chez Victor cost two shillings and sixpence — or would go back to Barbara's tiny Bloomsbury attic where she would cook something cheap but tasty. It was completely platonic. He was not the lifetime's partner she was waiting for, and he must have found her in some ways rather alarming, even domineering. This did not rule out — at least at first — a doglike devotion. They went away on weekends, walking across the hills talking endlessly about politics and books. Once they went to France, and asked *la patronne* for separate rooms. She gave them a knowing smile and thoughtfully provided rooms with a connecting door. Michael spent the night wheezing with a terrible attack of asthma; Barbara Betts, trying to sleep next door, anxiously rushed in, clad in a nightdress, as she heard his struggles for breath mount in an alarming crescendo.

Back in Guilford Street they would sit together on either side of the fire, like an old married couple, or in summer sunbathe on the Bloomsbury rooftop, each with a book, enthusiastically reading out passages to each other. Barbara conceived a great love for Dickens. They read *Das Kapital* page by page, the first time that Foot had read Marx. Teased by her about his "Why I Am A Liberal" essay, he read all the more keenly. Another crucial work for him at this time was *The Coming Struggle for Power*, the classic Marxist work by John Strachey, the former Mosleyite and former Communist who became War Minister under Attlee. (Foot was later to risk bankruptcy to defend Strachey's reputation in a libel action.)

Foot and Barbara went down to "Goodfellows" for political weekends with Cripps — they made conspiratorially cheeky remarks about him behind the Red Squire's back and irreverently outplayed him on the tennis court. They would take the tiny Austin 7 belonging to the Socialist League and set up a "mobile platform", a portable soap-box, at street-corner meetings in Mornington Crescent, or as far away as Wales. Foot used to visit Hyde Park for the other orators (his mother had urged him to go on Sundays to hear the Methodist Donald Soper, who was also a socialist). On those spring afternoons he would listen to Ben Tillett, Tom Mann, Jimmy Maxton of the ILP, and the famous anarchic actor and *littérateur*, Bonar Thompson, a working-class Ulsterman of whom Foot later wrote a charming short tribute in his 1980 collection, *Debts of Honour*. Foot listened entranced as Thompson explained why he had refused to join the Army because he had not been approached in the right manner. He warned his listeners against plain-clothes policemen. " 'By their boots ye shall know them', Bonar would gravely announce from the platform, and the whole audience would automatically look down at their feet, and at their neighbours' feet too, much to the embarrassment of the few plain-clothes spectators who naturally preferred his platform to all others."

Foot and his friends went to Mosley's New Party meetings, with their nauseating anti-semitism. Paul Reilly was with him once at the Albert Hall. They sat high in the gallery, Reilly whispering that this was the kind of rally, with its mass demagogy, he had seen in Hitler's Germany. Reilly recalls: "They were grim days. Michael was shouting, barracking Mosley from the gallery. People were being flung bodily downstairs, and we were both immediately pounced on by black-shirted stewards. They were toughs who pinned us to our chairs and ordered Michael: 'You will hear our leader out in silence'."

Sir Stafford Cripps now wrote, for Victor Gollancz's new Left Book Club, a tome called *The Struggle for Peace*. Foot helped him and it made a curious production, reflecting his undigested Marxism and his role as Cripps's acolyte. "For the convenience of readers," the foreword said solemnly, "this book has been divided into two parts. The first part contains the main text written by Sir Stafford Cripps, the second consists of notes upon that text written by Michael Foot."

Foot's contribution to the book was 4,000 words of detailed facts, figures and quotations, on the arms race, the League of Nations, the number of tractors used in the Canadian wheat fields, and forced labour in the African colonies. He had been reading the Communist theoretician Palme-Dutt, and the "knight-errant of socialism" as Foot thought of Noel Brailsford, whom he had just met in the Socialist League. Brailsford is another early hero later enrolled in *Debts of Honour* as a champion of women's rights ("Brailsford would not look upon any scene in our history without asking what the women were doing"); as a rediscoverer of the left-wing Levellers in Cromwell's army, and as an outraged supporter of all oppressed humanity. One of the greatest Marxist revelations, said Foot, was Brailsford's aphorism "Property Must Go Armed".

Another author approvingly quoted in 1936 did not survive into the later roll of honour: "Colonial peoples in revolt must be looked upon by a socialist movement in Britain as allies in the fight against the common enemy. This theory is fully developed in Stalin's *Marxism and the National Question*. The methods by which the Soviet government has dealt with colonial peoples reveal a real basis for co-operation with so-called backward peoples."

The Spanish Civil War began in 1936. To Foot, "It cut the knot of emotional and intellectual contradictions in which the left had been tangled ever since Hitler came to power. Suddenly the claims of international law, class solidarity and the desire to win the Soviet Union as an ally fitted into the same strategy." The war moved thousands of young men and women to passion and outrage. As Munich approached, the Tory government was if anything on the side of Franco, and the official Labour leadership under Attlee ambivalent. After the 1936 Labour Party Conference in Edinburgh, Cripps, bitterly upset by the attitude to Spain demonstrated there, swung the Socialist League into what was supposed to be a working-class umbrella group against the Tories and others — the rebellious Unity Campaign, linking the League with the

ILP and Harry Pollitt's (or Moscow's) Communist party. Foot saw it later as "the most ambitious bid made by the British left throughout the whole period of the 'Thirties to break the stultifying rigidity of party alignments". Later he wrote of the show trials: "How deeply the left craved to give the benefit of all the doubts to Moscow! No one who did not live through that period can quite appreciate how overwhelming that craving was."

The Unity Campaign was a fiasco. It was denounced by Transport House, and one of its few concrete effects was to destroy the Socialist League itself. But first, it gave birth to *Tribune*, later to become the house journal of the Labour left, and a magazine dominated almost throughout its forty-odd years by Michael Foot. Cripps put up £12,000 (from his monstrous legal income) and George Strauss £6,000. William Mellor was made editor, and Barbara Betts, by then on the League executive, worked for him in a close and admiring relationship. "She doted on him," says one of their colleagues. Foot joined the staff with her, and admired Mellor just as much. One of his tasks was to collect parliamentary sketches from a toiling and dishevelled Nye Bevan. "The Labour party has too much *reverence*," Bevan snorted over the abdication crisis. Mellor wrote the first ringing editorial: "It is capitalism that is piling up vast armaments now for the war whose shadow bestrides all our lives . . . the defeat of capitalism depends on the unity of the working-class." Foot and Barbara Betts wrote an industrial column together, as "Judex", partly about industrial disputes, partly about the need for the TUC to provide a strategy for the Labour movement. The unions were notoriously shy of strikes, spending much of the Depression in retreat. The 1937 "Coronation" busmen's strike was defeated. Quixotically, Foot took on the Labour nomination for the hopeless seat of Plymouth Devonport: his own home town.

Foot went on a trip to Finland with his brother Dingle in 1937, and while there they crossed the border for a couple of days to visit Leningrad. This is still the only occasion Foot has visited Russia. By the time the Cold War was under way, around 1948, he was strongly anti-Stalinist.

Within months, the Unity Campaign, which had always

threatened to break into its constituent parts, was crushed. Transport House disaffiliated the Socialist League, which decided to disband, with Barbara Betts telling a heated ten-hour meeting that this was "not a funeral, but a conscious political tactic". It led to the first great political crisis of the young Foot's life, and demonstrated vividly his personal loyalty to all those to whom he has given his friendship. He broke with the League and quit his job in support of Mellor.

Mellor had a raw puritan cantankerousness which often made him hard to bear; he and Bevan never really hit it off. Bevan would turn up late at board meetings, and deliver airy harangues which left Mellor growling. The paper had got nowhere near its planned 50,000 circulation and was losing money at a ruinous rate. On top of this, Cripps wanted to switch *Tribune*, already derisively known as "Cripps's Chronicle", to another line which the Communist party was peddling, and which had some grass-roots support because of Spain: a Popular Front, not of just left-wing organisations, but of all anti-Chamberlain political groups. Transport House's reply to this particular heresy was to throw Cripps, Bevan and George Strauss out of the party in 1939. Cripps spent the whole of the war without the Labour whip, although he was a prominent member of Churchill's own version of the Popular Front. Foot again took the lesson that it was generally the rebels in the Labour party who got issues right.

Mellor disagreed with the Popular Front, and truculently dug in his heels. Cripps, having gone on a tour of Jamaica, left Bevan to confront the bear in his den, and to fire him on the spot. Until then Foot had been campaigning for Arms for Spain, and peacefully churning out indigestible articles on behalf of the workers. One example conveys the flavour: "During the last four years, the number of workers in employment have increased by 16.6 per cent. During the same period the Board of Trade index of production has increased by 38.3 per cent. Output per worker therefore since 1932 has increased by 18 per cent. Since that date real wages have improved by only one per cent . . ."

Having arranged Mellor's sacking, Cripps offered Foot, his young protégé, the editor's chair. Foot, disgusted at the shoddy way Mellor had been treated, not only refused, but resigned himself. He had learned from his father never to hesitate on questions of principle. (Isaac, outside Parliament, was conducting a staunch campaign against Munich and appeasement, and even fought a hopeless by-election in St. Ives. Eva told John, "You boys aren't a patch on your father.") Brailsford gave Foot an important friendly warning about the "Liberal non-conformist tradition: one may . . . forget that to run a good paper matters more than to perform prodigies of conscience".

It was Bevan who bailed out Foot, and pitchforked him suddenly into an entirely new world which was to make his name as a journalist, and lead to another lifelong friendship which has appalled many of his Labour colleagues to this day. Jennie Lee, Bevan's wife, watched with interest as Bevan came home on the night of Foot's resignation, and dialled Lord Beaverbrook's number. "I've got a young bloody knight-errant here. They sacked his boss, so he resigned. Have a look at him."

5

LORD BEAVERBROOK CALLS

It was love. Everybody is agreed on that. Michael Foot worked hard for Lord Beaverbrook, proprietor of the *Daily Express* and the London *Evening Standard*, from the autumn of 1938 until 1944. Then their relationship cooled, resumed in 1948, and remained warm until Beaverbrook died in 1964. George Malcolm Thomson, Beaverbrook's political secretary during the war, describes the relationship thus: "It was a love affair. Beaverbrook and Michael was one of the most interesting of human relationships." The historian A. J. P. Taylor, another admirer of Beaverbrook, puts it this way: "The two men were bound together by a deep and enduring mutual love." Michael Foot himself says: "I loved him, not merely as a friend, but as a second father."

These are strange ways of describing a relationship. We can add glimpses from the war years which seem even more peculiar today. In the first, during the darkest time of the war, George Malcolm Thomson is arriving one night at Beaverbrook's country estate at Cherkley, near Leatherhead. Beaverbrook, in his Canadian rasp, introduces Thomson to a tall, scruffily-dressed young man, with an angular face, a mouth turned unsmilingly down at each corner, and a bad skin. "Get up and deliver a speech," Beaverbrook tells him, "anything you like." He does so. A stream of dazzling rhetoric pours from him, on arms for Russia or some similar topical theme; he works up to a torrential climax and finishes. Afterwards Beaverbrook takes his audience of one aside and asks, "What do you think of that?" Around the same time, Beaverbrook boasts to the Liberal Secretary of State for Air, Archie Sinclair, taking credit for restraining Foot from some especially strong newspaper outburst: "Michael is my man, as Dingle is yours."

A little later in the war, Foot is living — briefly — in a house on Beaverbrook's estate, which had belonged to one of Beaverbrook's sons who died. He is sharing it with a beautiful refugee ballerina, Lili Ernst, five years older than him. He is hopelessly in love with her, and when their friends see them going around together in London, they tend to assume they are lovers. In fact, she is in love with Beaverbrook himself, who does not advertise the relationship, and treats her badly. Foot appears, curiously, more happy all the time, as though this intense asthmatic young puritan with the vitriolic pen and the sudden flights of wit and repartee has been — the words his friends use is "re-born" — through Beaverbrook. He is working his way with a knife and fork through one of the rare treats of war-time England: once a month the ration allows them chicken. Lili is laughing at him. "Why don't you pick it up with your hands?" she says. "Don't waste it." "Can I really?" he asks shyly. He picks up the leg and gnaws it. Then he suddenly throws it over his shoulder, grinning: "It makes me feel like Henry VIII."

At other times, they turn up at Nye Bevan and Jennie Lee's London house, where the young Foot is one of the few politicians who have regular entrée: he is warm, and amusing, but sits silent for long, private stretches; the Bevans regard him as a younger brother in the family. Jennie Lee will come home, and find Foot squeezed round the refectory table with five or six of Bevan's other political and drinking companions, men such as Frank Owen and Wilfred McCartney, Owen, the charming and promiscuous carouser with his God-like high spirits (Foot's words), is a former Liberal MP and editor of Beaverbrook's *Evening Standard*. When he was called up Foot took over as editor. Wilfred McCartney having served a sentence in Dartmoor for giving secrets to the Russians, was now organising enthusiastic "Aid to Russia" mass meetings through the Soviet front "Russia Today Society".

Meanwhile Harry Pollitt of the CP, removed from his post in 1939 because his patriotism could not let him stomach the Nazi-Soviet pact, miserably haunted the pubs with these Fleet Street left-wingers until the day when Russia was invaded — and Pollitt, Beaverbrook, Stafford Cripps, Winston Churchill, Nye Bevan, Michael Foot and Joe Stalin suddenly found themselves all on the same side.

At Cherkley, on the day of the 1941 invasion, Foot, a guest at a weekend party, woke early and heard the news on the radio. He ran downstairs and rummaged through Beaverbrook's gramophone cupboard. The household, butlers and bleary guests, were blasted awake by the sound — at maximum volume — of "The Internationale". At the bottom of the stairs was Foot, excitedly telling them they were now allies of the Soviet Union.

One final snapshot comes from just before the war, and this is more of a composite of events at the Beaverbrook dinner table — a table, with its harangues, Pol Roger champagne, clashes of temperament, and wildly ill-assorted guests over which Beaverbrook, easily bored, by turns feline and earthy, mischief-making and intuitive, presided more like a ringmaster than a puppeteer. There was an invisible line, nonetheless, which was not to be crossed. His family went in abject terror of the monster, and his more craven employees allowed themselves to be cruelly baited. Charles Wintour describes one night some years later when Sir Beverley Baxter, former *Express* editor, Beaverbrook pensioner and a Tory, was taunted non-stop by a drunken Randolph Churchill about the *Express*'s appeasement line at Munich. "You wretched little Canadian piano-tuner," he shouted beerily, again and again, while Beaverbrook professed himself helpless to stop him. Baxter's wife made him leave in the end, saying, "We didn't come here to be insulted."

Foot was not craven. He liked Beaverbrook's provocations, just as he was fascinated by the offensive antics of that maverick Tory, Randolph Churchill. Randolph and he got on with each other, say their friends, "like a house on fire", and later Randolph assured the world that he would go tiger-shooting with Foot. Foot delightedly re-told some of Randolph's witticisms. (When a sub-editor once criticised a phrase in an article he had written, he riposted: "To the obscure, all things are obscure".) Foot was good at trading punches with Beaverbrook. "Michael used to stand up to him completely," says Thomson. There were lots of high-spirited disputes, and they used to argue all the time about politics — but it was on absolutely level terms."

At Cherkley, in the autumn of 1938, Beaverbrook was making himself notorious for a generation by backing appeasement. "Britain will not be involved in a European war this year or next year either," the *Daily Express* screamed. But contemporary evidence bears out what Foot himself says — that Beaverbrook kept an open line to the Opposition, and cheerfully listened to his views being denounced around his own dinner table. Robert Bruce-Lockhart, then running the "Londoners' Diary" column in the *Standard*, kept private diaries of the period when Foot was first introduced into the circle. They are full of attacks on appeasement by men such as his editor, Frank Owen, and Brendan Bracken, who became Churchill's lieutenant in 1940. Owen would begin a story and Beaverbrook, delighted, would make him finish instead of letting him have his soup. The soup would be taken away and there would be no more. "The rhetorical prize-fights . . . bore, I swear, little relation to the suffocations practised in Fleet Street," says Foot. He listened to his own idol, H. G. Wells, "in person, protesting against the playing of the National Anthem 'and all that Hanoverian stuff' in a fine Republican squeak which the near-Republican Beaverbrook was happy to applaud."

Ian Aitken, the journalist who worked at different times for both men, says the intriguing thing was the way Beaverbrook, with his famous 3,000-volt charm, loved Foot. "He loved to be made to laugh. Strangely enough, Foot educated him in a way: Beaverbrook had had a crabby Scots-Canadian schooling, while Michael talked ebulliently about a Homeric range of books."

These pictures of Foot in the Beaverbrook ménage raise one more question than those they answer. How could an idealistic anti-capitalist find himself in such situations? Should he not have swept Beaverbrook's Pol Roger crashing to the floor? There are answers — good answers even — and to find them it is not even necessary to delve into the Freudian pondweed and paint Beaverbrook as the "Bad Father", unconscious counterpart to Foot's virtuous father, Isaac. Foot himself has already written his own defence, a long, glittering apologia called *The Case for Beelzebub*. It is nice piece of work: candid, genuine, and funny. But it glosses over the question. Foot professes himself mystified as to why Beaverbrook was seriously considered by outsiders to be "engaged in some vast Faustian conspiracy against the human race". He writes, as if surprised: "Many other friends found this friendship absurd, inexplicable, discreditable and evil." A. J. P. Taylor, who was to meet them much later, wrote a Beaverbrook biography that takes the same line: "Many people regarded him as indescribably wicked, an evil man: I am totally at a loss to explain this."

The charge against Beaverbrook, of course, and as Foot, Taylor, and all the Old Man's other bewitched apologists know well, is that he was a great newspaper proprietor who had no respect for the truth. He used the *Daily Express*, as he was the first to admit, purely to broadcast his contemporary obsessions, true or false, brilliant or perverse, important or childish. He drew brilliant men to him, and kept them on a loose enough rein to hold on to their talents. He was not interested in lackeys, but delighted in the thought he could manipulate strong-minded and rebellious characters. Beaverbrook's influence on British journalism was malign: the *Daily Express* set an example of technical brilliance and unscrupulous content which has dogged Fleet Street ever since. This can be defended in some ways: better, perhaps, the openly propagandist sheet than a sanctimonious "objectivity" which merely takes the lowest common denominator of its chosen public's prejudices and serves it back. Beaverbrook was no worse than his fellow proprietors — Rothermere or Kemsley — simply more unpredictable. There is even a perfectly serviceable and cynical argument: the British public never believes what it reads in the papers and voted down Churchill in 1945 despite the mighty newspapers re-playing his charge that Mr. Attlee would institute a socialist Gestapo.

Beaverbrook was, in other respects, a great public man: like Churchill, he used his talents in the War Cabinet to do the state much service. Nevertheless, the charge is a serious one. Beaverbrook was not a socialist. He was a dictator. Foot was working for a man whose idea of journalism was to issue these directives to the editor of the *Express*:

Keep the Duchess of Sutherland out of the social column. She does not like to be mentioned.

Review a book for children by Mrs. John Buchan favour-
ably — the reviewer must do this for political reasons, and
must do it in a big way.

And this, four or five months before Foot joined the paper,
to Frank Owen on the *Evening Standard* (who, Taylor asserts,
took no notice whatever): "Frank, be careful of your attacks
on Ribbentrop. If you are making attacks on Ribbentrop, you
are going to disturb the immense efforts that are now being
made for an accommodation with Germany . . . We have got to
give over criticism of those foreign powers for the time being.
It is a great misfortune, a terrible deprivation that we face but
at the same time we must be big enough to do it . . . for the
benefit of our people."

Michael Foot has laid down the standards he wants to be
judged by, in his own defence of Beaverbrook: "Most of his
critics knew barely one per cent of the story, and the nearer one
approaches the whole truth, the more necessary it is to speak in
nuances, and to search for qualified judgments." What nuances
are there in Foot's own career?

When the phone rang for Foot and summoned him to
Cherkley in the autumn of 1938, he was twenty-five. One of the
principal things he knew about Beaverbrook was that his hero
Nye Bevan considered it perfectly all right to associate with
him; indeed he had organised the meeting.

When Bevan attacked Lloyd George and Chamberlain in
the Commons, as one newspaper put it, "like a storm attacking
a solitary tree", Beaverbrook fished for this talented young
socialist by getting him brought along to dinner as a friend of a
young Tory MP, Edward Marjoribanks. (Marjoribanks later
shot himself in the gunroom of the first Lord Hailsham, his
stern stepfather, fearing he was impotent.) Bevan loved
Beaverbrook's rumbustious dinner tables, where Brendan
Bracken, with his orang-utan arms, would trade witticisms
about Bevan, the "Bollinger Bolshevik". He described them to
Jennie Lee, as she went off dourly with Frank Wise to lectures,
as "slumming in the West End". Bevan gave Foot a biblical
text which he thought summed up his position — a garbled
passage from Ecclesiastes which Bevan read as, "Stand not
too near the rich man lest he destroy thee — and not too far

off lest he forget thee."

Bevan wrote to Beaverbrook in 1932:

> As one who hates the power you hold and the order of life which enables you to wield it, and furthermore because I know I shall never seek that power for myself, I feel emboldened to tell you that I hold you in the most affectionate regard, and confess to a great admiration for those qualities of heart and mind which unfortunately do not appear to inspire your public policy.

The *Express* cheerfully attacked Bevan a few months later for being "brilliant, proud, bitter, class-conscious . . . a dangerous fellow", and Beaverbrook offered him and Jennie Lee a cottage at Cherkley when they married, around the time Foot first came into the Bevan orbit. Jennie put her foot down. Bevan was apologetic. "In plain English we think it would be politically indiscreet." As late as 1942, Bevan could be seen anxiously hoping his name would be kept out of the papers when there was a small fire at Cherkley: he had been carousing there in honour of Bill Brown, former trade unionist and ex-Labour man who had just got in as an Independent at a Rugby by-election. That autumn Beaverbrook wrote mischievously to Roosevelt about Churchill's violent parliamentary antagonist, who even attacked Churchill's dress: "the more strange since Bevan himself is for the most part an untidy man. His hair is seldom brushed. He has no waistcoat and his belly is beginning to run over his breeches. He likes Champagne." After 1943, Bevan eased himself out of Beaverbrook's orbit, never to return.

Beaverbrook could offer Foot, however, much more than champagne. He made him into a celebrated journalist. That first breakfast-time at Cherkley, he ordered him to memorise the Sunday papers (like Isaac, his father, it was a trick he knew) and lecture the assembled guests on their contents. Having passed this test of fortitude, he was offered a job as a leader-writer on the *Standard* at the union minimum of £9 a week. It was soon raised to £12 and, when Foot became acting editor in 1942, Beaverbrook said he was paying him nearly £4,000 a year — an enormous sum. (MPs earned £600,

Cabinet Ministers £5,000, and Beaverbrook's personal expenditure was about £25,000 a year.)

Frank Owen, the editor, was a friend of Nye Bevan's too (the young MPs had shared a house together). He and Foot became close. Foot learned about nightlife, deadlines, liquor and — at a distance — women. He fell in with extraordinary characters, such as Tom Driberg, "William Hickey" of the *Express*. Owen and Driberg (the "cafe Communist" as Beaverbrook had him described in his other gossip column, "Londoners' Diary"), spent one night of the abdication crisis in a night-club called Frisco's, singing an impromptu calypso to the words of Mrs. Simpson's statement: "The situation is unhappy and untenable . . ." In the autumn of 1938, Bruce-Lockhart records: "At 12.30 a.m. took Frank Owen, Tom Driberg and Michael Foot to Sports Club. Huge talk on Russia with Driberg and Foot violently pro-Communist and Frank anti!" Foot puts it a little differently. Driberg was a Stalinist then, he says, and Owen liked to call himself a Trotskyist: "Tom would dismiss us as a couple of Trotskyist deviationists."

Frank Owen had taken over the *Standard*, the London evening newspaper about whose political content Beaverbrook was, most of the time, untroubled. Foot did not have to write anything with which he disagreed. As war broke out, Beaverbrook went into the War Cabinet and had even less time to bother with the *Standard*'s political line. When Russia and Britain became allies, Beaverbrook became a thoroughgoing enthusiast for the Second Front, the cause of all left-wingers. For a time the politics of Foot and Beaverbrook did not collide. What interested Beaverbrook was teaching Foot how to write. He went about it characteristically. In 1938 Foot, now lodging with his brother, Hugh, temporarily home-based in Battersea, and catching the bus in to Shoe Lane every morning, was whisked off — alone with Beaverbrook — to the South of France, and back via the Paris Ritz.

Beaverbrook urged him to study the American masters of the art of the column — such now-forgotten names as Arthur Brisbane, Westbrook Pegler and Heywood Broun. Foot's Beaverbrook style was jagged and highly coloured. One of his first pieces, in November 1938, was number six in a series on

"Murder in High Places." It explained the assassination of Walter Rathenau, the German foreign minister, in 1922:

Today 400,000 German Jews are persecuted while a disciplined people shout their approval. Sixteen years ago one German Jew was murdered . . . he heard the roar of a pounding engine behind him. A high-powered six-seater tourer shot alongside. It was almost a crash. Suddenly a muffled figure ripped out a revolver, rested it on his armpit and fired.

When the war came, Foot strung together a series of these sketches of inter-war European history into a book, *Armistice 1918-1939*, published in 1940, which now reads rather breathlessly. But then they were lurid times. Foot was beginning to develop skill at invective. On Spain: "Mussolini agreed to the Anglo-Italian pact on the explicit understanding that he should be allowed to murder the Spanish Republic in a corner." And, at length, on Baldwin:

The prophet of somnolence sucked a silver spoon from the day of his political birth . . . he entered the House of Commons with a safe seat and a large bank balance . . . He was left standing in lofty eminence like a hillock in the fen country . . . the master of eloquent irrelevancies . . . did his party ask for guidance on principle and policy? He was ready with a glimpse into the secrets of his heart, the dreams of his childhood, the hopes for his old age. . .

Owen reviewed his own friend's book in the *Standard*: "Here is a man writing like a man and not like a petulant old woman." The Conservative papers sniffed at it, for Foot had laid into their readers: "Unbiased historians are as insufferable as the people who profess no politics. (We know them so well. They are neither Tories, Liberals nor Socialists, but they intend to vote for Mr. Chamberlain and think something should be done about the unemployed who, of course, positively refuse to work.)" The *Cornish Times* deplored the way Foot "vilifies revered leaders", and pounced on the note of sorrow with which Foot felt obliged to condemn the Russian attack on Finland in the winter of 1939. "Thus as a mere 'prodigious blunder' is the rape of Finland accepted by this British socialist. What right has Mr. Foot to rave and rage against Japan, Italy and Germany for unprovoked aggression?" These were the days when Chamberlain was actively considering sending British bombers to Finland. It was still easier to attack Bolshevists than Nazis.

By 1940, Foot was continuing to read much of the situation aright. Just after the German invasion of Norway a large article by him appeared in the *Daily Express*, now claiming to be "the most popular newspaper in the world". Surrounded by an Agatha Christie serial, one of Beachcomber's droll columns, paragraphs of gossip by James Agate (one boosting Foot's own book), slanted news snippets about red tape and editorials attacking government grants for "culture" and exhorting people to cheer up, Foot warned dramatically that Hitler was on the brink of invading the Low Countries: "We must be ready for another blow from the Nazi hammer."

Life on the *Standard* was not entirely composed of grim warnings, of course. Foot wrote one pre-war leader in his best style about the railings round Hyde Park: "Someone ought to pull them down." When Captain Mike Wardell, the stuffy manager of the *Standard*, a right-winger and a philanderer, said it would lead to immorality, Beaverbrook squashed him: "No more of it, Captain Wardell; you have beautiful beds in Claridges and all over London where you can do your fucking; what about the rest of us?"

It was Dunkirk that made Foot's name. He, Frank Owen and Peter Howard (the same "Crossbencher" who had savaged "dry-as-dust" Dingle and Isaac in the past) concocted a pamphlet together, as the first news reports came in of the bitter troops straggling back from the beaches. Howard, then writing editorials, had already clashed with Beaverbrook's appeasement line in the phoney war. One night, emboldened by the company of Owen, Bracken and Nye Bevan, he told him, "The only hope is to put Churchill in and get rid of Chamberlain." Beaverbrook, shaking with rage, roared, "Get out of my house!", then pattered after him through the blackout, "a small asthmatic figure coatless and hatless trailing after me" to apologise. Howard even wrote in the *Standard*:

"Lord Beaverbrook, for example, is always decided and entirely cocksure that his views are right. I am bound to tell you however that sometimes he is wrong."

The trio spent a lot of time together, in the Café Royal and on the roof of the *Standard* building after edition time, waiting for The Two Brewers to open. By now, the Chamberlain government had fallen: Foot, Owen and Howard set out to repay the score against the appeasers with a series of truly vitriolic character assassinations. The author, they decided, should be "Cato", the man who cleaned out the sewers of Rome. Foot suggested the title, from a favourite life of the French revolutionary St-Just: "The leader of the angry crowd replied. 'The people haven't come here to be given a lot of phrases. They demand a dozen guilty men'."

Guilty Men was thrown together in a weekend, eight chapters each. This "instant book" is more interesting for its political impact than for any literary qualities. Peter Howard's hand can be seen in the picture of Sir Thomas Inskip, the ineffectual Defence Minister, as "that bum-faced evangelical" and "Caligula's horse". Foot's prose was sometimes comparatively high-toned: "As Foreign Secretary, Sir Samuel Hoare passed from experience to experience, like Boccaccio's virgin, without any discernible effect upon his condition." Sometimes it was the style he had learned from Beaverbrook: "Hitler came to power in Europe. His coming fell upon Europe like the crash of a great dam in the hills." And sometimes it was sheer invective: "MacDonald was thoroughly content provided he could *be* something. That something was Perpetual Prime Minister . . . Baldwin made no effort to restrain him. He allowed Mr. MacDonald to roam and spout all over Europe." The accusations were laced together with interviews from Dunkirk: "A Cornish able seaman said . . . 'eight Heinkels bombed the fifty men . . . The sergeant grabbed a Bren gun, stood his ground in the middle of the beach and blazed away at them' . . . one Bren gun and one hero against eight Heinkels."

Like all successful propaganda, *Guilty Men* caught a public mood, and amplified it into a legend. Victor Gollancz could not print enough hundreds of thousands of copies. It had the distinction of being briefly banned as dangerous by the

booksellers W. H. Smith: Gollancz sold it in barrows along
Fleet Street. The trio did not make much out of it, because
their agent ran off with most of the money. *Guilty Men* did not,
on its own, manage to take all the heat off the pre-war Labour
party and fix the blame for Britain's unpreparedness on the
"Old Gang". But it set the mythological outline for years of
wartime political discussion. Perhaps it even helped win the
1945 election for Labour.

One name not put in the dock was that of Beaverbrook.
Some people even thought he had written it, and he used
mischievously to talk about "my royalties from *Guilty Men*".
Others thought Bevan was the author. Beaverbrook never
directly asked Foot if he had written it, and the trio claimed to
have tried to put people off the scent. Howard wrote a review
himself in the *Express*: "I cannot do more than pay a tribute to
the powerfulness of the indictment brought in by Cato, the
mysterious author."

Foot tried to be more subtle. His signed review in the
Standard said:

> Pamphleteering is a forgotten weapon, yet once it was
> perhaps the most potent in English politics. A pamphlet by
> Swift broke the Duke of Marlborough . . .
>
> The weapon has now been drawn from its scabbard with a
> vengeance. *Guilty Men*, written by a mysterious and bashful
> Cato (Gollancz, 2/6) promises to become the most sensa-
> tional political publication of the war.
>
> It is a searing, savage, but documented attack on the men
> responsible for the failure to provide Britain with the arma-
> ments to fight this war. It is an amazing indication of the
> foresight of the present Prime Minister and it pays full
> tribute to the men who have intensified the war effort in
> recent months.
>
> The story is told by one who appears to have watched the
> drama from the floor of the House of Commons itself.
>
> Some of the judgments are unfair. It has some flagrant
> omissions. But whatever verdict is passed on the whole, no
> one can dispute the total effect is terrific.
>
> Who is this Cato MP? And why does he hide his fireworks
> under a bushel?

(Once again, Isaac's shadow crosses Michael Foot's history. He was the one who told the young Michael about Swift's pamphlet, "On the Conduct of the Allies", and eventually persuaded him to write a long history of that affair.)

The three authors of *Guilty Men* all came to strange ends. Foot eventually became leader of the Labour party. Frank Owen became editor of the *Daily Mail* after the war, but ended a long career of drink, printers' ink and women by suddenly collapsing into premature senility. Howard, of whom Beaverbrook must have had his suspicions, was banned from writing political leaders. While he was hanging disconsolately about the managing editor's office, trying to get the ban lifted, the middle-aged office secretary, Edith Ducé, converted him to religion. He finished up actually running Moral Re-armament. This led to a row with Foot: Howard produced a tract of his own called *Innocent Men*, which Beaverbrook — always the tease — promptly showed to Owen and Foot. Foot rang up Howard's wife in Suffolk and bawled her out for twenty minutes. Then the enraged pair saw Howard and tried to persuade him — unsuccessfully — that since he now professed to believe in "absolute unselfishness", he should give up his share of the royalties from *Guilty Men*.

When Frank Owen was called up into the Army, Foot was made editor. The two of them claimed to have transformed the "political tone" of the *Standard*, while Beaverbrook was immersed in the War Cabinet: "Day by day our tone became more exhilarated and revolutionary," says Foot. He wrote leaders saying, "We are fighting this war to uphold the principles of the French revolution." *Tribune,* which had emerged from a Communistic period, and was being written by men such as Bevan, and the Swiss socialist Jon Kimche, became an unofficial annexe of the *Standard.* Foot was involved in one of his frequent car-crashes when Beaverbrook tipped him off that Frank Owen's notorious *Tribune* pieces attacking Churchill's strategy over the name "Colonel Rainsboro", were under investigation by MI5. Foot roared down to Andover, where Owen was serving in a tank regiment, collected the final instalment, and careered off a humped bridge. Mechanics from an Army camp mended his car.

Later the Conservatives tried to blame Foot (and Beaverbrook) for generating socialist propaganda in his paper. After the 1945 general election the defeated Tories organised an exhibition called "How the people were told a story". They had a rogue's gallery of propagandists — Hannen Swaffer of the *Daily Herald*, Allen Lane, owner of Penguin Books, and Foot. The Tory chairman, Ralph Assheton, wrote to Beaverbrook, following the 1945 fiasco, to complain about the long-term anti-Conservative work of men such as Low the cartoonist, and the "vitriolic propagandist" Michael Foot. Beaverbrook had hired "some of the ablest and most consistent left-wing propagandists of the day", he said. Beaverbrook, never short of an answer, riposted, "Owen and Foot never gave a left turn to the politics of the *Evening Standard*. This will surprise you. . . There was considerable agitation in the *Evening Standard* for a Second Front. This may have been misunderstood as a movement to the left."

From about 1943, the question of the political shape of postwar Britain began to arise. The Commons hotly debated land nationalisation. To Beaverbrook's displeasure, his *Standard* welcomed the system of national insurance proposed by Beveridge. Foot and Beaverbrook's views began to collide.

As Foot tells the story, Beaverbrook circulated a form after *Guilty Men* ordering all employees to notify the management about books they were going to write. When Mussolini fell in 1943, Foot, highly delighted, sat up all night to produce a souvenir edition of the *Standard*, and then wrote a new pamphlet.

This time, Gollancz's little yellow book was by "Cassius" and called *The Trial of Mussolini*. It was a mock trial in which Foot set out to show that the British establishment had their own guilty record in backing Mussolini. Counsel for the defence quoted Sir Austen Chamberlain, Foreign Secretary in 1924: "Signor Mussolini is a wonderful man"; Lord Rothermere, the newspaper proprietor: "He is the greatest figure of our age"; Sir John Simon: "I was not prepared to see a single ship sunk . . . in the cause of Abyssinian independence"; Sir Samuel Hoare: "We were obsessed with the urgent necessity of doing everything within our power to prevent a European conflagration". On he went through the guilty men, again: Chamberlain, Halifax, the odious Hore-Belisha.

> The England of the Conservative party . . . condoned fascism, consorted with fascism, connived at imperialist war, abandoned any hope of building a sane and secure international society . . . yet there was still another England . . . this was the England of the left, the England of Labour . . . it was the resurrection of this other England which saved the world, and the hopes of the European revolution . . . will depend on which England rules as the fighting subsides.

Beaverbrook was not having this. Foot was swiftly moved out from the *Standard* and put into limbo on the *Daily Express*. In November Kingsley Martin of the *New Statesman* tried to get Foot to write for him. Foot told him to ask Beaverbrook, who pointed out how much he was paying Foot on retainer: "I can well understand your desire to make use of the fine talents of Michael Foot . . . I sympathise with your difficulties, but could not possibly entertain it." Foot carried on for another seven months, and then wrote Beaverbrook a resignation letter. He wanted to leave without a row.

> Your views and mine are bound to become more and more irreconcilable. As far is this socialist business is concerned, my views are unshakeable. For me it is the Klondyke or bust, and at the moment I am doubtful whether I am going the right way to Klondyke. There does not seem to be much sense in my continuing to write leaders for a newspaper group whose opinions I do not share and some of whose opinions I strongly dissent from. I know you never ask me to write views with which I disagree. But as this works out it is good business neither for you nor for me. The leaders which I now write are hardly worth writing since they are non-committal and from my point of view I am associated with a newspaper group against whose policies (but not against the proprietor) I am resolved to wage perpetual war. Somehow things were different before. The compromise worked, and certainly greatly to my advantage. But I do not see how it could work very much longer. The business of maintaining allegiance to my own political ideas and to a newspaper which must be fundamentally opposed to them is too difficult. . . . It seems foolish to raise a personal

matter like this at a time when much bigger things are happening. But it would also be foolish to disguise the fact that my feeling is I am wasting my time and there is so much I want to do and accomplish. Your kindness to me has given me great advantages in this world. I do not forget them. But I am sure it is right for me to make a change and I dearly hope you will understand my reasons.

In terms of political integrity, Foot's professional relationship with Beaverbrook between 1938 and 1944 thus seems to have taken a perfectly decent course. The Tory party certainly seem to have been the very last people who thought Foot had sold his soul to capitalism. Foot went out of his way after the war to attack the great newspaper proprietors, and spoke and testified against his old mentor to the Royal Commission on the press — he fought a public battle against all the *Express* stood for, just as he had promised.

Foot and Beaverbrook's personal relationship was more subtle than the professional one. There was a third person involved. Foot had met Lili Ernst, the refugee ballerina, on the first night he was summoned to Cherkley for dinner. She was beautiful, delicate and fragile; the most exotic of the exotic species the young socialist was suddenly surrounded by. Lili watched, impressed, as Foot performed his memorising feat for the guests — she had to read and summarise French and German newpapers for Beaverbrook, and knew just how difficult it was. She was Jewish. Beaverbrook had helped her get out of Vienna: he liked women and they liked him. He was so embroiled with her that Foot was urged to write long articles in the *Express* backing the Jewish cause. He also later wrote an article in the *Standard*, attacking the crass way the authorities were locking up alien refugees. Lili, as a refugee, felt grateful. She wrote to him. Foot immediately rang her up. From then on, he never left her side. When Lili realised how seriously this shy, asthmatic young man felt about her, she told him, their intimates say: "My life is just one man." This did not make the twenty-seven-year-old Foot at first hostile to Max, as Lili called him. On the contrary. As Foot himself puts it: "The best thing I knew about Max Beaverbrook was that Lili Ernst had truly loved him." Foot was like a younger brother to Lili, sympathetic, even adoring. With Frank Owen and Nye Bevan he could carouse all night; with Lili Ernst he could wander abstractedly through the estate at Cherkley as she pointed out the beauties of the sunset. He could write, talk books and politics to his heart's content, share with Beaverbrook their favourite authors, well-remembered Bible stories, (both were nonconformists by origin) — and even their asthma. Beaverbrook had it too. Beaverbrook was a man who could make anyone feel it was his special gift to bring them alive, and it was natural enough that Foot should give him the credit for all the unbuttoning going on inside Foot himself. Beaverbrook was the fount from which all blessings flowed. Or so it seemed at first.

Like the professional relationship, the personal one became too much of a strain by the middle of the war. Foot never made a sexual advance to Lili, never even kissed her. Her life got darker as time went on. After the period of the exhilarating Second Front meetings, with Foot making passionate speeches, and then all of them singing the Red Flag, she became unhappy and ill. Her family had disappeared in occupied Yugoslavia. Beaverbrook was — and this was not only Foot's impression of the way he behaved to women — hard, demanding, possessive, and wayward. Lili was installed in the cottage at Cherkley, and by all accounts Foot behaved in an extremely selfless way. He stayed there with her. Lili would urge, "You must find a young woman and go and get married", and Foot would reply, "Don't worry: as long as you don't mind, I want to stay with you." He seems to have been able to talk to Lili in a far less inhibited way than with others: intellectually he was highly developed, emotionally he was private and shy. But he did make one professional remark to Lili which stuck in her mind. She was anguished about the Nazis: "How can you explain the success of Hitler?" she demanded. "We watched him in the early days in Austria, and his speeches were so low and evil and just *nothing* that everybody laughed at him. How did that fool achieve this?" Foot said, "You go to Marble Arch and try and make a speech about goodness and love. You won't have a soul listen to you. Try good, juicy hatred, and you'll get an audience of hundreds."

The private and the professional relationships with Beaver-brook both became unmanageable by the end of 1943. Look-ing back in relative old age, Foot is candid enough to say openly that perhaps he was jealous of him over Lili, as he attacked him and the other proprietors just after the war. Lili stayed with Beaverbrook until 1946 and then broke with him too. (She went on to marry happily, and still thinks affection-ately of Foot.) Foot, meanwhile, did go off towards the end of the war and propose to someone else. This was Connie Ernst (no relation to Lili), a fizzy American from a wealthy New York radical family. She turned him down flat. It was not until Foot met his future wife, Jill Craigie, in 1945, that his emotional life really matured. It was under her influence that he moved right out of the Lili-Beaverbrook planetary system.

So, neither of the possible charges against Foot — that he was under Beaverbrook's political thumb, or under his personal thumb, really stand up. Later, towards the end of the 'Forties, he again became friendly with Beaverbrook, who even gave a covert subsidy to *Tribune*. Foot became book-reviewer on the *Standard* towards the end of Beaverbrook's life, and used to spend what his fellow socialists thought was a disproportionate amount of time being rung up by that growling Canadian voice, now elderly, or writing his books at Beaverbrook's Riviera villa, Cap d'Ail. He and Jill even moved into a cottage on Beaverbrook's estate at Cherkley when they were temporarily homeless — after consulting Nye Bevan as to its propriety. Beaverbrook in his old age needed a son who shared his interests in books, the Bible and political intrigue; Foot always needed strong, rebellious characters to look up to. A socialist who is fascinated by strong characters, and who takes great pleasure in human idiosyncrasy, may be difficult to explain. But Foot would no doubt say that those who attack him have too narrow a definition of socialism.

When he quit Beaverbrook, he was hired by the *Daily Herald* to write a political column and spent the rest of the war energetically campaigning for a Labour victory at the next general election. He produced, under his own name this time, another yellow Gollancz booklet called *Brendan and Beverley*. This was sarcastic, in a slightly elephantine way, about the Tory party's disarray. Casting Brendan Bracken, the Tory

Information Minister, and Sir Beverley Baxter MP, the former editor of the *Express*, as Tadpole and Taper, the two unprincipled string-pullers in Disraeli's *Coningsby*, Foot has them searching around in desperate fashion to counter the propaganda of men such as the authors of *Guilty Men*. After rejecting in panic any idea of appealing to the Tory record in the 1930s, they decide to invent the idea of continued coalition, in order to dish Labour. Foot invents a moving Churchillian wireless broadcast, which might possibly bamboozle the voters. And then he delivers himself of his own socialist election broadcast: "Our faults are pygmies in the shadow of their great crime . . . these men are unfit to govern . . . England can recapture the moral leadership among the nations which she commanded in the nineteenth century." He called for an Anglo-Soviet alliance and the freedom of India. He quotes Tom Paine, and the fall of the Bastille: "We can stand on our own feet and make a society in which wealth, so often acquired by means which leave whole communities destitute, shall not be the test of worth . . . we are asking, not for office, but for power . . . the next twenty years must be ours."

In the *Herald* in late 1944, he returns to the idea of the "two Englands" and accuses Churchill of trying to put the petty kings of Europe back on their thrones. He also savages the "National Liberals": "No outward mark of the influence of this coterie on the national life remains, except for one or two beacons at the pedestrian crossings." This was a gibe at Hore-Belisha, his father's old enemy, down in Devonport, the seat for which Foot had been adopted six years previously. As the war ended, Foot was turning his mind to becoming an MP.

Above: Isaac Foot the elder and his wife Eliza, Michael Foot's grandparents.

Below: The Foot tribe: *back row, left to right* Christopher, Michael, Hugh, Dingle, John; *front row, left to right* Hugh's wife Sylvia, John's wife Anne, Isaac Foot, Eva Foot, their daughter Sally, Dingle's wife Dorothy.

Above: Summer with the Cripps family, Scilly Isles 1934: *left to right* Peggy (later to marry Joe Appia), Foot, Theresa, Lady Isobel and Geoffrey Wilson (later to head Oxfam as Sir Geoffrey).

Below left: The undergraduate, 1933: tennis at "Goodfellows", home of Stafford Cripps. *Left to right* Foot, Geoffrey Wilson, John Cripps (later Sir John).

Below right: 1936: Foot and Sir Stafford Cripps with *The Struggle for Peace.*

Above: 1945: the Labour candidate for Devonport (*second from right*) at his family's election headquarters at Pencrebar.

Below: Isaac and his five sons setting off to support Plymouth Argyle football club: *left to right* John, Dingle, Isaac, Christopher, Michael, Hugh.

Above: Jill Craigie, the film producer, when Foot first knew her in 1948, making a documentary about Welsh miners — *Blue Scar*.

Below: The young MP joins in a tug-of-war with Labour supporters at Calstock, near Plymouth, in 1949.

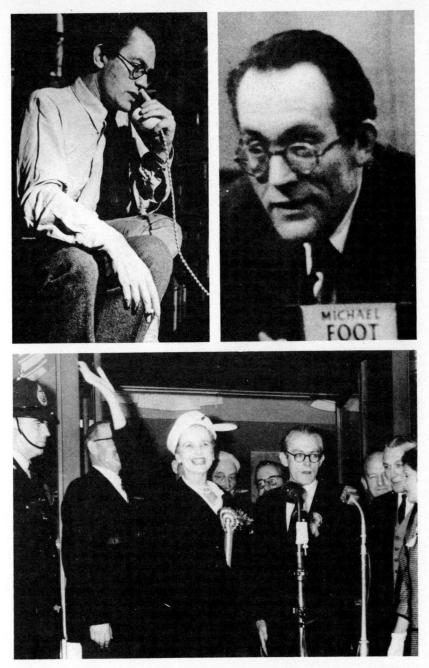

Above left: Foot, the former editor of the *Evening Standard*, in his London flat at the end of the war. Note he is still afflicted by eczema.

Above right: The early TV personality: "In the News", BBC 1950.

Below: 1955: Joan Vickers defeats him at Devonport.

Above: CND: Foot on the 1958 march from Trafalgar Square to Aldermaston.

Below: Foot addresses the 1957 *Tribune* meeting at the Labour Party Conference at Brighton. Bevan has already decided to make his speech against unilateralism later in the conference, forcing Foot to break with him. *Left to right* Foot, Claude Bourdet, editor of *L'Observateur*, Ian Mikardo and Bevan.

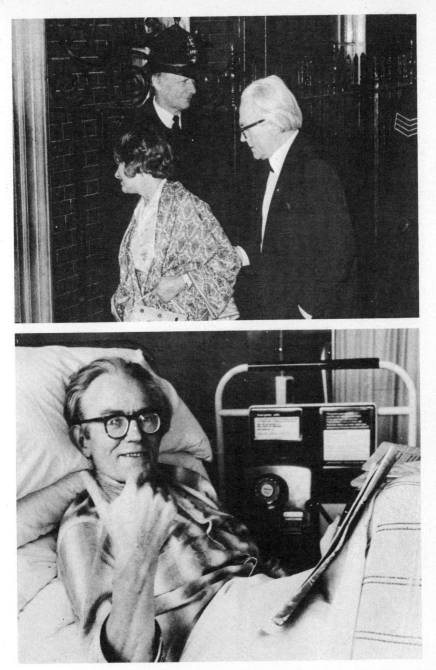

Above: 1976: Harold Wilson's farewell dinner for the Queen at Number 10. A rare agreement by Foot to wear a dinner jacket.

Below: A thumbs-up from his hospital bed after the car crash in 1963 which cured his asthma.

Above: 1964: Foot about to address the CND Easter rally at Trafalgar Square.

Below: With the eighty-five-year-old Lord Beaverbrook, shortly before his death, at Cap d'Ail in the south of France in 1964.

6

LABOUR COMES TO POWER

Foot's life changed utterly at the end of the war: he won his election at Devonport, Labour swept to power, and he met Jill Craigie. The exhilarated new MPs, some anticipating a blissful new dawn of socialism, sang the Red Flag together on their first day in the Commons Chamber; Foot sat there with his old friend Barbara Castle, with Tom Driberg, with the young Ian Mikardo, the business efficiency expert of the Labour left, the saintly anti-colonialist Fenner Brockway, Richard Crossman, Jennie Lee and a triumphant Nye Bevan, who became the Cabinet minister charged with establishing the National Health Service.

Jill Craigie, soft, intelligent, strikingly pretty, turned Michael Foot from being a talented yet somehow two-dimensional man into something much richer. His friends and family are unanimous about this. She needed his capacity for unselfish affection, and to an extent his greater feel for the world of affairs (he still addresses her pleasantly, though sometimes a shade curtly, as "my dear child"). He needed her grasp of a range of human feeling beyond the rather limited masculine attitudes of the thirty-two Beaverbrook-nonconformist-semi-Stalinist years of his life. He also needed her practical help. Over the years Jill, the first woman film-maker in wartime Britain, dropped out of the film world and concentrated on a supporting role, renovating their houses, cooking meals, and making what efforts she could to send him out looking a trifle less scruffy. By 1980, when he became party leader, she settled for buying six suits at once, and put him into a fresh one each day. She still does some journalism, and is writing a book about the Suffragettes. Jill is also an important source of political strength to her husband; instinctively and solidly on the left, she sees herself as a "William Morris

socialist". She taught Foot feminism, and his writing shows
that he has striven to be a good pupil. They would like to have
had children – Foot's nieces and nephews testify how much he
enjoyed their company when they were young — but it never
happened. So they lavish affection on a series of hairy dogs,
with which Foot has usually been seen on his early morning
walks, yelling exasperatedly for them to come out of a pond in
Regents Park or Hampstead Heath. First there was Vanessa,
who when thirteen gave birth to a mongrel, Roxana, who lived
until she was twelve. Then came Dizzy, a Tibetan terrier. Foot
may well be the only leader of the Labour party with a dog
named after a leader of the Conservative party.

Jill Craigie's early life was often lonely. Her father died in
the First World War, and her mother married a member of a
Sudan plantation syndicate and moved abroad. Jill bumped
around a series of boarding schools, cheap or expensive,
depending on the fluctuations of the Sudan dividends, and in
the 1930s was living alone in London on two pounds ten
shillings a week answering the letters on *Betty's Paper*. It was
not an easy life, but she read a lot — Shaw's *Intelligent
Women's Guide to Socialism* — and studied art, because
galleries were free. She remembers trying to buy Marie
Stopes's *Married Love* from a disapproving shop-girl in
Bayswater so she could learn about the facts of life.

She attracted a series of men and some of them fell in love
with her. She married, briefly, and had a daughter, Julie,
before divorcing. During the war she persuaded the British
Council to take a documentary script of hers on war artists
such as Sutherland and Henry Moore; the Foots still have a
Moore drawing bought from the then unknown sculptor for
ten pounds. By the time she met Foot, she had been noticed for
this twenty-minute documentary, *Out of Chaos*. She had been
steeping herself in the works of Lewis Mumford and the
idealistic, socialist town planners of the 1940s, and was
working on a full-scale documentary for Rank about the
rebuilding of Plymouth. It was Paul Reilly, the architect's son,
who introduced her to "Plymouth's next MP".

Both were working on their visions of the new Jerusalem
amid the rubble of the worst-blitzed city in Britain, when Foot
returned from a UN conference in San Francisco. He found

her installed with a camera crew and only too willing to show him round his home town. At lunch together he typically offered to lend her a book.

"I fell for him straight away," she now says. "I liked that myopic look in his eyes and I liked what he had to say. I felt he was honest, and integrity means a lot to me in a chap. His eczema gave him an inferiority complex and was sometimes so bad he couldn't show his face out of doors, but he didn't have it the day I first met him. He was a little shy, didn't make a pass at me or anything like that, but he was such a good listener, always asking questions."

The Plymouth Plan was a great local issue. Where the Labour party saw broad avenues in place of the old slums, village precincts and great arts centres, the Conservatives saw a plot against private property. Labour won, but it is hard to see now, confronted with the dreary cut-price layout of Plymouth today, why the battle was worth fighting. Jill's documentary was a great critical success, but got her into trouble with the monopolistic film tycoon J. Arthur Rank, and would probably look hopelessly idealistic if it were shown today. Foot extolled social and urban planning to the voters: "We really can have the most beautiful city in the world."

The Plymouth Labour party did not have much hope that Foot could oust the elderly Hore-Belisha, a man whose name lives on in the "belisha beacons" he introduced. Hore-Belisha had been a dockyard institution for twenty-two years, and was now the Minister of National Insurance. Men like Ron Lemin, an electrician at the huge naval dockyard, remembered him at the 1935 hustings, the last time he won the seat. Lemin's father was unemployed for fourteen years. He would take his seven-year-old son down to the dole queue when he signed on, and Hore-Belisha would arrive to orate to the long line of shabby men and children: "Look around!" he would cry to his captive audience. "Look at you, and you, and you! Able-bodied men without work!" He promised them jobs through the Liberals, though the jobs never came.

Plymouth's Labour men did their best to teach the candidate their store of local low cunning. His teachers were Methodists and teetotallers. Harry Wright was a boilermaker at the dockyard, and became a Labour council candidate at the age of twenty-one, something which took a degree of courage in the atmosphere of the times. He was on his way to becoming Chairman of Plymouth's Finance Committee and a considerable local boss. A machine right-winger himself, he always stuck by the left-wing Foot and would put him up in his house. There were men such as Bert Medland, another boiler-maker who was elected for the neighbouring constituency, and the straitlaced Alderman Harry Mason, the son of a Methodist minister. They liked Foot; he was a fanatical supporter of Plymouth Argyle, like the rest of his family, and he later formed a "Dockyard Group" of MPs. He campaigned successfully for pension rights for dockyard workers. He liked them, although he always found it easiest to unwind with the workers over a few drinks. When he went out campaigning, he would set up a loudspeaker in the street, and orate to the passers-by, rather than lever himself, tongue-tied, into people's homes. Bob Edwards, then working on *Tribune*, remembers one night at a street-corner meeting in the 'Forties: "We went to a working-men's club and drank a hell of a lot of beer. I got very drunk. On the way back to Harry Wright's house, where we were staying, Michael whispered, 'I shouldn't mention what we've been doing all night'."

During the campaign, Foot naturally went to Pencrebar to pay his respects to the clan. Isaac, who had stumped the West Country before the war preaching "England Arise!", was standing for Tavistock; John for South-East Cornwall (where he told Liberal commuters to vote for his brother Michael in Devonport), and Dingle, a junior minister throughout the war, was defending Dundee. Michael had told his father that he had met their mutual enemy Hore-Belisha at Cherkley and that he did not seem such a bad chap. Isaac snorted: "You didn't commit yourself to a clean fight, I hope." Eva was more reserved, but then just before Michael's eve-of-poll meeting she sent him one of her home-baked Cornish pasties which he ate on the platform to the cheers of the crowd. During the campaign he stayed with John and his wife Anne; their housekeeper gave notice rather than clean for a socialist.

Throughout the campaign the meetings were huge and the atmosphere electric. Nye Bevan came down to speak for Foot, who was by now hoarse with passion. Bevan was more relaxed, but his message was the uncompromising class struggle for power. Jill went to every one of Foot's political meetings: when the astonishing result came in and he had turned an 11,000 Tory majority into a win by 2,000 votes, Foot was so drained and pale that he could manage only a few platitudes before being carried off to the victory party. Jill, to her chagrin, was not invited.

All three Liberal Foots lost. The seven-year-old Paul Foot burst into tears at his grandfather's defeat, and Isaac, shocked out of his normal sunny disposition, was unapproachable for days. He became Lord Mayor of Plymouth. There were no more theatrical renderings of the great parliamentary occasions on the family hearth, and he disappeared further into his books.

Back in London, Jill phoned Michael to invite him to see the Plymouth film and they began to meet regularly. Foot (he had read Bertrand Russell) was now sufficiently familiar with the ways of the world to begin an affair, and they were formally married in 1949. Jill had been making an independent living — she directed *Blue Scar*, a documentary about miners, and wrote the script for *The Million Pound Note*, which starred Gregory Peck. Their circle became film people, artists, and relatively few politicians. The MP Hugh Delargy was a frequent visitor, and so was J. P. W. "Curly" Mallalieu. Barbara Castle tended to assume Jill knew little about politics, which did not go down well. Lili Ernst had the occasional lunch with the couple, but it was not an easy relationship. Foot had taken a pokey flat in Mayfair during the war, at a rent of thirty shillings a week, but when they married, they found a small house in Hampstead on a short lease. Bevan and Jill got on well; she thought there was no better company in England than the ebullient Welshman, and he was almost vulgarly direct about her personal charms. They went to parties together; Foot took her to the Castles' at Christmas to show her off to his friends, and she promptly buttonholed the young President of the Board of Trade, one Harold Wilson, to harangue him about the film industry. Barbara would skylark with the guests, and they would all jockey for the chance to sit near Nye Bevan.

Their political enemies sometimes call the Foots

'Hampstead socialists", which of course they are, but the phrase misses their unassuming personal habits. When the lease ran out on their Hampstead house they lived for a while in their car. With £1,500 saved as a deposit, they bought a house in St. John's Wood for £6,000. Ten years later, when Foot was sacked from the *Daily Herald* he was given £6,000 redundancy money. They had inherited little from Isaac except books. They sold the St. John's Wood house for £13,000 and bought their roomy Victorian villa near Hampstead Heath, in a rundown state, for £12,000. Foot's only libel action — against the *Daily Mail* — brought them £500 which they spent on a new hall carpet. They have a tiny cottage in his constituency, and like to go to Italy, especially Venice, for their holidays — but did not go to Spain, until Franco died.

In the 1945 House of Commons, the new MP was facing for the first time the sad collapse of his hopes for the new government. In his *Herald* column his own caution about the appalling difficulties ahead could not at first dampen his euphoria: "Now, at last, for the first time in a great industrial state, power is granted to embark on the task of achieving socialism by full parliamentary and democratic means."

For months his *Herald* column had been pouring scorn on the Tories who wanted to sweep away the controls which had been essential to win the war and which he saw as equally essential to win the peace. The column contained some of his most savage writing, tailored carefully for a mass readership of millions. It was a blend of cynical irony, ferocious vendettas, a great deal of humour — some sour and some good-natured — and quotations from the vast breadth of his reading. Any work of literature, *Alice in Wonderland,* the Bible, the *Arabian Nights*, Greek and Roman legends, the pamphlets of obscure eighteenth-century radicals, provided the timber with which he hewed cudgels for his opponents. He could be bitingly satirical: "The task of most economists during [the past fifty years] was to invent plausible excuses to enable the statesmen, the financiers and the industrialists to go on doing what they were going to do anyway. This is known as Applied Economics."

When Foot arrived at Westminster in the crush of Labour MPs, he was already a substantial figure within the party. He lost little time in making it clear how he intended to carry on. In October, at the first full meeting of the new Parliamentary Labour Party, he seconded a motion moved by Barbara Castle, worded in feline fashion to call on ministers "to preserve the unity of the party" by consulting the PLP before they took decisions which went against the annual conference. Foot wanted to know why the government had ignored party policy by not appointing a Minister for Housing — a crucial issue after the war — and added with his usual injured innocence that the motion had been tabled merely to avoid trouble and not to create it.

In November 1946, a key left-wing rebellion came. Dick Crossman, the Oxford don now an MP, had returned from Palestine heavily critical of Bevin's policy as Foreign Secretary; he had tabled an amendment to the King's Speech asking the government to recast and review its foreign policy. This is a daring gauntlet for a backbencher to throw down, and Attlee complained bitterly at the party meeting, saying that the amendment was "unreasonable". Why hadn't the rebels given him notice? Foot backed Crossman in this typical parliamentary row — hugely important to those involved, puzzling and insignificant to the electorate outside. But it was the most important early shot across the government's bows.

Left-wingers of like mind had been meeting informally for some time, but after this they decided to group together in a more coherent fashion. In January 1947, after a gloomy chat in the small hours during the passage of some interminable Bill, they decided to write a pamphlet, and Foot, Crossman and Ian Mikardo travelled to Crossman's home near High Wycombe to do it. They liked the title *Keep Left*, a familiar road sign before continental blue arrows replaced it. Mikardo says that Foot was the most energetic ideas man of the group: "He was full of sparkling ideas, a tremendous political analyst and a hell of a good writer." Woodrow Wyatt, then thought of as a left-winger, added a section on defence.

Keep Left reads mildly enough today, though it created an enormous stir in its time. Many of the arguments it laid out reflected the disputes in the Cabinet, though in those strict days there was almost no leaking. Foot insists that there was no liaison between the rebellious ministers and the backbench left. Bevan was rigid about never giving away Cabinet secrets, a practice which Foot later observed punctiliously himself.

The introduction to *Keep Left* said that its fifteen signatories agreed (barely a year after the government had begun work) "about the need for a more drastic socialist policy if we are not to drift to disaster".

It lashed out at Bevin's anti-Russian and pro-American policy, and at home it warned that swift action would be needed to prevent the disasters which might follow the exhaustion of the American loan. It attacked the view that it was too much socialist planning which had left the country weak; on the contrary "the difficulties are the result of not enough boldness and urgency and too much tenderness for vested interests. You cannot make socialist omelettes without breaking capitalist eggs." There was a streak of austerity: the government had got its priorities wrong, making "electrical heaters and taxis plentiful". We had spent our "shrinking store of dollars on tobacco, films and chewing gum".

The section on defence was especially gloomy, pointing out that Britain could not survive for more than the shortest period against either of the two superpowers. Bizarrely to modern eyes it outlined, without any trace of irony, the possible course of a war against the United States: "These islands would be starved into submission within a few months, and the Commonwealth would disintegrate."

Keep Left led to the Keep Left group, forerunner of all the line of left-wing ginger groups within the Labour party. It was a talking shop, though in the view of its surviving members, a particularly good one, creating serious analyses of the government's problems and investigating practical solutions. One backbencher tempted to attend was a former naval rating called James Callaghan, who used to sit in on some discussions — usually held in a corner of the Smoking Room, a bar where MPs traditionally plot undisturbed. Callaghan, a working-class lad who had not gone to University, found the sessions "an intellectual treat", which he always gratefully remembered. But in the end he fell out; in particular he could not stand Crossman's donnish habit of arguing a case passionately one day, then the next day arguing the opposite. Foot, quite as shy and withdrawn as ever, was lured out in this atmosphere of constant debate and threw off ideas.

Foot, Crossman and many of the others had never done a stroke of manual work in their lives. In those days the horny handed sons of the trade unions tended to take a cautious right-wing line and had something near contempt for the clever young men in the Smoking Room. Mikardo says bluntly now that the right felt it completely safe to ignore them: "They saw us as a lot of amiable nuts, not as a source of danger," he says.

Around this time Foot's attitude to the Soviet Union and to Communism was changing. In a celebrated speech in March 1946, he said that the Russians were actually eager to destroy the Labour government, seeing social democracy as a powerful alternative to Communism. He backed Bevin's anti-Russian policy at this stage; if the Soviets were going to attack the new government, then Britain's first job must be to make it stridently clear that British socialism was here to stay.

On *Tribune*, where Foot took over the editorship in 1948, his anti-Stalinism became so fierce that he picked a quarrel with the ninety-two-year-old Bernard Shaw, and Ian Mikardo felt driven to resign from the *Tribune* board. Foot told his readers: "Bernard Shaw stopped thinking about 15 years ago . . . collectivisation, forced labour, diplomatic secrecy and bureaucratic tyranny — all these are mere trivialities . . . he has nothing to offer now but the same fulsome flattery for Sovietism he once lavished on Italian Fascism." But *Tribune* defended the Nato Pact "which serves only strictly defensive purposes".

Foot was never guilty of a naïve anti-Americanism. He had travelled there just after the war, when the United States had abandoned all controls with the same thoroughness which the Tories demanded in Britain. Even then he had been hard put to find too much at fault, though he pointed to their failure in house building. Later *Tribune* supported American intervention in Korea, another sign that Foot had given up all hopes of Russian diplomatic innocence. And later of course, just as vigorously, he hurled himself into the fight against United States policy in Vietnam.

All this time, Foot remained fundamentally loyal to the government, clear in his own mind that a Tory replacement would be a thousand times worse. He toured the country boosting the morale of constituency workers, depicting every setback in the most optimistic light. The glow from 1945 still lingered, and two years later, when the government had begun to sink into deep unpopularity with working-class as well as middle-class people, a Labour rally could be a cause for great celebration. There is a touching account of one such rally which Foot addressed in July 1947, held to commemorate the second anniversary of the election. It was held in Ashton-under-Lyne, Lancashire. There was a "Rally Queen" on a horse-drawn lorry, sports for the children, a tug-of-war and a Punch and Judy show, and afterwards a whist drive and dance. Foot made what was described as "a rousing speech". In fact it was the same speech he made in every corner of the country, in Carlisle, Kirkby-in-Ashfield, South Shields, Bletchley, Ilkeston and Weston-super-Mare, where he began, "I would not expect to find Weston-super-Mare a centre of revolutionary activity."

The speech had three basic elements: it praised the government for demobbing the Army quickly, for rescuing the most important industries from collapse, and for its "magnificent" start in housing. He admitted that he was known as a backbench critic of the government, but said that all governments needed criticism. He slipped neatly out of the noose by saying that Labour had been faced with such a "down-at-heel, despairing and miserable Opposition that the Labour party had not only had to provide the government, but the Opposition as well."

In fact the Opposition was not "despairing" at all, but was mounting a sustained attack on a government which seemed to be tottering from crisis to crisis. Now Foot's speeches and columns often look like a desperate attempt to find a silver lining. In the freezing winter of 1947, when fuel shortages led to blackouts and power cuts, he found "a lesson in socialism . . . the miners have got to the pit faces even though their villages seemed blocked with snow . . . The railway workers have been loading and despatching their precious cargoes with frost-bitten fingers in the face of blizzard and fog."

He was especially infuriated by what he saw as a wicked Tory attempt to depict Britain as an island of lazy workers, sinking fecklessly into a slough of socialist controls. In 1947 he wrote that the country was going to the local elections to defeat "the biggest, most brazen, most shameless lie ever told about our country". His optimism was misplaced, and the government's unpopularity reflected in disastrous results. Yet at the PLP Foot said that this was largely a failure of public relations, and the government should learn to believe in itself. This thread of naïveté ran through many of the speeches at that inquest: George Thomas, later the Commons Speaker, blamed the cut in the sugar ration. Mrs. Jean Mann of Coatbridge asserted the two-ounce reduction in the ration was not really a cut, merely a discontinuation of a previous increase.

By now, Foot was everywhere. If you didn't read him in the *Herald* or in *Tribune* you could hear him on a public platform. Hugh Gaitskell met him at one of these endless speaking engagements, at the Northumberland Miners' Gala of 1948. He found Foot "rather strange. He never seems to talk except when making speeches, and was most silent and reserved all the time."

The torrent of public words endeared him mightily to the Labour constituency activists. They were troubled by the government's laggard attempts to usher in the millennium, and angered by the unremitting assaults of the Conservatives, who found a ready response in a country fed up with rationing and austerity. Foot recognised the dual strain on their loyalties.

In the elections of the Constituency section of the National Executive, always a beauty contest for popular Labour figures, he came seventh at his first attempt in 1948. The next year he soared to second, taking 644,000 votes — more than half as many again as in 1948. The NEC has always been an acrimonious body; as a happy band of comrades it is a miserable failure. Nominally confidential, its proceedings are systematically leaked by all sides as they try to establish their version in the press. Foot found the atmosphere horribly oppressive, and conceived a strong dislike for Emmanuel Shinwell, then Minister of Fuel and Power. The two quarrelled angrily at the monthly meetings. In 1950, after a series of bruising rows about nationalisation and the public ownership of assurance funds, Foot thankfully left the NEC to concentrate on *Tribune*. It was twenty-two years before he returned, to find the atmosphere had changed only little.

Earlier he had begun a campaign against the Tory press and Beaverbrook. With Fleet Street hands such as Driberg and Hannen Swaffer, he successfully fought for a Royal Commission on the press. Lord Kemsley and his chain of provincial papers were his chief target: Kemsley's papers, he said, distorted the news, suppressed evidence, and acted purely as a vehicle for Kemsley's own political views. "Among newspaper proprietors, megalomania is an occupational disease." He taunted Kemsley for fearing to sue *Tribune* for libel, "because he is afraid too much dirt will come out". (Kemsley did not forget this taunt. Four years later he did sue, in curious circumstances.) Independent editors, he said with the experience of having once been one, were becoming "stooges, cyphers and sycophants".

He testified about Beaverbrook's specific malpractices to the Commission. "I expected no better from that fellow Driberg, but I never thought Michael Foot would do this to me,"

" WE'VE COME FOR THE WASHING "

Beaverbrook lamented. But the Commission never got to the bottom of the old man and his "blacklists" of people he did not care to see boosted in his various papers. He flabbergasted his critics by announcing, "I ran the papers purely for propaganda." He mused expansively on his protégé: "I did issue very many of what were called directives, really advice, particularly to Michael Foot. A very clever fellow, a most excellent boy, and then suddenly he was projected into the editorship of the paper before he was really ready for it . . . Michael Foot himself believed I made him a journalist. He took the view I allowed him immense freedom of speech." Foot was able to wound but not to kill — he told the Commission, for instance, that the high-spending advertiser and Moral Rearmer, Austin Reed, had had an article critical of MRA taken out of late editions of the *Standard*. Frank Owen, who had been editor at the time, was obliged to testify that Reed had indeed complained that morning, but that the piece had been shifted between editions in the normal way. Examples of exaggeration like this weakened the case, while a succession of newspaper executives filed into the Commission, depicting themselves as saintly men harassed by unbelievable pressures. The Commission Report was a damp squib: it thought local monopolies were in little danger of getting out of hand, there were no significant blacklists as far as it could see, and a sufficient slap on the wrist for Fleet Street could be administered by setting up a Press Council, which still exists, slapping wrists to this day.

The Tories were delighted: "Socialist attack thrown back," crowed the *Standard*. Beverley Baxter needled Foot in the debate on the Report in July 1949, accusing him of an obsessive bitterness against Beaverbrook. Foot calmly stood up and said, "I have great personal affection for Lord Beaverbrook, who has done great service to me. I have never made any personal attack on him."

The year before they had resumed their friendship. Foot made a speech at Beaverbrook's seventieth birthday dinner, and he pulled out one of his father's old debating tricks. He quoted Milton: "Princely counsel in his face yet shone . . . sage he stood, with Atlantean shoulders, fit to bear the weight of mightiest monarchies" — he paused — then announced that

Milton was, of course, writing about Beelzebub. The breach was healed.

Foot held Devonport in the 1950 general election, though Labour's overall majority was reduced to the fatally low figure of six. He fought a rumbustious campaign against Randolph Churchill, possibly the most disgraceful of all Foot's disgraceful friends, and increased his own majority. Randolph was even ruder about the local Tories than about Foot himself. He hung about Foot's election meetings: Jill and Michael, convinced that he was lonely, went drinking with him afterwards. After the vote, Churchill toured the streets in a loudspeaker van, supposedly thanking local citizens for their support. Omitting to switch off the microphone, he demanded to be taken to a pub, and en route delivered a long, offensive tirade against the incompetence of the petit-bourgeois local Tories.

A few miles away, in Callington, Isaac remarried. (Eva had died in 1946.) He consulted Jill anxiously beforehand: did she think the family would mind? "How long have you known her?" Jill asked. "A week," he confessed. Jill suggested they might get to know each other a little better. "But I can't wait," declared the seventy-year-old Isaac. "I'm only flesh and blood!" The marriage was a success.

If the government was sinking fast, so was *Tribune*. Foot moved from the editorial board to the co-editorship in 1948, with the battle-cry: "*Tribune* will spend the next twelve months fighting for socialism, lambasting the Tories, exposing humbugs, discrediting frauds and generally upholding together the claims of the community and the rights of heresy in the fields of arts, science, literature and politics." *Tribune* was relatively highbrow — George Orwell was literary editor, and Sean O'Casey, William Empsom, John Berger, Stevie Smith and Roy Fuller all appeared in its pages. But it was going broke. The paper came out fortnightly instead of weekly to save money, and raised a little cash through a string of pamphlets. Foot went to desperate lengths. He put in his own fees from broadcasting, and even enlisted Isaac to guarantee the overdraft. Peggy Duff, who later became famous as a leader of CND, was business manager; they had worked together on the 1946 "Save Europe Now" campaign, which aimed in Christian fashion to send food to starving Germans. Since Cripps's days there had been no rich patron, and by the beginning of 1951 Foot was confiding to Peggy Duff that *Tribune* might fold.

On top of all this, Lord Kemsley was suing them for libel. Now not only the paper itself but the Bevans faced bankruptcy. Jennie Lee was on the Board, and much of Bevan's savings were in her name since he ran such a risk of libel actions himself. This one began when Foot took an outraged swipe at the *Evening Standard* (notwithstanding the new rapprochement with the paper's owner). When Fuchs, the atom spy, was arrested, the *Standard* ran a Cold War smear about John Strachey, then a member of the government. "FUCHS AND STRACHEY: A GREAT NEW CRISIS", the headline said: "War Minister has never disavowed Communism. Now involved in MI5 efficiency probe." Strachey himself was advised not to sue, so Foot leapt into the breach. "LOWER THAN KEMSLEY," *Tribune* shouted.

At this crisis, Foot consulted Jill, who had a gift for dealing with Beaverbrook. She was the only person who knew that he went to ask Beaverbrook for £3,000, arguing that he had never had any redundancy payment from him in 1944. Far from bearing a grudge about the "Lower than Kemsley" jibe, Beaverbrook gave him the money and charged it to the *Daily Express*, saying, "What would we do for recruits without *Tribune*?" Kemsley hired a battery of lawyers, but Foot fought the case stubbornly and riskily all the way to the House of Lords. The Lords ruminated slowly to the sound of a dozen legal taximeters clicking, then announced that the words "Lower than Kemsley" constituted "fair comment".

It was in 1950 that Foot really began to acquire his public image as a savage fanatic. He became a television personality. Edgar Lustgarten, who had produced a US Forces discussion programme during the war, persuaded the BBC to launch "In The News", the first regular political debate on British television. Foot and A. J. P. Taylor, freebooting representatives of the left, were matched against Bill Brown and Robert Boothby, equally irrepressible mavericks of the right. (Boothby was so often at odds with his leadership that when a *Herald* reader asked Foot why he was a Tory, Foot replied, "Search me".) The programmes were, embarrassingly for the timorous BBC, a tremendous success. On television his trademark became the phrase: "That's absolute tripe, and you know it!"

The show had a large audience. "The regular team . . . seemed in combination to provide a remarkable effervescence of wit, common sense, intellectual honesty and political passion," says Grace Wyndham Goldie, who became Head of BBC Talks. They made Foot a famous personality, though his image was not necessarily the one he would still like to have as a party leader. Foot does not smile while arguing; he is too keyed up with the tension of the rhetorical cut and thrust, and friends say that he will not hesitate to use underhand debating tricks even in private conversation. He is ill-at-ease in the less formal atmosphere of present-day political television; he refuses to wear make-up under the bright lights, and he looks drawn and tense.

His political colleagues noticed that he seemed to be getting rather a lot of the limelight. Almost as soon as "In The News" began, the BBC was subjected (though it kept it a secret from the public) to pressure from both the Labour and Tory machines, which wanted to get rid of these outspoken independents and replace them with safe party men. The pressure worsened after the 1951 Bevanite split in the Labour party, and the programmes were filled with tame MPs from party lists until they became too dull to watch. After four years the team went over to the ITV as "Free Speech" and "In The News" died an unlamented death.

What happened in 1951 was the great watershed of post-war Labour politics. It is the source even today of tribal incantation which puzzles anyone under the age of thirty-five: "teeth and spectacles". There are two versions of Foot's role in the Bevanite split, which came when Nye Bevan, Harold Wilson and John Freeman resigned suddenly from Attlee's tired government and, in effect, set up a left-wing opposition.

The Gaitskellite view, put by Philip Williams, his biographer, goes like this: Foot falsified history in his own account of Bevan's life, written twelve years later. Hugh Gaitskell, a noble young Chancellor of the Exchequer, responsibly insisted on some trifling cuts in the National Health Service Budget to finance post-Korean War rearmament. Bevan, a monstrous egotist who was probably conspiring to win the Labour leadership, plotted with his friend Foot and his wife Jennie Lee to discredit Gaitskell, and in the process fatally damaged the Labour government. Not that he cared. Bevan and Foot were backed by Beaverbrook gold, in order to turn *Tribune* into a strident factional organ which would hurt the really responsible figures in the Labour movement. Foot was glad to use the row to give *Tribune* a new lease of life when it was on the brink of collapse. Bevan insisted on resigning, in spite of Gaitskell's patient attempts at compromise, and then blamed the Cabinet for all sorts of other decisions which had nothing to do with the resignation issue. His fellow Labour MPs were disgusted, and these men, unlike the misguided constituency activists and his deluded henchman Foot, could see through him. Foot himself deliberately began the Bevanite schism with a notorious article in *Tribune* assailing Gaitskell's Budget, savagely attacking the Chancellor personally, comparing him with the 1931 "Judas" Philip Snowden, and calling his measures "contemptible; timidly and squalidly inadequate".

Williams sums up: "This was the journal which, on 20 April, 1951, ended several years of reasonable harmony in the Labour party and resumed the fratricidal civil war which has lasted on and off ever since."

The Bevanite view, of which Foot is the most persuasive exponent, naturally differs greatly. It says that the left sweated out the first five years of a disappointing government in loyal fashion. They did no worse than laugh in the privacy of their own homes as Bevan delivered hilarious lampoons of Attlee's small suburban mind. Disappointment turned to justified anger with the promotion of Gaitskell, a rigid Chancellor who embarked with a stubbornness, explicable only by a desire to drive out Bevan, on a grotesque programme of impractical defence expenditure, totalling around £4,700 million. Gaitskell wanted to slice off a trifling £23 million of this sum from the National Health Service, by charging half the cost price for teeth and spectacles and so destroying its greatest principle — that it was free. Bevan said that he would be obliged to resign if Gaitskell and his friends persisted, but they did not care. He might have behaved somewhat temperamentally afterwards, but then he was a Celt. Foot's relationship with Beaverbrook had nothing to do with it, and PLP meetings were notorious for behaving with moronic hostility to anyone who broke ranks: "Like a load of damp cement," in Jennie Lee's words. Michael Foot, *Tribune* and the left, as so often in the party's past, were the lonely torch-bearers of the true faith, against the flinching cowards and sneering traitors.

Both sides exaggerate, of course. It is disingenuous for the Bevanites to pretend that Bevan was acting purely from socialist principle. There is plenty of evidence that he could be offensively egotistical, as well as a brilliant and kindly charmer. Equally, Gaitskell had a paranoid streak and tended to imagine serpentine left-wing conspiracies where none existed.

The split marked another great break in Foot's life, another shift in the pattern of his loyalties. He had quit the Liberals, quit *Tribune* in support of Mellor, quit Beaverbrook from principle and because of Lili Ernst. Now he was breaking with the Labour government he had so passionately welcomed, and from the same mixture of high-flown principle and personal loyalties.

At the junior ministers' table in the Members' dining room, George Strauss recalls, the muttering rose until, after 1951, when Labour had been thrown from office, it became a chorus. Foot was untrustworthy. He had let his colleagues down. It had been the great post-war government, making great achievements. Foot was so left-wing, so violent, so . . . personal. He was a traitor, unstable and unreliable. One MP summed it up at lunch: "If there is one person who is *intolerable* in the party, it is Michael Foot."

7

TRIBUNE FIGHTS: GAITSKELL WINS

The three resignations, and Labour's narrow defeat in the 1951 election, set the scene for the fiercest struggle the fractious party has ever seen. The participants' animosity to each other went far beyond any enmity they had for the Conservatives, who looked on this epic fratricidal feud with amusement and delight. The struggle to capture the helm of the Labour party will no doubt always be waged, yet it would be surprising if it were to continue in so bitter a fashion.

The two main lists in this tournament were the PLP meetings of MPs and the National Executive Committee. People can still recall vividly the poisonous atmosphere at the NEC. Ian Mikardo, who had been voted on in 1950, says the meetings were "absolute torture" and describes his friend Driberg leaving them "looking like a dishrag, absolutely shattered by the horrible atmosphere". Richard Crossman, who in 1952 incurred the special wrath of the right wing by getting elected with Harold Wilson and so knocking off Herbert Morrison and Hugh Dalton, gives the impression that the meetings were an endless blend of tedium and spite. "An appallingly dreary atmosphere of subdued bickering," he said of one meeting. He left another with his "entrails acid with anger. These meetings really do turn your stomach."

Foot had had enough in 1948–50 and did not wish to return, though he kept in touch with each awful twist in the feud. Mikardo blames the acrimony on a small group, mainly women, who were "supreme, world-class haters. The world champion was Edith Summerskill." The left-winger the right hated most was Mikardo, the cunning and efficient organiser.

In 1955, the NEC was considering whether to expel Bevan from the party for challenging Attlee in the House over Labour's nuclear war policy. Mikardo's daughter was due to be married in Israel, and she brought the date of the ceremony forward by one day so that her father could get back to London and vote against the expulsion. His side won by one vote, so preventing Mrs. Summerskill from using her casting vote as chairman to clinch Bevan's fate. She never forgave Mikardo, and indeed could not even bring herself to use his name. "Referring to the remarks made by the man in the brown suit," she once said, and the phrase stuck, whether Mikardo was attired in brown, blue or grey. He says: "If I had moved a motion that the sun rises in the east, Gaitskell would have said, 'That looks all right, but there is clearly a sinister political motive here'."

The meetings of the PLP which Foot often found "gruesome" could be just as unpleasant. MPs still trade poisonous personal abuse, but more often in private, and on occasion right- and left-wing Labour MPs may be seen drinking together. But it is still true that many left-wingers are more at home with a Tory MP than a Labour man of the right, and the struggles of the 'Fifties remain undimmed in many memories. It is still possible to hear, in some bar or corridor, during a dispute about a modern issue or tactic, a raised voice declare scornfully: "That's not what your lot did in 1955!"

Both sides remain convinced that it is only their opponents who stoop to personal abuse. Two small examples illustrate this: in a famous speech at Stalybridge in 1952, Gaitskell attacked *Tribune*, and by implication Foot, for "vitriolic abuse of the party leaders". In a phrase which long haunted him, he declared of Foot and his friends: "It is time to end the attempt at mob rule by a group of frustrated journalists . . ." He said he had been told at Conference that "about one-sixth of the constituency party delegates appeared to be Communist or Communist-inspired". This insinuation infuriated the left, which had always been proud of its independence from the Communists. Philip Williams, in his biography of Gaitskell, says merely that the speech was "injudiciously phrased", adding that others beside the Bevanites resented him for "hitting back — after eighteen months — at those who had systematically denigrated him and his colleagues".

Foot, in his biography of Bevan, takes a quite different view: ". . . Senator McCarthy himself had never attempted a vaguer, more unproveable, and therefore more despicable smear." The speech, he wrote, "spread a sense of boiling outrage against the leadership throughout the party". It certainly spread a sense of boiling outrage through Michael Foot, who never lost an opportunity to assail Gaitskell's leadership until his death in 1963. Foot's friends insist that the attacks were not personal, as Gaitskell was never attacked in public for anything except his political behaviour. Be that as it may, the attacks were directed at one individual, who had come to epitomise Foot's loathing of a Labour party which seemed to be in full cowardly retreat from socialism.

Of course when the left did make personal attacks, they struck the left as good-natured banter, the result of intolerable goading, or slight and easily excused lapses. But politicians, like anyone else, remember insults. Once Bevan antagonised many MPs, especially women, when he turned to Mrs. Jean Mann, a member of the NEC, who was interrupting a difficult speech he was making at the PLP, and growled, "Contain your bile, woman". It was a crass mistake for any politician to make. Foot, however, says that Bevan had been "fearfully provoked"; Bevan's widow, Jennie Lee, in her book *My Life With Nye*, says that it was "very silly of Nye" who had not remembered that "a little bit of soft soap can go a long way". "But," she adds airily, "you cannot have everything. That was Nye!" Both sides fervently believed that it was only their opponents who were unworthy, conspiratorial, deliberately disloyal and motivated by spite and ambition.

Foot was already famous. One day in 1950 Elizabeth Thomas, later to join him and work on *Tribune*, looked across the Strangers' Cafeteria at the House. With a start she thought: "My God, that's Michael Foot!" Thanks to the *Daily Herald* and television, he was already a star to the general public. He used his position to the full, never hesitating to plunge into the hottest party controversy.

In July 1951 *Tribune* produced a pamphlet called *One Way Only*, largely written by Foot, which tackled head-on the defence issue, accusing the West of basing its policies on a "gross overestimate of Soviet strength and a cringing inferiority about Soviet political warfare". United States pressure had imposed not only impractical and excessive rearmament which was threatening our economic recovery — our foreign policy across the world was also being warped. Above all, there was "the reckless, ruthless pressure to secure German rearmament". Foot, relishing the effect of his words, said later: "*One Way Only* was bitterly denounced as a near-treacherous document in Britain, as an imperialist war cry in Moscow, and a sinister charter for appeasement in Washington."

In 1952, *Tribune*, which had become a fairly sober fortnightly, burst forth in a new shape. It returned to being a weekly, dropped its price to fourpence, increased its size to tabloid and filled its eight pages with pictures, cartoons and large black headlines. It went boldly on to the attack, lashing out in every direction, reacting swiftly to each tumultuous row with language which excited and agitated the reader. In 1952, Foot handed over the editorship to Robert Edwards, but stayed on the editorial board, taking on the editorship again in 1955. He nursed his paper doggedly, while a parade of talented young recruits came, learned the job, and went on to higher, or at least better-paid, positions. Edwards was to become editor of the *Daily Express* (twice), before becoming editor, first of the *Sunday People*, and then the *Sunday Mirror*.

The paper has never had a high circulation, only rising to around 18,000 during newspaper strikes. It sells considerably fewer copies than that now. But its keenest buyers have always been Labour activists, and there is no doubt that it was *Tribune*'s tub-thumping support of the left against the "official" party leadership which helped the extraordinary spread of Bevanism in the constituencies. This could be charted through the annual elections to the constituency section of the NEC. The seven people elected to these places were among the very few on the Executive not chosen by the vast union block votes. In 1951 four Bevanites were elected, in 1952 there were six, and in 1956 for the first time they managed a clean sweep.

Foot was always at the centre of the political whirl. People who worked on *Tribune* remember him sitting at his desk in the middle of the appallingly dusty warren of rooms at 222, The Strand, scribbling out his notes in a handwriting so vile that only Elizabeth Thomas could read it. The offices, in the Outer Temple, consisted of a string of interconnecting rooms, gloomy in the middle of the day. The liftman had been a drayman and still lived in a stables, so that a smell of horses hovered pungently.

Foot's asthma might have had physical origins, but it was certainly linked to the turmoils in his mind: colleagues used to say that they could detect the state of the Labour party and tell how near Bevan was to being thrown out by the frequency with which they heard Foot's adrenalin spray in action. Now and again the phone would ring and Beaverbrook or one of his minions would be on the line. Foot would stalk into a private room to take the call. Reproached, he would do what he usually does when a distasteful subject is raised: say nothing at all. Beaverbrook often asked him which promising journalists Foot had spotted and could recommend.

Board meetings were held on Monday mornings. These were often fairly heated, particularly just after 1957, when Bevan had renounced unilateralism. Jennie Lee was constantly watching Foot — colleagues say perhaps she was a unilateralist at heart and was trying to hide her divided loyalties — and conceived a deep dislike for Edwards. The meetings could be scrappy, ill-humoured affairs quite different from the smooth and well-oiled machinations imagined by their opponents.

Those opponents were everywhere. Though Gaitskell, who became leader at the end of 1955, received their fiercest anathemas, the most powerful enemy in the early 'Fifties was Arthur Deakin, the right-wing General Secretary of the Transport and General Workers' Union. Deakin, Foot later wrote, "was a fierce, breezy, irascible stout-hearted bison of a man who genuinely believed that any proposition he could force through his union executive was the will of the people . . . leaders must be loyally followed; that was the Deakin dream of democracy . . ." Deakin helped build up his protégé Gaitskell, now eager to pursue the fight against the left. Williams's description of Deakin is, for once, close to Foot's. "He was one of those vigorous, boisterous, extroverted and intolerant working-class characters whose bullying and crudity are readily excused by intellectuals who like their politics but never forgiven by those who do not."

The one thing Deakin and his union did not like was strikes. Williams argues that the restraint such people exercised, fighting hard against a "militant or demagogic minority", had been essential in the difficult post-war years. In any event, in 1954 some 40,000 London dockers had come out on strike, led by the small National Association of Stevedores and Dockers, known, because of the colour of its membership cards, as the Blue Union. The strike was against compulsory overtime and had been joined by many Transport and General Workers' members, frustrated by their union. Ian Aitken, who had joined *Tribune* and wrote about industrial affairs, said that whenever trouble loomed, the job of the TGWU docks officer was to go down and tell the lads to get back to work. Deakin, speaking in Birmingham, claimed, without producing any evidence, that the strike was "a Communist plot".

Meanwhile a different row was going on at a tiny organ called *Socialist Outlook*, run by two men: Gerry Healey and John Lawrence. Healey, now the boss of the Workers' Revolutionary party, had been carefully infiltrating the Labour party until in 1954 he was expelled. The NEC also tried to proscribe his magazine. Foot, spotting a danger, spoke in defence of *Socialist Outlook*; he told 300 people in Holborn Hall that if the NEC got away with this "they will look around for the next one on the list". Healey was at perpetual loggerheads with Lawrence, who was going Stalinist, and, ironically, supported the TGWU in the docks dispute. Their quarrel took the form of vast attacks on each other, spread over the paper's centre pages. After the proscription, Healey decided to close it down, and the two men quite literally raced each other to 222, The Strand, to get a toehold in *Tribune*. Lawrence was a fairly flatfooted Marxist, and it was the engaging and fluent Healey who won the fight for Foot's ear. *Tribune* rushed into print with an artillery barrage by Ian Aitken against Deakin, who was accused of betraying the dockers. His speech had shown that he "did not understand the dockers and had little interest in finding out". This called forth a chorus of abuse against *Tribune*, and even some of the Bevanites, such as Harold Wilson, Hugh Delargy and Crossman, felt that Foot had gone too far. Deakin might have been an opponent, but that did not provide an excuse for what was seen as an attack on the whole trade union movement.

Foot and the rest of the editorial board — Jennie Lee and

"Curly" Mallalieu — were censured by the NEC for a "scurrilous" attack — the word was Gaitskell's — and they replied with a 6,000 word article, a sort of *Tribune* Magna Carta, claiming its right to criticise without being charged with disloyalty. "Trade union leaders are not a special breed of humanity, always to be shielded from the rough breezes of democracy, rare birds to be protected by special game laws. They are there partly to be shot at — like all other elected persons who must run the risks of public life if they aspire to hold the prizes and the power."

The row was typical of many; blown grossly out of proportion by both sides, the cause of endless wranglings, damaging to the Labour party and counter-productive in almost every way. Deakin's boorishness (he had called the Blue Union leaders "a moronic crowd of irresponsible adventurers") was matched by Foot's hot-headed rashness, his sudden emotional attachment to the cause of the moment. One of his main reasons for supporting the Blue Union was his belief that it was intolerable for someone not to be allowed to join the union of their choice; not a view he took so readily when a successor of Deakin, Jack Jones, was one of those asking for legislation on the closed shop.

Shortly after this dispute, Crossman had a discreet meeting with Gaitskell, and warned the future leader that he was beginning to look like a stooge for the trade union forces outside. Gaitskell replied, according to Crossman's diaries, with a speech in which he declared that Bevanism was "a conspiracy to seize the leadership for Aneurin Bevan. It is a conspiracy, because it has three essentials of a conspiracy, a leader in Bevan, an organisation run by Mikardo, and a newspaper run by Foot." Crossman asked him how he could take *Tribune* seriously since its circulation was so low. "He said, 'It's read everywhere in the constituencies. It's the single most important factor which our people on the right complain of.'"

The Bevanites were certainly not efficiently organised to grab power. After the 1952 Conference in Morecambe, when Morrison and Dalton had lost their NEC seats, and after Gaitskell's Stalybridge speech, the PLP moved to ban their weekly meetings. Attlee made a strong speech in which he said that the previous year had been the unhappiest of his seventeen years as leader. "I do think that where you have a continued stream of articles all directed in support of an organised group, it does give the impression in the House and in the country that we are divided." The thing that had distressed him most had been the "exceptional amount of personal animosities; I am not going to say who by . . . the Movement is far greater than any individual, and really anyone who says he is a real socialist ought to have a fire within himself that would burn up all the straws of hatred and ambition." The Bevanites decided to disband.

They did not, however, disappear. They began to hold weekly lunches at Crossman's house in Vincent Square, open to a small group of their leading lights: the six who belonged to the NEC with Foot and the others on the *Tribune* Board. The lunches were simple, buffet affairs; each member paid six shillings and sixpence, and Crossman provided the wine. They were far more concerned with immediate parliamentary problems and tactics than the old Keep Left meetings had been. One problem was that most of the participants were "more Bevanite than Bevan". Crossman exasperatedly recorded how Bevan was incapable of giving any kind of leadership or organising anything, and quite often did not bother to attend. Mikardo says now, simply enough, that he was "lazy". If there was a conspiracy, then Bevan was a most inept conspirator; nor, as their opponents sometimes thought, did they take their orders from Bevan. Foot describes the lunches: "None of the participants in these rhetorical orgies suffered from a poor appetite, and each, if need be, was ready to take on the rest. Far indeed from reality was the picture of 'the great man' surrounded by his tongue-tied sycophants."

It is indeed difficult to imagine any group which included people such as Foot, Barbara Castle, Tom Driberg and Harold Wilson taking their political orders from anybody. Yet it is clear that even in his absence, the fire, the spirit, the intellectual power Bevan possessed and the excitement he engendered, the fact that he was genuinely "charismatic" meant that he dominated all their meetings. Foot, admittedly — with Jennie Lee — his greatest admirer among the group, quotes Sir Robert Stopford, one of Nelson's commanders: "We are half-starved and otherwise inconvenienced by being out of port, but our reward is that we are with Nelson." And although they were never half-starved at Crossman's No. 9, Vincent Square, so it was with the Bevanites.

Their influence was inevitably weakened by the ban which meant the exclusion of dozens of sympathetic backbenchers. Mikardo looks back on the year and a half they had before the banning as a kind of golden age: "It was a very serious discussion group; people wrote magnificent papers. It was the best political education I ever had in my life, and that is what we lost by its banning."

Foot and *Tribune* were in the forefront of the continuous attack on the right. In 1954 he wrote *It Need Not Happen*, a pamphlet attacking German rearmament, which the left opposed on the grounds that the Germans were not yet to be trusted. They disliked the motives of the right, which backed the Americans in their efforts to bolster the Western alliance against the Russians. *Tribune* asked, "What makes Germans different?" and published an article suggesting that Nazism was merely dormant and would one day awake. The issue quietly died when this proved not to be the case, yet it is odd to read Foot in 1960, in the course of a massive attack on Gaitskell, saying in *Tribune* that the party's decision to commit itself in 1954 to German rearmament was "an appalling error which powerfully contributed to the party's defeat in 1955". This seems an extraordinary suggestion now, yet it reveals how ingrown the party's disputes had become.

Attlee and his successor, Gaitskell, believed that the party's electoral failure — it lost three general elections in the 'Fifties — was largely due to its factional fighting and the fear of Bevanism, particularly Bevanite views on the bomb and nationalisation. The left alleged that it was Gaitskell's milk toast brand of socialism which dismayed the voters; there was little point in voting for a party which merely claimed, on the basis of scant evidence, that it could operate the capitalist system better than the Conservatives. It has always been an article of faith among the Labour left that the public sometimes vote Conservative because Labour's policies are not sufficiently bold and left-wing, and the argument may not be as absurd as it sounds. Labour actually won in 1974 on a programme more left than its 1964–70 government had been. In fact, the public may not necessarily choose between 'left' and 'right', but, instead, seek leaders who offer thoroughgoing solutions, a commodity of which *Tribune* and the Bevanites had no shortage. The left has always argued that elections can only be won if the party's constituency workers are motivated by enthusiasm for the leadership and the programme it is fighting for.

Gaitskell, Foot argued in the charge sheet he brought against him in 1960, had a set of political ideas and outlook "so far out of sympathy with those of the great bulk of the Movement that the attempt to force them down our throats as the official doctrine of the party was bound to be a persistent source of division and disillusion among the rank and file".

The most bitter dispute with Gaitskell came in March 1955, when Bevan challenged Attlee in a defence debate to say whether the party leadership could envisage Britain being the first to use nuclear weapons in a war. Foot and fifty-six other Bevanites abstained on a Labour amendment at the end of the debate. The right finally saw their chance to get rid of Bevan, and Gaitskell was prominent among the group which tried to administer the coup-de-grace. Though Bevan lost the Labour whip in the Commons, the right failed to get him out of the party altogether. By now the NEC knew that Bevanism was such an enormous force in the constituencies that his expulsion would have wrecked the party for good. As it was, it made a poor prelude to the 1955 general election, when the Conservatives increased their majority, taking 344 seats to 277. It was the first Parliament for twenty-nine years which did not have a single Foot sitting on its benches.

Michael lost in Devonport by a mere hundred votes to Joan Vickers, a Conservative social worker. Ron Lemin, his agent, recalls: "All the local party hierarchy was down there at the count — Bert Medland, Harry Wright, and Jack King the housing chairman. I knew his 2,300 majority was down. Bert said, 'It'll be 1,500', Harry, 'nearer 2,000', and Jack said, 'If he's got 800 I'll be thrilled'. My argument is that he never really lost that election — he would have been allowed a second recount, but he accepted the result. Jill sat there transfixed and I was shattered. If they said, 'Let's all get in our cars and go and jump off the Tamar Bridge, I'd have been the first. I cried all night!" Outside, elated senior policemen ran across the yard, peaked caps in hand, shouting, "She's in! She's in!" Officialdom had always regarded Foot as a dangerous firebrand.

Isaac sent Michael a consolation prize: a Swift first edition, inside which he had written:

> This book (from my library at Pencrebar) is given, with my love and some reluctance, to my son Michael, as a token of consolation on his defeat at Devonport in the General Election, May 26, 1955. I recall defeats at Totnes, Plymouth, Bodmin, St. Ives and Tavistock, in the years 1910, 1918, 1924, 1935, 1937 and 1945. On the whole, these defeats were more honourable than my five victories.

Michael took the hint his father was giving him about Swift, the man who had broken the Duke of Marlborough with a pamphlet, the eighteenth-century equivalent of *Guilty Men*. He told Jill: "Now I can write that book." He turned to and produced a work of scholarly history.

The Pen and the Sword traces the work of Dean Swift as a pamphleteer in the single year of 1710, when he wrote *The Conduct of the Allies* as a propagandist in the service of the Tories. Against a backdrop of obscure hopes that the Jacobites could one day be restored, Tory grandees, led by Henry St. John, intrigued against Whig grandees and the Duke of Marlborough, then conducting the War of the Spanish Succession. Press censorship had fallen into disuse and the modern system of government by Prime Minister and party was solidifying out of what looked, close to, more like a chaotic swirl of intrigue and Grub Street assaults on public opinion. It was obviously a fascinating period for a politician and a political journalist such as Foot. The thesis he was trying to prove was that Swift's pamphlet, *The Conduct of the Allies*, had been such a brilliant propaganda coup that it turned vague grumblings about Marlborough into a swelling chorus of public opinion. "Marlborough Must Go!" His lowered prestige gave the Tories the chance to end the war. Ergo, Swift was the first master of Fleet Street polemic, and the book is a blow by blow account of the interplay between events and a rowdy press.

"As a historian," says A. J. P. Taylor, "he has this great quality of enthusiasm, and I think he gets carried away. He starts out with the idea that the Swift pamphlet did the trick and ended the war. Then you read on and discover that it was really done by the manoeuvrings of St. John. It's brilliantly written and presents Swift so well, but it's like going for a walk along an old railway line. There are bumpy bits where the track simply isn't there." Yet Foot wrote scrupulously.

When, later, Foot wrote a long essay about Disraeli, he admitted that the most serious charge made against him was implied by Disraeli's biographer, Lord Blake: "For politicians to devise myths to help shape the future may be part of their stock-in-trade. For politicians to apply comparable methods to the art of historical writing is to trespass and to vandalise." Foot half-believed this, although he went on to paint a picture of Disraeli as a true radical, rather like himself — he had a bibliophile father, also called Isaac, who taught him to "love books, the best gift of all". Disraeli too had asthma.

And this is a picture which all Foot's own friends would recognise:

> One of his most attractive characteristics was his capacity to honour an opponent, his freedom from malice, his readiness to forgive insults and injuries. He had plenty to avenge, but he would not waste his spirit on such self-destructive pursuits. But he could not be expected to forget, and mockery was an instrument which his good nature did not require him to discard. It is poured forth in a ceaseless flow on the head of one particular victim.

Gaitskell became leader of the Labour party in 1956, leading a Parliamentary Labour party without Foot. The *Sunday Express* remarked: "There is only one prospect more embarrassing than having Mr. Foot in Parliament. And that is having him out of it." On some things Gaitskell and Foot were on the same side. The Suez invasion in 1956 was courageously attacked by the Labour leader. On "In the News" Foot and

A. J. P. Taylor were so outraged that they refused to address a word to the two right-wingers over lunch beforehand. "Even to a humble 'pass the salt'," says Taylor, "we responded as though they weren't there. Michael and I felt at that moment Suez was not just wrong, but genuinely wicked."

Elsewhere he contrived to embarrass not only his own leadership, but even the French government. He wrote an article in *Tribune* describing President Coty as "the Great Nothing of the French Republic" and in June 1958 was expelled from France. He wrote a stinging letter to *The Times* complaining about the feeble efforts made by the British Embassy to save him. The ban was lifted in 1961, and he could visit again Beaverbrook's villa near Nice.

Foot respected Gaitskell for his ability and his courage, but nevertheless the leader was the nearest he got to a real personal enemy. In 1959, Bevan covered up for Gaitskell getting monumentally drunk during a trip to the Soviet Union, but had himself been described by the *Spectator* as being inebriated in Venice two years before. Foot used to say indignantly, "Gaitskell was drunk. He was drunk!"

When Labour lost in 1959 Foot, himself defeated for the second time, was the furious Savanarola of the subsequent inquest at the party Conference. As Gaitskell tried to rewrite Clause Four of the Labour constitution, the Clause which enshrined nationalisation, hoping to move the party in a social-democratic direction, Foot was the one, his voice pitched high, his arms flailing, who denounced "the evil, the rotten, the disgraceful society" in front of the television cameras.

Gaitskell and his friends disliked Foot even more than he disliked them. Douglas Jay thought he was "obviously egged on by Beaverbrook". On one occasion Foot and Jill were holidaying in Portofino, Italy. Suddenly Gaitskell walked into the restaurant with a party, including Maurice Bowra, a don and a friend of Foot's from Wadham days. Foot waved a greeting. Gaitskell stonily ignored his existence. At the coffee stage, Bowra sheepishly came over saying, "I'd better not talk for too long, or I'll get into trouble."

As the 'Fifties ended, however, there was one issue more than any other which gripped the entire Labour movement.

The anguish went well beyond the squabbles between the Bevanites and the party leaders. The issue was known to everybody simply as the Bomb.

8

BEVAN AND THE BOMB

"Michael was like a priest!" Jennie Lee says, holding up her fist and clenching it: "Like that!" Foot quarrelled spectacularly with Nye Bevan over the H-bomb, and would go on to become prominent in the Campaign for Nuclear Disarmament protests, which enlisted, and eventually disappointed, thousands of decent, idealistic and impotent citizens. At the head of the marches, trudging from the nuclear weapons design station at Aldermaston, with his flowing hair, his walking stick and his dog, Michael Foot stood out as the English Radical Conscience personified. This was the same man who had been making the Quaker case for unilateral disarmament of all kinds twenty-five years earlier, and who, twenty years later, would complain in the Cabinet about nuclear tests. He has been a disarmer all his life.

Yet what A. J. P. Taylor, his fellow campaigner, says is also true: "Michael is a middle-of-the-road man. He is a compromiser." Right-wingers, who saw Foot's election as Labour leader in 1980 as an open invitation to the Russians to invade, missed the real point. What Foot saw in the special circumstances of the years 1957 to 1963 was a chance to shift events in Britain — then striving to get into full-scale H-bomb manufacture — at a specific point when political pressure might just have worked. Even in CND he proved to be a compromiser.

CND was a failure. It did not "Ban the Bomb". (Though there was eventually a partial test-ban treaty, it did nothing to stop the increase in weapon stockpiles.) Worse, from the point of view of the Labour party, was the ill-will it caused. Idealistic people went sour on the Labour party, and a genuine public tide of moral feeling was broken on the unyielding rocks of the Labour leadership. What CND did leave behind was a glow of exhilaration and then nostalgia among those who had supported its cause. For Foot it was the second out of three such great causes: Spain was the first, and Vietnam was to be the third. Each time his final loyalty remained with the Labour party, and — apparently — none of the moral energy left him.

Ever since it had become clear, in 1954, that the British government was moving towards making its own H-bonb, there was gloom on the left. The Attlee government had produced the atomic bomb without any public or even Cabinet discussion. A line of Tory prime ministers followed this precedent. They developed the H-bomb, they secretly constructed an expensive series of rural bolt-holes for administrators, and they tried to build a British system of missiles to deliver the bomb. When Blue Streak failed, the US sold Britain missiles for the Polaris submarines. These, ageing but refurbished, were still cruising in northern waters, when Foot became Labour leader. They constitute the "independent British nuclear deterrent".

The theory is that, should the Russians wish to obliterate Britain on its own, they will be discouraged by the knowledge that Polaris will survive to exact revenge on Moscow (the missiles are not accurate enough to aim at military targets). A variant of this theory is the belief that if there were a "conventional" Soviet attack in Europe, Britain could insure against any American faintheartedness by threatening to begin a nuclear exchange on its own. Yet both of these notions of the "balance of terror" are considered by many as somewhat academic in a context of the giant arsenals of the two super powers.

A third idea is that the possession of these H-bomb systems constitutes some kind of bargaining counter with which Britain itself can encourage the process of disarmament and non-proliferation — it would carry a seat at the conference table for the honest broker, the sophisticated voice, the potential moral leader. The evidence to support this theory is, as yet, scant.

However, to the unilateralist, these ideas seemed not merely questionable but terrifying and obscene, much as in the 1930s, it was thought that rearmament would lead to war, and war would bring the end of civilisation. In the mid-1950s many perfectly sensible people in the worst days of the Cold War thought not that they were living in a post-war but in a pre-war period.

Tribune published in 1954 the story of the *Lucky Dragon*, a boat whose crew was sprayed with radioactive fall-out from a US H-bomb test in the Pacific. The first parliamentary campaign against the bomb was a fairly damp affair, a petition and public meeting, in which Tony Benn was prominent. Later sixty-three left-wingers signed an amendment calling on Parliament to be given a veto over the making of H-bombs. A greater rebellion came the following year, a classically Bevanite imbroglio, in which the problems of policy on the bomb were drowned in recriminations about Bevan's supposed misconduct, indiscipline and lack of proper respect for his leader. On this occasion he was almost expelled from the party. He, and fifty-six other MPs refused to vote on an official Labour amendment which contained the phrase, "It is necessary as a deterrent to aggression to rely on the threat of using thermonuclear weapons." This, they thought, implied that Labour was prepared to countenance using the bomb first in order to deter a "conventional" Soviet attack. And no doubt this is just what it did mean, but as Labour had nine more years in Opposition it had little practical importance, though the dispute was rich in political symbolism.

This row did, however, stake out a position to which Bevan clung, as the debate on the left grew more radical and neared the unilateralist position. Bevan did not object to Britain manufacturing the bomb, though he wanted tests suspended. What he could not tolerate was the idea that this country might deliberately escalate a war they were losing and turn it into Armageddon.

By 1957 he had sobered into a rapprochement with Gaitskell. He was the party's spokesman on foreign affairs, and was assumed by most Labour MPs to be the next Foreign Secretary. By now Britain had begun to test its own H-bombs, on Christmas Island in the Pacific. The Federation of American Scientists warned that "future H-bomb test programmes by several atomic powers will reach a level that is a serious threat to the genetic safety of all the people in the world." An early Quaker-dominated campaign with a unilateralist policy had begun and was attracting support. Bit by bit the unilateralist cause was gaining ground, and had won over most of the Bevanite group. At the Labour Conference in Brighton that autumn there were more than a hundred unilateralist motions on the agenda. Foot, of course, was a unilateralist too, and the question that he and his colleagues were waiting to see answered was whether Bevan would join them and lead them.

That summer Bevan had been to Russia, and his talks with the Soviet leaders obviously impressed him — like many others before and since — with a somewhat inflated idea of Britain's potential role in world politics. Sam Watson, the miners' leader on the NEC, also spent a good deal of time urging conciliation and "responsibility" on Bevan. At the NEC meeting which precedes the Conference, and where the serious horse-trading over resolutions and motions takes place, Bevan said that the full implication of accepting the unilateralist resolution scheduled for debate would mean "the dismantling of international alliances and commitments, dismaying the Commonwealth, and reducing Britain to complete negation in the counsels of the world". He told Foot what he had done just before the *Tribune* meeting at the Conference, where they were both to appear: "Since he made it clear his choice was irrevocable," Foot said, "there was not much more to be said."

The *Tribune* meeting was a miserable affair for Foot. "They cheered when I said the way to peace was for Britain to renounce the bomb," he recalls, explaining how subdued and apprehensive the audience were as they waited for Bevan. "Everybody at the Conference under forty", was there, Crossman wrote. He painted a picture of Foot gallantly banging away "at his most blaringly demagogic", and Bevan making a speech which gave away nothing of his own intentions, "truisms and platitudes curling round his lips in a very serene way". Foot was to carry on at *Tribune*, while the rest of the Bevanites were quietly put out to grass — or so the centre and the right of the party hoped.

Between the *Tribune* meeting and the great foreign affairs debate on the Thursday morning, Foot was one of a crowd of left-wingers who clustered round Bevan beseeching him to think again. In the back room of English's fish restaurant, and up and down the sea-front, Geoffrey Goodman of the *Daily Mirror*, James Cameron, the journalist, and Vicky, the cartoonist, were given the painful news. Foot clung to some slight optimism that Bevan might not renounce unilateralism totally. He has always overestimated his ability to persuade; he is much better at inspiring the converted than getting people to change their minds.

That night, on the eve of the debate, the Bedford Hotel, where the Bevanites and their supporters were staying, was a scene of utter misery, as keen young left-wingers burst into tears when they learned the news. Foot himself gives a moving account of Bevan's speech the next morning. Stung by hecklers, he roared back at them, pouncing upon those who wanted security, yet who wanted to tear up all Britain's international agreements for the sake of their moral superiority. Unilateralist resolutions, he said, "will very greatly embarrass a Labour government". He told the incredulous audience that the sudden lack of British moderating influence would probably provoke the Third World War. Britain would be put into "diplomatic purdah". The unilateralists were guilty of — and he spat it out — "an emotional spasm". Worst of all, the resolution would send a British Foreign Secretary "naked into the conference chamber".

Elizabeth Thomas, working at *Tribune* with Foot, is one of the people who then worshipped Bevan: "I remember sitting in the *Tribune* offices listening to his speech over the radio and hearing the boos. I was thinking, 'This can't be true.'" Crossman on the other hand was smug. He recorded in his diary: "Nye . . . just floundered round and round in circles . . . it was a ghastly performance. And yet it was immensely impressive directly they started heckling him, for at this point the old bull turned . . . that vast blue-suited figure and bright red face and the iron-grey hair angry — and he's terrific when he's angry — mortally offended and repudiating with violent indignation the suggestion that he was grooming himself as Foreign Secretary." Crossman saw a Gaitskell-Bevan axis curbing the "extremists" on both nationalisation and the bomb. He thought that "doctrinaire faith in pacifism" had been crushed.

Vicky, the cartoonist, a friend of Foot's, published a drawing of Gandhi. He captioned it: "*I* went naked into the conference chamber." That weekend, A. J. P. Taylor says: "We were due to have a 'Free Speech' programme on nuclear weapons. We were discussing it at Edgar Lustgarten's flat when the bell rang. There was Michael, shaking all over. He said: 'I can't go on today — you'll have to get someone else.'"

Back in the Smoking Room, the Bevanites were scattered. Bevan himself sat boycotted by all but a few of his faithfuls: Harold Davies, Leslie Hale and Foot himself. He suffered vituperative attacks and poison-pen letters, not from Tories but from his own left-wingers. By 1959 and the election he had cancer and died the following year; there are a few close to him who think bitterly that the "emotional spasms" of some of his old comrades helped to kill him.

Even Foot, whose enemies have never been able to detect a streak of personal malice in him, was sufficiently shattered to have the occasional personal quarrel with his old hero. He could not understand how Bevan could have made this terrible misjudgment on an issue about which he felt far more deeply than most. Bevan could not understand how Foot, of all people, refused to appreciate his position. Delegates waylaid Foot at Brighton and asked, as he describes it, "over and over again. 'Why has he done it? Why? Why? Why?' I myself never asked him why. It would have been an insult."

At *Tribune* he continued to campaign for unilateralism. He was tender to Bevan, and ran the speech at length as "what Bevan really said". In his own article he wrote in answer to it:

> Britain has only had a tested H-bomb for a matter of months . . . were we not members of all these alliances before we had the bomb? And does not the same apply to many other nations who, fortunately for the world and wisely for themselves, have no intention of attempting to make one? . . . Of course, it would be hypocritical to surrender our own bomb and merely be content to shelter behind someone else's. But it would not be immoral to abandon our own bomb and seek the best diplomatic means we could to ensure that others did the same. The power of example might be one of the best ways of securing that end . . .

When Jennie Lee, still on the *Tribune* board, complained angrily, Foot dug in his heels. The truth was that he was receiving so many anti-Bevan letters that he was reduced to secretly making up and printing a few in his favour. Foot describes the period delicately in his Bevan biography, but it had ugly moments. Jennie Lee was sufficiently bitter at the time to want to see *Tribune* close rather than have it go on as "the Paper that leads the fight against the H-bomb". She and Bevan could have done so; its chief 'angel' at the time was the socialist property magnate, Howard Samuel, a close friend of Bevan. "You must defend Nye's honour," she scolded Foot. Foot was impressed by Bevan's fortitude in the face of the storm but was no longer his disciple.

The following July they nearly came to blows. Foot and Jill met Bevan and Jennie at a Polish Embassy reception. They went back to St. John's Wood for more drinks, and quickly started an argument about the Labour party in general, and the mentality of the NEC in particular. The strains suddenly became too much: Foot records that there was "a blazing bonfire of a row, with much ill-considered obstinacy from me and some more eloquent and even four-letter responses — I had never heard him use them before — about my 'sterility' until he picked up a Sheraton chair and smacked it to the ground as if he almost wanted to throw that onto the polemical flames. It was a horrific occasion."

Jill made peace between them the next morning, but it was a long time before they became warm friends again. Almost a year later, Foot, arriving for what must have been a curious dinner party with Crossman and Henry Kissinger, told Crossman as the guests arrived, that he had spent only one cautious afternoon with Bevan since the beginning of 1959. "People like you and Barbara and Tony Greenwood had better talk to Nye," he said, "I'm no good nowadays." Crossman was trying to start up a group to discuss nuclear weapons again. "Michael told me that never in his whole life had he felt more depressed about the party."

While the Labour party was trying to get itself into shape to face the electorate in 1959, Foot was involved elsewhere. As the Labour party closed the door against the unilateralists, CND had begun.

In the spring of 1958, a few months after Bevan's speech in Brighton, Kingsley Martin, the editor of the *New Stateman*, asked Foot to a meeting at the house of Canon John Collins. Martin had been publishing articles against the bomb written by J. B. Priestley and Bertrand Russell, and had already done preliminary work to sound out the idea of a mass movement. At the meeting there were people such as James Cameron, who had actually watched nuclear explosions, and A. J. P. Taylor, both of them nowadays united in their belief that CND was the one thoroughly decent venture into which they had ever thrown themselves. Collins had just organised a vigorous campaign against capital punishment, which Foot had supported, and brought with him from that campaign Foot's old *Tribune* colleague, Peggy Duff. (She had been fired as business manager of *Tribune* in 1955, detecting in him "a ruthlessness which others discovered". Some, like Barbara Castle, have always claimed to see an autocratic streak in him, though Bob Edwards, who was falling out with Peggy Duff at the time, says Foot was "not a good firer" at all, and was if anything too nice to his friends to make the perfect editor. Peggy Duff did not bear him much ill-will; Foot was one of the people to whom she dedicated her memoirs.)

Foot gives Martin the credit for getting CND on the road: "He could seize the moment to inspire a new departure. It was his flair against the advice of most of his *New Statesman* colleagues that made possible the conjunction of ideas and people that launched CND . . . no doubt he regarded himself as the leader of a great crusade, but mingled with the deed was also the matchless timing of the journalist born and bred." Not that Martin saw, at first, the campaign as out-and-out unilateralist.

The campaigners did not want MPs on their executive; this was not a party venture, though obviously if CND's supporters saw a practical outcome for their efforts it was to convert the Labour party and get it into power. How else could the bomb be banned? Foot, then out of Parliament, was an obvious choice for leader, and he was the first to push Lord Russell and the whole campaign firmly onto the unilateralist road.

CND's first meeting, in the Central Hall, Westminster, was

one of the landmarks in British "protest politics". People rushed to buy the sixpenny tickets: four overflow halls were filled. Foot was billed first, and made a slashing denunciation of the British bomb. "Michael was supposed to be the impassioned orator," Taylor recalls, "and then I would come on later as the cool academic. But when he made his big speech, he had terrible trouble with the Empire Loyalist hecklers constantly interrupting. Michael did his best, saying, 'All right, fair enough, let's hear them. Speak up!' but I thought with this heckling, I'd better be aggressive." He tried to work on the audience: "Who'll push the button?" he kept asking. The pro-bomb MPs, he declared to wild applause, were "murderers". The hecklers had all gone home; what Taylor's speech did was to excite the audience to the point where many respectable persons rushed up the road to Downing Street, where some were arrested.

From then on, the energies of the Labour left — with thousands of other pacifists, youngsters, Communists, house-wives, students — went into the campaign. The Aldermaston marches began and were soon a British tradition, marchers trudging through the Home Counties, sleeping in schools and halls organised by the indefatigable Peggy Duff, on into Trafalgar Square, 100,000 strong by now; then, with a shade of anti-climax, Foot would deliver the final speech: "This is the way of showing the government what the sane people of this country think." He walked the full march, but returned to London each night to sleep. "Then we all finished up at Michael and Jill's house with an enormous party," Elizabeth Thomas says. "There were people like Spike Milligan there, everyone nursing their blisters, lots of food and drink — it was a wonderful end to the march. You really felt you were achieving something, everyone having a marvellous time marching through London. All the people cheered you."

Now the big unions with their block votes were falling to unilateralism as well. Frank Cousins, the new left-wing leader of the Transport and General Workers' Union, had become a great friend and ally of Foot. He was narrowly overborne by the rest of his delegation from voting against Bevan at the 1957 Conference, but by 1960 he had cajoled and enlisted TGWU activists throughout the country. Foot made endless speeches in London and in Plymouth, where he was still the candidate. Taylor toured the big cities. In Nuclear Disarmament Week in 1959, forty speakers appeared simultaneouly all over the country. Gaitskell and the Labour leadership were still adamant against them.

Foot, the great loyalist, pinned all his hopes on converting the party. Even before the general election in 1959, there were noises being made about a "Voters' Veto" campaign against pro-bomb candidates. The argument was that this tactic might force the party into rethinking its policy before the election. Foot said in the CND bulletin that this tactic was mistaken: "Only through the election of a Labour government and the political pressure which we may exert afterwards can we succeed. A renewed mandate for a Tory government which has shown itself adamantly opposed to any concession . . . would be a serious and possibly fatal set-back to our campaign."

Labour duly lost its third election in a row, and it was left to Macmillan to abandon Blue Streak and to buy Polaris. Foot's reputation as a unilateralist did not help him in Devonport, where thousands of the voters worked in the naval dockyards. They had a strain of both working-class jingoism and real fear for their jobs. "He'd have these dockyard meetings," Ron Lemin, his agent, wearily recalls, "and he'd talk about the manifesto up and down, backwards and sideways, education, housing, the lot. Then some clot at the back would always say, 'What are your views on the atom bomb?' Well he couldn't wrap up about it, so next day there it would be all over the paper again: the bomb, nothing but the bomb." The seat was marginal in any case, and in 1959 the Tory majority rose from a hundred to 6,454. He had always refused to leave it and find somewhere safer, although after 1955 there had been approaches from Northumberland and Aberavon. The local party tried to construct good-natured conspiracies to drop him; Lemin remembers Foot arriving on the doorstep and hauling him down to the Pear Tree for a pint: "No, I said, you don't brainwash me! I felt it was a complete waste of his ability to be in the wilderness. I said I'd canvassed everyone on the General Management Committee. We went to the meeting, I moved the resolution, he got up and in three minutes he had them all in the palm of his hand. I only got three votes! He loved Devonport."

Foot and Bevan were reconciled by now, but Bevan was already a sick man. The climax of every Devonport campaign since 1945 had been Bevan's arrival to speak. He set out to the station, but felt too ill, and had to turn back. Jennie Lee urged Foot to visit him in hospital. "Take a few books. Have a good rough argument, make him feel that everything's normal." They gossiped cheerfully, and Bevan told him two significant things. Nothing they wanted, he said, could be achieved outside the Labour party. "Never underestimate the passion for unity, and don't forget it's the decent instinct of people who want to do something." (Twenty years on, newly elected as Labour leader Foot quoted this.) Reproving Foot's "quixotry" in running again and again for Devonport, Bevan also said, "Now you'd better look properly for another seat. Perhaps you needn't look further than Ebbw Vale."

In 1960, CND, vilified by the "respectable" elements in the Labour party, spurned by Gaitskell, mocked by Fleet Street, managed, largely due to Cousins, to generate a majority at the Labour Party Conference. After they had won the key vote, Gaitskell electrified the delegates by his promise to reverse the vote: "There are some of us, Mr. Chairman, who will fight and fight and fight again to save the party we love." The right-wing were already mobilised to fight back with the Campaign for Democratic Socialism, a highly efficient ginger group run by William Rodgers, with help from Dick Taverne, Brian Walden, and Denis Howell. They overturned the conference decision in just a year.

In 1960, just after Foot had got back into Parliament, he became involved in an elaborate plan of Crossman's to produce a compromise document on the bomb which would somehow unite the party. This turned out to be a confused paper, and Crossman's own interest seems to have been to devise it in such a way that Gaitskell would be forced to reject it so as to appear unwilling to unite the party. Crossman wrote at the time about Foot: "I got the impression from him that his commitment to CND is really an embarrassment, since he knows in his heart that the party can't be a completely unilateralist party."

CND continued to hold marches and executive meetings. "Michael didn't contribute anything constructive to those meetings," says A. J. P. Taylor. "What could anyone contribute anyway? Propose another march?" There was nothing CND could do, as the next party Conference trampled on its dreams and overturned the 1960 decision.

The idea of the "Voter's Veto" was renewed. A few marginal votes cast against right-wing Labour candidates could cost Labour up to fifty constituencies. James Cameron agreed to stand, if he was sure he would not win. At a rowdy meeting at the 1961 Conference, Foot said again that the idea was "poison". Progress could only come through the Labour party.

The other possible way out of the impasse for CND was tougher action on the streets. Foot set his face against Gandhian "direct action". He said that he was not prepared to incite people to go to prison. If he did not get jailed himself, it would be immoral, and if he did it was equally immoral to use his example to egg on people whose careers or lives might be much worse affected than his own. CND split, with the "Committee of 100" and Lord Russell engaged in a sulphurous row with Canon Collins and the official CND.

The campaign became confused and rancorous. By 1963 politicians such as Judith Hart and Anthony Greenwood, who had come on to the executive in response to the threat of CND independent candidates, withdrew. Foot himself resigned. In August 1963, *Tribune*, edited by Richard Clements since Foot had returned to Parliament, dropped its "anti H-bomb" masthead. Foot was back in the fold. Labour had a new left-of-centre leader in Harold Wilson, and another election was approaching. Foot was preparing, with dogged optimism, for yet another painful disappointment — the Wilson government of 1964, and Vietnam.

9

THE ROMANCE OF EBBW VALE

After that, Foot was always to have a solid political base. He finally abandoned his beloved Devonport and, following Bevan's deathbed hint, successfully applied for the nomination at Ebbw Vale. The constituency, with its massive Labour majority, is set high in the valleys of South Wales. As well as Ebbw Vale itself, it contains two other towns: Rhymney, and Bevan's own home town of Tredegar.

The people of Ebbw Vale had often felt a trifle neglected by Bevan, who was not the most devoted constituency MP Westminster has ever known. They admired him and even loved him, but knew his habit of making unnecessary opponents. He did not suffer fools gladly; indeed he did not always suffer sensible people gladly either, if they happened to disagree with him. A favourite saying, as liberally employed as "blockhead", was, "The trouble with you, boyo, is that you have nothing between your ears." Nevertheless, the gap he left behind seemed huge. The constituency party wanted either someone who was local or of similar international standing to replace him.

Ten people offered themselves as candidates, and Foot, Bevan's loyal henchman, had far and away the most nominations from the ward parties and trade union branches, a total of seventeen. More important, he had the backing of the Bevan family. So it was all the more astonishing when the party's executive committee met in September 1960 that Foot was not on the five-man shortlist they had drawn up after a secret ballot. The news amazed not just Ebbw Vale, but the country as a whole, which had taken it for granted that the nomination was Foot's. Bevan's brother William said that he was "shocked" like the rest of the family. He said he could not interpret the committee's decision, since he had seen Foot as the natural heir to Nye. The universal belief, that the various supporters of the lesser candidates had clubbed together to keep the strongest candidate off the list, is not an unknown device in local Labour politics. Jennie Lee, Bevan's widow, intervened at once, telling his old agent, Archie Lush, that she wished to see Foot's name on the shortlist. A fortnight later the Management Committee met and the names of Foot and the miners' nominee, Frank Whately, both appeared on the list. Foot led from the first round of voting, and won easily on the third round.

" HERETIC ! STILL BELIEVES IN WHAT WE USED TO PREACH..!"

For thirty-one years the election workers of Ebbw Vale had been doing little more than piling up votes for a candidate who, for the most part, was away touring the country. But the 1960 by-election campaign left a glow of excitement and exhilaration still remembered by those who took part. The campaign was hardly directed against the Conservatives at all. Brandon Rhys-Williams, the forgotten Tory candidate, put it succinctly: "Does the so-called Labour candidate think it honest to use the Labour organisation here, built up over so many years, as a platform from which to launch his campaign, the only object of which is to smash the leadership of the Labour party and to pour scorn on its policies?"

This was precisely what Foot was doing. The by-election was a crusade against one man, and there was scarcely any attempt to pretend otherwise. For example, in mid-October, after the "fight and fight and fight again" speech at Scarborough, Foot said in Ebbw Vale: "I shall not make an issue of Mr. Gaitskell's leadership, but I am bound to be asked questions on it. I will answer them. I will not enter into personalities." A week later he wrote one of his fiercest attacks on the leader. Labour, he said, had reached the point of crisis under Gaitskell. He had failed to weld the varying elements of the party into a cohesive and enthusiastic force. "On this test Mr. Gaitskell's leadership has failed. If he persists in the course he proclaimed at Scarborough it will be extremely difficult, if not impossible, for that disunity to be quickly repaired."

The size of Foot's majority was to be the symbolic indicator of the success of left and right in winning the voters. Bevan's majority in 1959 had been, in a straight fight with the Tory candidate, just under 21,000. Now Foot faced a Liberal candidate and a Welsh Nationalist as well, both of whom were bound to cream off some votes. A majority of 12,000 became the imaginary watershed for press and politicians; anything more was a victory for Foot, the left and the unilateralists; anything less a win for Gaitskell.

The struggle attracted enormous attention. Bevanites poured in to address packed and enthusiastic meetings: Barbara Castle, Richard Crossman, Ian Mikardo, Harold Wilson and several lesser known figures such as John Stonehouse. The most surprising visitor was Foot's old opponent, Jim Callaghan, who was to vote for his expulsion from the PLP in 1961. Callaghan was due to speak at two meetings, in Ebbw Vale itself and Tredegar. During the first speech he said that he opposed Foot's policy on defence and, according to Michael Parkinson, then a reporter on the *Daily Express*, was rousingly cheered by part of the audience. The party workers were appalled at this lèse majesté: Len Evans, who had been given the job of driving Callaghan to the next meeting, remarked as they passed the small lake at Waun-y-Pound: "I've a good mind to dump you in it after the speech you made." When they arrived, safe and dry, at Tredegar, someone whispered to the chairman that Callaghan had attacked Foot and it was smoothly arranged that, though he should stay on the platform, he would not be allowed to speak.

Foot stomped happily through the valleys, beginning a love affair which has never ended. The pictures of the period show him with striking wings of hair on each side, like a mad professor. Two middle-aged ladies promised: "We'll vote for you, bach, provided you get your hair cut." He took his dog Vanessa out canvassing, and would appear at a door wet and bedraggled — it rained almost ceaselessly throughout the campaign — accompanied by four or five curious strays, curs and mongrels. Conversation often took the form of electors chatting cheerily on while Foot barked the odd word of greeting or encouragement.

The election came alive at night when Foot spoke. He gave his listeners the pure, undiluted grain spirit of socialism, and in particular his belief in nuclear disarmament. Certainly most of the constituency activists were unilateralists, and many belonged to CND. But this feeling was not so strong among the ordinary voters, and while the subject cropped up, it was not — according to those who remember the campaign — the only important topic. This did not deter Foot from writing in the *Daily Herald*:

> Defence, nuclear weapons and foreign policy push all else into the shadows: . . . we have held packed village and schoolroom meetings late into the night where every question without exception has turned to these topics. At 10 o'clock on Saturday night at a workmen's club, after the housey-housey session was over, 400 miners, steelworkers and their wives were quite ready to debate the same matter . . . people stop you on the doorstep to ask you about Polaris . . . A new and explosive element has been imported into British politics.

The fact that a substantial portion of his voters disagreed with him was irrelevant. It was crucially important for him to win the seat on an unashamed unilateralist platform, and nobody in Ebbw Vale could have been left in the slightest doubt about that.

It is the tradition in by-elections that candidates receive public letters of support from their party leaders. Tories waited eagerly to see what Gaitskell would write, and the week before polling day the leader found a form of words he could send. It appealed to Labour voters to avoid complacency and

'*That's torn it—a real one's got in!*'

to make sure that every Labour vote was recorded on the day. It did not burke the issue: "You and I disagree strongly on some important issues on defence and foreign policy, and neither of us would wish to gloss over these differences. There is no need to exaggerate their scope, and I am sure you would not wish to do so."

The *Daily Mail* saw the candidate "with his wild, questing eyes, his straying hair and his perpetually undone overcoat. He looks like a man who has just discovered that he has lost his ticket." The *Evening Standard* reported a meeting one freezing night in a small village hall, packed with a hundred people:

"Jill Craigie, in a red shortie coat with a black Hussar hat set rakishly on the side of her head was gazing up at her husband . . . occasionally she interpolated the speech, so that when he declared that the Soviet Union spent more on education than Britain, she quickly added 'per capita'." She too developed great affection for the people: "The Welsh often laugh that they may not weep," she said. "I think now I understand that the people of the valleys have emerged from the years of Depression so effervescent and yet so serious a people."

The campaigners met after hours at a pub called the Castle in the village of Cwm. Foot relaxed over a drink and joined in the jokes and the singing. Party workers from Devonport made the long journey to help, and at the end of each session they would sing the Red Flag, long after closing time. At the evangelical eve-of-poll rally Foot made a speech which some say was one of the finest of his life. He told them: "The flame of socialism will never be extinguished as long as it lasts in Ebbw Vale."

Foot won, with a majority of 16,729, much more than most of his supporters had dared to hope. His agent, Ron Evans, wanted a recount, hoping the Tory would lose his deposit, but Foot had heard that Isaac was ill, and wanted to tell him the result. He shouted it down the phone, and the old man, now two weeks from death, said gleefully: "When they fight the Foots, the Tories bite granite." When he returned a reporter asked him if the result meant, "God help Gaitskell", and Foot replied: "You said it." He added: "We have demanded a foreign policy which repudiates entirely a nuclear strategy. We have stood out for those things demanded by the Scarborough conference. We have kept the Red Flag flying here." Vicky drew a cartoon showing Gaitskell reading the news of Labour's defeat in six other by-elections that same day. Foot's face glowered up from one paper, and Gaitskell was saying gloomily, "Oh dear, we've won."

Three days later he was introduced into the Commons. All six Conservative winners wore black jackets and striped trousers. Foot wore an ageing and unpressed suit. As he stepped forward, the Conservatives cheered him on and mockingly waved Gaitskell to join them. The Labour leader managed a smile as crumpled as his newest member's clothing.

Foot was enchanted. Not only had he won the by-election on an uncompromising unilateralist platform, but he had discovered in Ebbw Vale a community which fitted all his most romantic notions about how the working-classes existed. To a man who grew up in the southern middle-class, Ebbw Vale and the valley towns seemed a kind of socialist Shangri-La, untouched by the tawdry horrors of the outside world. He wrote an encomium to his new constituency in the *Herald*:

What is it that South Wales and more particularly the constituency of Ebbw Vale has got which others haven't got? The short answer is that the people of industrial Wales are proud of their working-class tradition, proud of their working-class achievements and still as proud as ever of *being* working-class. Against this rock all the prissy values preached by the BBC, all the tinsel tuppeny-halfpenny ideas filtered through television, all the snobbery and smug complacency associated with a Tory-directed affluent society beat in vain. For the people of these valleys, after a century of tumult and struggle, there is more in heaven and earth than the threadbare dreams which our society purveys as a substitute for living . . . in South Wales the spirit of class-consciousness suffuses the whole community. Men and women still believe that it is better to live in a real community than to set before themselves the idea of rising out of their class, spurning their great ancestry and kicking away the ladder . . . the Ebbw Vale election was for me more exhilarating than any political experience in my life precisely because it revealed how strong and indestructible are the sinews of British democracy. Here were people, masses of them, old and young, and plenty of the young to dismiss the sneers against them, eager and determined to debate the major challenges to British society and the world. Certainly they were not content to be palmed off with trifles and trinkets.

Soon afterwards the Foots bought a tiny run-down miners' cottage in the middle of Tredegar, a small victory in the town's continual rivalry with Ebbw Vale. The roof was falling in, yet Jill managed to restore it to a smart, attractive, slightly austere home for their visits to the constituency, which they try to visit at least once a fortnight. He holds his surgeries in the living room of the cottage, often phoning people with problems and inviting them down. The local people are not pleased with his down-at-heel garb; some of them complained to Jennie Lee that Nye had always dressed smartly, and they expected their MP to be well groomed. But they greet him in high good humour and their affection is obvious and genuine.

In 1972, Foot unveiled the memorial to Bevan at Waun-y-Pound on a hill overlooking all three towns, on the spot where Bevan addressed the great rallies of his constituents who walked up from their homes, from the mines and the steelworks to hear him. The memorial is four limestone pillars, one for each town and a central one with the inscription: "It was here that Aneurin Bevan spoke to the people of his constituency and the world." It is a moving place though not an idyllic one; the stones face a few small advance factories and a filling station; some people have stopped by only to scrawl graffiti on the stones.

The love affair between Foot and Ebbw Vale has continued to this day, but not quite uninterrupted. In February 1975 the Labour government to which Foot belonged announced that some half of the 8,600 steel jobs in Ebbw Vale were to go by 1979. All steelmaking in the area would end, and the remaining plant would concentrate on tinplating and galvanising steel brought in from Llanwern. Foot knew of the decision in advance, and arranged to address a public meeting on the Saturday night after the announcement. On Friday he arrived with John Morris, the Secretary of State for Wales, to meet the local council and discuss plans to get new industry to the towns. The Labour government had agreed to spend £12,600,000 on this operation.

But the steelworkers came out on a one-day protest strike, and several hundred men marched on the civic centre where Foot and Morris were talking to the council and stood outside yelling abuse. Foot grabbed a loud-hailer and went downstairs. Any hopes that they would be calmed by promises about the future quickly disappeared. They shouted "Judas", "Give Foot the boot", "Traitor" and "Get back to Devonport" at him, as he repeatedly told them that they could trust him. "We can save Ebbw Vale," he shouted back. "You can do it if you are prepared to face the future with guts and confidence . . . I will tell you the truth although you won't like the truth."

Those who saw him immediately afterwards say that he was shaken by the hatred he had faced from part of a community he virtually hero-worshipped. Some of the striking workers said later that they had been ashamed, yet the anger remained at the meeting the next night. When Morris described the many firms preparing to bring work to the constituency, the secretary of the works council said, "We don't want to work in marshmallow factories or make eyes for toy dolls."

Thanks in part to Foot's efforts, some new factories eventually opened and there are more advance factories built waiting for the end of the recession. But the steelworks closure left a bitterness which has not been entirely erased, a sense of having been betrayed by their own. Many unemployed steelworkers find that the breadwinner in the family is a wife or daughter earning good wages in one of the small light industries now dotted around the valleys. In a society where men are expected to support their own families by hard physical labour, it is painful to live off money that a nineteen-year-old daughter brings home from a bra factory.

These events seem to have done Foot little lasting harm. The swing against him in 1979 was five and a half per cent, very marginally higher than the nearby Labour constituencies. With a majority still over 16,000, this is hardly a cause for panic. And still, as he stalks about the constituency in a battered old tweed jacket, or driving an even more battered car, waving his stick and shouting, "Hello, yes, well, how are you? Good, good," the local people smile back gently and chat about the council, or the steelworks, or the weather.

Two days after re-entering the Commons, Foot was into the political swing signing a motion which deplored the plight of Britain's professional footballers. If Gaitskell and the Shadow Cabinet imagined that he would spend his days on such blameless sporting interests, their illusions were swiftly shattered. His first meeting of the PLP rapidly degenerated into uproar. Calling for unilateralists to be added to an NEC-Shadow Cabinet meeting to discuss defence, Foot was constantly heckled, by no one so loudly and frequently as Mr. Joseph

Symonds of Whitehaven, who shouted, as Denis Healey had done at the 1959 party Conference, "What about Devonport?" Foot had the satisfaction of being able to shout back: "What about my thumping majority at Ebbw Vale?" Gaitskell moved the closure after only twenty minutes, and Anthony Greenwood yelled: "These are the methods of National Socialism!" George Brown bawled back, "You're calling us Nazis!" and a general mêlée ensued. To no one's surprise, Foot lost by ninety-nine votes to twenty-seven.

A fortnight later he heard that his father had died. That day the House was to debate a motion of censure tabled by George Brown which asserted the "paramount need for multilateral disarmament". Foot walked sadly into the Chamber for Question Time, sat through two long front-bench speeches, and then spoke himself. It was not one of his best performances; Crossman heard that he had been "diffuse and a little vague". It was hardly surprising. Nigel Birch, the right-wing Tory, made a warm and sympathetic reference to Isaac in his own speech, and those close to Foot saw his chin fall to his chest. He bit hard on his lower lip, and his eyes glistened over. In his speech, his second maiden, he said that CND was a surge of democratic protest against the system of dictatorial controls of the weapons and of their destinations which had been too lamely accepted in certain quarters.

Less than a fortnight later, he returned to the attack on Gaitskell with a furious article in *Tribune*. He cited again German rearmament, nationalisation, lackadaisical opposition, and, of course, the bomb, in a long list of the crimes which could be laid at Gaitskell's door. He wrote that all these

initiatives and attitudes are supposedly to be regarded as triumphs of statesmanship . . . according to the same theory the designs of an immaculate leadership have been upset by the wicked, irresponsible, obstreperous activities of a minority which engineered the final affront at Scarborough by turning itself into a majority. In short it is the rank and file of the movement, or a very bulky section of it, which is the source of all the trouble. Now anyone who believes that will believe anything . . . we tried it out at Ebbw Vale. We fought openly and proudly on the basis of the Scarborough decisions about peace and public ownership, while demanding tolerance for all sections of the Movement. And we had a wonderful victory.

Next February he was attacking "the leadership" (his euphemism for Gaitskell) at the PLP again, this time demanding that Labour should not take up its share of the new life peerages, which had been introduced in 1958. He denounced the "whole new field of patronage" which the peerages opened up for Prime Ministers and Opposition leaders. Until the party decided its attitude to the Lords, no party member should accept ennoblement. He was defeated as usual, after Gaitskell had said that it was necessary to keep up Labour numbers in the Lords: "As long as the House of Lords exists, it is necessary to keep the party represented there" — almost exactly the arguments Foot himself used in 1981 when he nominated his own first batch of Labour peers.

In 1961 came his complete break with his parliamentary colleagues. There is an occasional tradition of some MPs, generally pacifists and unilateralists, voting against the defence estimates, which provide funds for the Armed Services. It is purely a gesture, though if by some awful mischance the estimates were not approved, the Services would lose all their income. In 1961 the PLP had decided not to vote against them and to abstain instead. Foot, not entirely willing to court disaster and knowing Gaitskell's truculent mood, did not at first incline to defy this ruling. But he was egged on by William Baxter, another unilateralist, and the two of them, together with Sydney Silverman, Emrys Hughes and S. O. Davies, marched into the lobby against the estimates.

The right, goaded as they thought beyond reason at Foot's onslaughts, acted swiftly. Less than twenty-four hours after the rebellion, the party meeting heard the Chief Whip, Herbert Bowden, move that the five should have the Whip withdrawn, the parliamentary equivalent of excommunication. Bowden said he had given them full warning; a similar revolt a few days before had been overlooked. Two Bevanites, Crossman and Walter Padley, asked for a postponement in the hopes of cooking up a compromise, but the MPs voted them down. Then Foot defended himself. He said that he had fought his by-election campaign clearly in support of the Conference decision on the bomb, and it was right for him to uphold these principles in Parliament. To interfere with this right, he said, could only do irreparable harm to the House of Commons and all democratic institutions. Several MPs tried to ward off the evil day. Sir Lynn Ungoed-Thomas pointed out that only half the party was at the meeting. Gaitskell said briefly that there was a three-line Whip that night, and that a supplementary notice had been sent out to remind MPs of the meeting. Nothing could now stop the vote going ahead, and the five found themselves drummed out by ninety to sixty-three.

The loss of his party's Whip makes little real difference to an MP. The unwilling independent may find himself invited on fewer trips abroad and not sitting on committees, privations which in Foot's case brought him no inconvenience at all. His friends are as eager to talk to him, his salary remains unchanged, and by and large life goes on as before. Ten days after the rebellion, Foot's management committee in Ebbw Vale gave him unanimous backing for acting "in full accord with his election pledges". Any official candidate put up against Foot and the local Labour party would almost certainly have suffered a humiliating defeat, a fact which doubtless weighed heavily in the minds of the Shadow Cabinet when two years later they grudgingly restored the Whip.

Meanwhile Foot was touring the country offering not an apologia but a new crusade. A *Tribune* meeting in Birmingham, called to demand the reinstatement of the five, was attended by 500 people. Foot declared, "They can withdraw the Whip from me, or expel me from the party. But they cannot, by legislation, or edict, or decree, prevent me from continuing to be a democratic socialist." George Brown had alleged that they had been expelled for voting against the country having an Army and Air Force at all. "I hope we will hear no more of that quibble — the most polite name I can think of — from Mr. George Brown." The same day Harold Wilson said that any thought of the NEC expelling all five from the party as a whole was "plain daft". Two days later, in the *Daily Herald*, Foot launched into the rigid authority of party meetings. These were conducted in private: "Yet this is the assembly, according to the 'discipline' theory, which should have the right to settle everything, including matters which may affect life and death." Since voting lists were not published, "a constituency cannot even discover whether an MP stands by his election pledges or the general policies he had advocated when he seeks election".

It was not until their old friend and partner Harold Wilson had been elected leader that they even formally applied to get the Whip back. The subject could have been discussed at the 1961 Conference, but the preceding debate was filibustered in order to prevent it being raised. Foot could be seen angrily pacing to and fro at the back of the hall as the discussion dragged on.

Meanwhile he kept up his attack on the binding, secret party meeting. In 1961 the PLP reimposed standing orders, in effect obliging all Labour MPs to support all PLP decisions. "If such standing orders had been enforced and accepted by the Conservative party in 1940," he wrote to the *Manchester Guardian*, "the overthrow of the Chamberlain government and the salvation of the nation would have been excluded." He returned to the subject again the next month, this time tacking his complaint on to an attack on the "guillotining" of debates. This, he said, prevented "free and open debate", though years later he himself was to cause five Bills to be guillotined in a single day.

One subject on which both Foot and Gaitskell agreed was the Common Market. Both were vehemently opposed to Britain joining, though even here Foot found a chink into which his sword could be inserted. In July 1961, he wrote that Gaitskell and his friends had believed Macmillan's assurance that he was negotiating merely to discover whether satisfactory arrangements could be made with the EEC; but five MPs, including Foot, had warned him that Macmillan intended to go in, come what may. "We trust that Gaitskell and his friends will never display such innocence again."

In January 1963 Gaitskell died of a rare viral infection. In spite of the constant struggles and skirmishes with the left, part of a war which Foot acknowledged Gaitskell had finally won, the Labour leader had come to be seen as the almost certain next Prime Minister. Foot wrote a guarded, but nevertheless generous obituary in *Tribune*. He paid tribute to Gaitskell's bravery, and to the respect, devotion and loyalty he had commanded among those who knew him best. "No one but a fool would doubt that strength of character as much as intellect was responsible for his growing reputation." But he concluded that Gaitskell had failed the "final test"; he lacked the "single supreme quality of political imagination . . . and this was the profound reason why he often found himself in such deep hostility to the aspirations of those he hoped to lead".

Without the Whip, Foot could not vote for Harold Wilson in the leadership election which followed. Foot greeted the new false dawn buoyantly. Crossman found that he had "a wonderful sense that the incredible has happened" and just before the poll he met Foot "genuinely and enormously excited by the prospect of Harold's victory". A few days after the election the five rebels applied for the Whip to be restored.

Even then, two years after their exclusion and with an election due in no more than a year, the Shadow Cabinet was unwilling. Every member of the Shadow Cabinet had voted against them in 1961 and against Wilson in 1963. Wilson himself complained to a small group of former Bevanites that they were causing "every kind of difficulty about the readmission of the rebels" and added graphically that he was "running a Bolshevik revolution with a Czarist Shadow Cabinet". According to Crossman, Wilson was not prepared to put himself out for the five, saying that it was "their own fault that the rebels are in their present position". Wilson's own version is that he finally had a row with George Brown, who had taken his defeat badly, and who was extremely angry when he saw that Wilson had brought the question of the five to the top of the Shadow Cabinet agenda. Finally Brown said, "All right, you won the election, I'll support you," and the five were readmitted to the parliamentary party. The Shadow Cabinet had wanted Foot to write a grovelling letter, but Wilson managed to tone this down too. He did not offer him any front-bench spokesmanship, reasoning that Foot would not have wanted a position to which he had not been elected. (When in Opposition, Labour elects twelve members of the Shadow Cabinet; other front-bench jobs are appointed directly by the leader.)

Foot's career as a writer reached a peak in the four years which saw the deaths of the three most influential men in his life: Bevan, his father Isaac and, in 1964, Beaverbrook. When Bevan died, Foot was more than a friend and comforter to Jennie Lee. He urged her to write a memorial to her husband, but she wanted to leave the job to him. He embarked on his own, without research assistants and while still an active MP. So great was the mass of Bevan material, much of it provided by his widow, that he soon decided to make it a two-volume work, and had written the first part, *Aneurin Bevan 1897–1945*, in less than two years, by July 1962. The second volume was mainly written in 1972–3. For much of this time he was watched, hawk-like, by Jennie Lee, and friends say that this pressure accounts for the long gap between the two volumes.

After becoming a Cabinet Minister himself, Foot said, "If I'd known what it was like, I would have written it a little differently." The biography is less a simple political biography than a vast medieval fresco with a religious theme: "St. Nye and his band of followers confront the Forces of Darkness during their thirty years in the wilderness." It is also, indisputably, a great work, of tremendous depth and sweep, a powerful invocation of the political life of the times, superbly written. It was attacked as a literary Big Bertha brought out to win the last battle against Gaitskell. Attlee reviewed the first part, and thought Foot was quite wrong about the 'Thirties: "The refusal of the Labour party to be beguiled into joining the Popular Front was fully justified." Ben Pimlott in his book *Labour and the Left in the 1930s* says Foot made far too many excuses for the self-defeating antics of his old friend Stafford Cripps. A. J. P. Taylor, further to the left, still says that Foot exaggerated Bevan's political importance during the Second World War and the coherence of his thinking. Philip Williams, Gaitskell's biographer, pounces on dozens of ideas and conclusions which he claims distort the record in Bevan's favour. But biography is not always the same as history: Foot used his power as a writer to erect another monument to his hero.

In 1963, Foot and Jill, while driving their car near Ross-on-Wye, collided head-on with a lorry. They were in hospital for several months, and Foot in particular sustained appalling injuries, leaving him with his splayed walk. Yet the crash had one extraordinary side-effect: it cured him of his asthma. It also persuaded him to give up smoking; he had been a chain smoker, and the couple would buy a box of 200 Gold Flake every morning. This had not caused the asthma but had certainly not helped. His eczema, which had also dogged his life, had been cured in the 'Fifties, thanks o Bevan. After consulting Jill about the pattern of the attacks, Bevan announced that Foot needed Vitamin C through the skin. He produced a sun-ray lamp, under which Jill persuaded her husband to sit regularly. His skin began to clear, though the complete cure took two or three years.

While he was ill, the *Daily Herald* had sent Foot bouquets of flowers. On his return home, he set off for the office, and came back in two hours. "I've been fired," he told Jill. He bore no grudge. "Perhaps it's as well," he said, "I expect I was getting stale." Later he was given a £6,000 cheque, which helped them to buy a house Jill liked in Hampstead, where they now live. Beaverbrook had just got rid of Malcolm Muggeridge as chief book-reviewer for the *Evening Standard* — Muggeridge had dared to write disrespectfully of him — and was delighted to give Foot the job. His first article was in praise of his father Isaac and his love of books. He included at the end one of his own favourite aphorisms. "To read and to act is not achieved by many. And yet to act and not to read is barbarism." Foot has a love for the well-turned phrase and will use a good one time and again over the years, in speeches, articles and books: "stabbed to death in the open forum"; a "seraglio of eunuchs".

His next book contained little that was memorable, which proved to be reason for gratitude. Genuinely hopeful about his old Bevanite colleague and eager to help win the coming election, he provided the text for *Harold Wilson — A Pictorial Biography*. Foot throws some of himself into the picture of the new Opposition leader: Wilson too came from an earnest, non-conformist, Tory-baiting household: "Life had a purpose. It was unimaginable that civilised beings could contract out of ... the good fight which must be fought." He stressed Wilson's debating skills, his academic achievements, his courage in backing the Bevanites, and his ability to heal the wounds in the party. If he was worried that Wilson was rather more concerned with tactics than principles, then it showed only fleetingly. He could not resist quoting Wilson's Tory biographer, Dudley Smith, who said that he would need more than "a glib tongue, political ingenuity, and an awareness of party expediency for the future". Foot added, "True. But Wilson has fully revealed other qualities in the past."

As the election approached, Wilson successfully tried to persuade Frank Cousins, the left-wing leader of the Transport and General Workers' Union, to stand for Parliament and accept a Cabinet post. It reveals much about his enthusiasm and optimism that one of the loudest voices urging his friend Cousins to accept the offer was that of Michael Foot.

10

HAROLD WILSON'S CONSCIENCE

Labour won the 1964 general election with a majority of only four seats, and a disappointing margin of just 100,000 votes over the Conservatives. But the government's precarious strength was enough to send a wave of excitement sweeping through the party. After thirteen years of opposition, there was a euphoric sense of anticipation, and nobody was more exhilarated than Foot. Friends say that he received the result with the same delight with which he had welcomed the Labour win in 1945, and even more pleasure than he had marked the elevation of Harold Wilson in 1963. Now, he and many others believed, Labour would not toss its opportunities away.

By 1970 that mood had utterly changed, and it was Wilson whom the left blamed personally for what they saw as the failures and miseries of the previous six years. Even then, Foot refused to despair. In his blackest moments, he held firm to his belief that the greatest need was to keep the Tories out, or, should they be by some frightful mischance returned to power, despatched back to the Opposition benches as speedily as possible. Through the whole period he remained ambivalent; in public his onslaught against the Wilson government grew in its intensity almost from month to month. In private he was conciliatory and spent much of his time and effort restraining the substantial band of left-wing MPs who were as depressed and despairing about the course of events as he was himself. Looking back now, he sees the government, especially the 1966 to 1970 period when it had a safe majority of a hundred seats, as a "bloody catastrophe", the worst failure the party has ever suffered and the cause of lasting damage to the Labour Movement. Wilson he thinks was principally, though not exclusively, to blame, and privately he heaped anathemas upon his leader's head in the immediate aftermath of the 1970 election.

However, in 1964, Foot would have accepted a government job, if one had been offered. Instead he saw his less left-wing brothers installed. Dingle, who had switched to Labour and had entered Parliament after a by-election in 1957, became Solicitor-General. Hugh was ennobled and, as Lord Caradon, was appointed a junior minister representing Britain at the UN. In 1965 Cousins, following Foot's advice, accepted the job of Minister of Technology. He was keen to have Foot as his junior minister, but all that came Foot's way was a message from his old Bevanite friend George Wigg, now an intimate of Wilson, hinting that he might expect preferment later. Wilson afterwards maintained that he felt Foot would prefer to avoid the constraints of office and would have refused. Wigg got a more cynical impression: he thought that Wilson feared that Cousins might resign on principle at some point, and the Prime Minister did not want to risk two simultaneous resignations.

The left in 1964 faced a delicate problem of judgment. For thirteen years it had enjoyed the luxury of total opposition to the Tories and often much more passionate opposition to its own side. It had been able to take part in a bruising internal conflict, secure in the knowledge that it was not putting the survival of a Labour government at risk. It now had to decide how far it could criticise the new administration without threatening its survival and so re-admitting the Conservatives. Foot wanted a compromise. They should press their own policies strongly, while bearing in mind that others held different views; they should not whine every time they failed to get their way. People who disagreed should, if possible, be persuaded. "We have to do this in such a way that we do not destroy the possibilities of the Labour government. For it would be an outrage to throw away these possibilities by foolish action on our part," he wrote in *Tribune*. At the same time, it would be an "outrage" if the left failed to sustain its constant pressure for a change in policy.

Even months later, in March 1965, Foot remained optimistic. Wilson's superiority, he wrote in a Welsh newspaper, had been one of Labour's chief assets in the election. "But the proven drive and capacity of Labour's leading ministers is a

new advantage. The hoariest old piece of Tory snobbery —
that Labour was not fit to govern — will not serve any more."
He predicted that "the fate of the Wilson government depends
on what develops in Vietnam." Vietnam would determine
what happened in the arms race, and, "A Labour government
would find it hard to survive if the worldwide arms race were to
be renewed. All its ambitious plans for social advance and
national economic regeneration could be eaten up by the
avaricious arms budget."

The Parliament of 1964 had changed in several important
ways. Until then the left in its various manifestations had a
distinctly middle-class air. It did have working-class supporters, but the intellectual drive came primarily from highly
educated people, often from public schools. They sensed
themselves to be in opposition to the trade union right wing,
the nondescript bulk of Labour MPs loyal to their union
bosses and deeply suspicious of the smart-Aleck, clever-clever
left which they, sometimes quite justifiably, thought hopelessly
out of touch with ordinary working people. But in the 'Fifties
and 'Sixties there came a new generation of trade union
workers and officials, more militant, better educated, and less
inclined to accept the law as laid down by autocrats such as
Arthur Deakin. The TGWU was now led by Frank Cousins, a
left-winger, and was succeeded by another, in Jack Jones. The
Union gave money to *Tribune*, and Jones went on the paper's
board. The TGWU Executive minutes recorded optimistically
that *Tribune* was "the last major national newspaper firmly
committed to the Trade Union and Labour Movement" — not
a sentiment with which Deakin would have found himself in
agreement.

Meanwhile, this new generation of self-educated union
officials were becoming MPs, and many entered Parliament in
the 1964 and 1966 elections. Eric Heffer arrived, as did Stan
Orme who went on to become a Cabinet minister, Albert
Booth who replaced Foot as Employment Secretary, Norman
Atkinson, later Treasurer of the Labour party, Norman
Buchan, Russell Kerr, Sydney Bidwell, Roy Hughes, and
many other names, famous and unfamiliar, who are now
firmly bedded down in the active Labour left. These men were
Foot's natural allies; they had looked up to him and drawn

inspiration from his speeches and writings. At the same time Foot has always had an exaggerated respect for self-educated men. A friend says, "Michael thinks that they laboured under such dreadful disadvantages that if they've managed to read a few books and can marshal an argument, then they must be absolute geniuses, intellectual Titans." Naturally Foot formed links, and often close ones, with these new members, though it is true to say that some of them found him a shade disappointing. As the government moved from crisis to crisis, and as each successive compromise caused further agonies, it was Foot who held back the enraged left-wingers. Stan Orme, one of Foot's closest political friends, says that Foot was often blamed for the left's rebellious abstentions, and nearly always wrongly. Under Wilson, who was determined to bury the poisonous feuds of the 'Fifties, party discipline was much laxer. Rebels were cajoled, criticised and hectored where it was thought worth while, but nobody was deprived of the Whip.

In March 1967, after a series of rebellious votes, which appeared to be bringing the whole government into public contempt, Wilson made the mistake of haranguing the PLP in what he thought to be a tough, uncompromising speech, fit for a leader to make. In a well-remembered phrase, he said, "Every dog is allowed one bite, but a different view is taken of a dog that goes on biting all the time. He may not get his licence returned when it falls due." "Dog licences" could only mean the party Whip. The speech had a sinister whiff of the bad old 'Fifties, and Foot replied with some vintage 'Fifties invective. The speech was "deplorable", he said on television. The MPs had not arrived on Wilson's coat-tails, and he would have to learn that a growing body of MPs opposed him. A few days later in *Tribune* he went, as so often, over the top, comparing Wilson to a "Führer". He conjured up an image of a leadership which demanded unthinking loyalty before it permitted people to stand as Labour MPs: "To have a grand parade at Transport House of all those who would pledge five years of unblushing devotion to the Führer would be one of the most contemptible scenes in British history."

All this puffing and blowing helped to conceal the fact that the unpleasant days of the 'Fifties were indeed over. But it did not conceal the abiding misery of the left. By now Foot might

have been expected to know that the socialist millenium was
not around the corner. But the young left-wingers who had
arrived in 1964 and 1966 were too young to have become
cynical. After each setback they would drink together in the
Smoking Room, the old Bevanite haunt, and it would be left to
Foot to summon up some semblance of good cheer. They
would troop off glumly for a meal — usually, following
Bevanite tradition, a good one. Foot, Driberg, Kerr, Mikardo,
and whoever was about and needed brightening up would
come along to gossip and talk about books, politics and old
friends. When the youngsters became too depressed, Foot
would tell them that their job was to fight for the policies in
which they believed inside the party. There should be no talk
of splitting, of destruction, of bringing the government down.
At all costs, Foot said, they had to keep the party together in
order to win the next election. By this time, however, some of
them felt that the next election might not be worth winning.

The honeymoon had been short. In September 1965, less
than a year after Wilson's victory, *Tribune* said, "So deep is the
frustration and despair that in some cases members of the
Labour party are unwilling any longer to take part in its
activities." There may well have been some exaggeration, since
its claim to represent and motivate the party's true activists is
the only way in which the left can present its policies as vote-
winners. That said, Vietnam, and Wilson's support for the
Americans, came as a stunning blow — the more so because it
was an archetypal left-wing issue: real, moral, and urgent, but
concerning a country tens of thousands of miles distant. In the
Hull by-election of 1966, which Wilson saw as the barometer
for success in a general election, an independent socialist,
Richard Gott, stood against Labour solely on the Vietnam
issue. Foot agonised about his own position in two long
Tribune articles. Gott's decision, he wrote, was logically the
same as if twenty, thirty or forty MPs had voted in Parliament
to bring down the government, as some left-wingers had been
urging. An election would have followed in which Labour
would have suffered possibly overwhelming defeat. A handful
of left-wingers would scrape back, in effect an independent
party. The resulting feud would be as deep and as lasting as
anything in Labour's history.

The following week, Foot summed up the reasons why, in spite of every fresh blow, he would carry on loyally supporting the government, many of whose actions he "detested".

Despite Vietnam, despite the immigration policy, despite many other deeds which have stuck in electoral gullets, there is a widespread determination throughout the rank and file of the party to do everything to win a fresh electoral victory, to do nothing to put it in jeopardy . . . if the Labour party turns away from power at this critical moment, or if it tears itself to pieces for the convenience of the Tory enemy . . . we will be condemned for generations to ridicule and ineffectiveness."

In 1964 the left had formed itself into another group, the Tribunites. It was hardly likely that an old Bevanite such as Wilson would try to bar this new group, which has more or less flourished from that day to this. The group has no formal or financial connection with the magazine, though its editor, Richard Clements, is invited to its meetings. These take place on Monday evenings when the House is sitting. The group does not try to exert discipline on its members, many of whom are in frequent disagreement with their colleagues on issues of policy and tactics. Throughout this period of Labour government, Foot would have been their unquestioned leader had he shown any desire or propensity to lead. He invariably refused to bind the group together to deliver what might have proved a fatal blow to the government.

Shortly before the 1966 election, Foot was approached by Ernest Fernyhough, the MP who was then Wilson's parliamentary private secretary. He was asked whether he would like to become Minister of Technology in place of Cousins, who, it was thought, was on the brink of resignation. Foot was more than a shade indignant, and much surprised that his old colleague Wilson should have misread him so badly. It was absurd, he suggested to Wilson's envoy, to imagine that he might take over after the resignation of his friend Cousins, with whose criticisms of government policy he agreed — on Vietnam, on incomes policy and many other issues. To spare Wilson any embarrassment, he wrote to him privately explaining why he would refuse such an offer. Wilson himself is strangely vague about the whole affair. He says that the incident "figures", though he cannot recall whether he wanted to use Foot in place of Cousins, or to make him part of a "three-man move", one of the games of musical chairs Prime Ministers enjoy playing.

Yet Wilson remembers Foot in this period with affection. He detected the change in him. Foot was "maintaining an equipoise against the right wing" while simultaneously "doing nothing to embarrass us". He says, perhaps with the glow of their later co-operation in mind, "One didn't really mind trouble from Michael Foot." At this stage Foot was clearly beginning to suffer from the affliction of all politicians who stick to their beliefs — they can be safely ignored. As long as Foot refused to lead the left in a destructive campaign and as long as his speeches and writings had that predictable quality, he remained, in the last resort, harmless.

Not that there was any shortage of causes to be fought. In 1966 he was one of a group of left-wingers who opposed the Chancellor's deflationary package and the Prices and Incomes Bill. This contained the controversial Part IV, which included fines for employers and unions who broke the wage freeze. Some twenty-seven Labour MPs abstained on this clause, claiming, justifiably, that they were following party policy and the manifesto against the intolerable changes imposed by the leadership. The party's old-fashioned disciplinarians, including Foot's old enemy Manny Shinwell, wanted the twenty-seven to be thrown out of the Parliamentary Party — which would have made them the instant heroes of the party Conference. Crossman, who was just about to take on the job of Leader of the House, pushing difficult legislation past a frustrated and increasingly fractious mass of Labour MPs, rightly spotted that in many respects the left could instead be isolated and so largely ignored. "The twenty-seven are now regarded as unrepentant, and in that sense the separate left-wing has become an accomplished fact," he wrote. Foot defended himself and his colleagues: "My primary concern as a Member must be to discharge as best I can the obligations I have to those who sent me here"; as always, when at odds with his party leadership, he invoked the presumed views of his constituents. A few months later, he told the *Observer* that it was the job of the left "to support a Labour programme, not a Labour government".

The list of complaints against the government grew longer by the month. He attacked the government over its failure to act resolutely in Rhodesia, over its decision to postpone cuts in the British Army on the Rhine, over the Letter of Intent which the Chancellor had been obliged to write to the International Monetary Fund at the end of 1966 as a condition of its support for sterling. He continued again and again to assail the government over Vietnam: "The excuses for American conduct become more pathetic and dishonourable every week."

Yet even in April 1967 he found time to praise the government's achievements: Labour was facing local government elections, and, hoisting himself up on to a platform in Hampstead, Foot managed to unearth something he could offer his listeners: "The government has carried through a Rent Act which has transformed the pattern for some houses . . . pensions are still miserably inadequate, but that does not alter the fact that the government did increase them." It was not an inspiring or exciting list, and it did not prevent a twelve per cent swing against Labour in the GLC elections. Foot identified the cause of this unpopularity as the new vogue idea in politics: consensus. "We were assured by the pundits that the triumph of Harold Wilson and his Cabinet was to have captured the middle ground. The floating voter was finally hooked. Well, maybe Labour did capture the middle ground, and lost the rest. We had the consensus on our side, everybody else stayed at home." He drew from this the same lesson that the left has always drawn: "Once again, your leaders must learn: you can't run the Labour party without a militant rank and file, if they are reduced to the status of hewers of wood, door knockers whose views about policy expressed at party Conferences and elsewhere can be safely dismissed and derided." Too many people in the party thought it could run on discipline, in effect as a piece of machinery. "It is not more machinery we want; it is light and heat."

In June 1967 he was prevailed upon to stand for the party treasurership against Jim Callaghan; a forlorn hope, but a gesture necessary to show that the left was in there fighting against the Wilson-Callaghan axis. The Labour treasurership is another of the party's many beauty contests and is determined entirely by wheeling and dealing between the big unions. It has nothing to do with the ability to add up or even to raise sums of money. The *Daily Telegraph* found it a "cause for wonder" that he should even have stood. "To confront him with a ledger, much less the task of forming a government, would be tantamount to torture," the paper said, claiming that Foot was an "artist" rather than a leader. Foot himself said that he was standing in order to offer a choice; if he didn't stand, there might be no election. This is precisely the argument which Tony Benn put forward in 1981 when, against Foot's most earnest entreaties, he decided to stand for the deputy leadership.

Foot welcomed the devaluation of the pound in 1967. He even hoped that it would lead the country out of the recession. "I trust now that the pace of our escape from this recession will be guided by the interests of the economy and not by the esoteric calculations of unnamed persons . . ." By this he meant the bankers whom he saw as exercising a baleful and unjustified control over the economy. The day he made this speech, Crossman noted his naïveté: "Poor Michael Foot thinks that the bankers' control was ended by devaluation. It is, I fear, a pure illusion."

Crossman had no reason to thank Foot when, as Leader of the House, he tried to put through an ambitious plan for the reform of the House of Lords. It was a complicated scheme by which the Lords was to be divided between voting and non-voting peers, mostly hereditary. The voting peers would be, in effect, appointed by the parties and their numbers would be so distributed as to give the government of the day a small majority. Foot, who has constantly campaigned for the total abolition of the House of Lords, opposed the bill because, he felt, that by giving the House a semblance of legitimacy, it would make it far more powerful. It would also create a new seam of patronage for the party leaders which they could mine to manipulate their back-benchers.

Ranged on the same side were a number of ultra-conservative Tories who opposed the Bill because they resented any change at all in the Constitution. Crossman had obtained the grudging support of the Opposition front bench for his Bill, and against Wilson's cautious advice, plunged ahead.

Constitutional bills are a minefield for any government. Their committee stage, instead of being parcelled away to a small group of handpicked MPs sitting in a room upstairs, have to be debated on the floor of the House, where all MPs may speak. They are generally so rich in minor diversions, elaborate side issues and fine legal technicalities that an opponent does not even need to filibuster; he can talk for hours without once straying from the subject. A tiny group of opponents can wreak havoc unless the great majority of MPs are committed and enthusiastic. In this case they were not. For example, the Labour left and the Tory right managed to spend four and a half hours, during one session in March 1969, purely devoted to points of order on the question of whether past House of Lords attendance records should be deemed confidential. In 1969, the government bowed and abandoned the Bill. It was one of the very few concrete successes Foot was able to celebrate during the Parliament.

Although Foot has continued ever since to call for abolition of the Lords, he has in fact subsequently obtained several peerages for people in the unreformed chamber. Two were acts of political charity which allowed old political friends to stay at Westminster. Foot asked for a peerage for Tom Driberg — who shortly afterwards died — on the grounds, according to Lady Falkender, Harold Wilson's political secretary, that Driberg was getting old and going blind. He asked for a peerage for Lena Jeger, a long-serving Labour MP, on the grounds that it would be pleasant after her retirement for her still to have the use of a library and political work to do at Westminster. After Foot became leader he created a number of Labour peers, including John Mackie, former Labour MP and old colleague of both him and Nye Bevan. (His brother, Lord Mackie, is a Liberal peer.)

These last creations were to satisfy the complaint that Labour had so few "working peers" that they were becoming exhausted. Much to the disapproval of purists such as Benn, Foot argued that the Lords had not been abolished: only a Labour government with a good majority could do it; and meantime there was no point in letting the existing machinery of the Lords collapse. To do so, he reasoned, would only give the Tories an opening to launch another unsatisfactory "reform" of the system. Foot's attitude is not in the least corrupt, but it shows once again how little of the impersonal revolutionary there is in his character.

Crossman, sitting wearily in on the endless and futile Lords Reform debate, said that the "story was a concerted plot between Robert Sheldon [the Bill's most active Labour opponent], Michael Foot and Eric Heffer on the one side, and Boyd-Carpenter, Enoch Powell and his gang on the other". In fact there was no planned conspiracy; there didn't need to be. All they had to do was to keep talking. Foot says that there was no concerted plot. He had had nothing to do with Powell for two years after his notorious "I see the Tiber foaming with much blood" speech on race relations in April 1968.

Foot's own record on race is pretty well unimpeachable, and he had a genuine loathing for Powell's remarks. Powell himself is the exact opposite of the "hail fellow, well met" style of politician, and it would have been surprising if he and the painfully shy Foot had struck up a warm friendship.

Yet each fascinates the other. They are both passionate opponents of the Common Market, and for largely the same reason: because they believe EEC membership reduces the sovereignty of the British Parliament, for which both share a deep and romantic attachment. They dislike prices and incomes legislation because it usually delegates legal authority to extra-parliamentary bodies. They are both men who could have been in government and risen swiftly to the highest counsels of their parties, yet for years refused to do so on principle — Powell after and Foot before being in government. The two men clearly see a reflection of themselves in the other, and are not entirely displeased by what they see. Powell once said, "I will tell you who my pin-up is. Michael Foot. I suspect he likes me too for we have many similarities. I admire Michael Foot because he speaks beautiful English. He is through and through devoted to the House of Commons. I think he has the same combination that I have of logic and passion."

Foot is not quite so ready to pat himself on the back by praising Powell, and he is appalled by Powell's views on monetarism as well as race. The racial opinions he sees as a "tragedy", though he remains impressed by Powell's decision not to stand in February 1974 because of his objections to Heath's policies. Foot now says: "It was absolutely fantastic; this exotic act, the ultra-insistence on his honour."

Foot's last great fight against Wilson was over the failed attempt to bring the trade unions into line through Barbara Castle's "In Place of Strife". These proposals, with their sanctions against unions, appalled the TUC and many ordinary Labour activists. Foot wrote hyperbolically in *Tribune*: "Harold Wilson and the Labour Cabinet are heading for the rocks, loudly cheered along this course of navigational disaster by a huge assorted company of well-wishers and ill-wishers. It is the maddest scene in the modern history of Britain." "In Place of Strife" did indeed die a sudden death, and there was an important lesson for Foot here. It perished not because of the outrage of the left, but in large part because it had been knifed by James Callaghan, who had not had a left-wing thought in his head since the early days of the Attlee government. Unlike the left, Callaghan was in the thick of the action, his hands soiled with power, while they stood unsullied and impotent on the sidelines.

Edward Heath won the election of 1970, and Foot was enraged. Those close to him said that he went "wild, absolutely wild" with anger. Wilson had been given, with his hundred-seat majority, an unparalleled opportunity and had thrown it away with astonishing speed. "What are we left with now?" he would shout. Second only to Wilson as chief culprit was Roy Jenkins, the Chancellor, who had obviously failed to produce a give-away electioneering Budget. Austere economics have never found favour with Foot.

Nevertheless, around this time, the changes which had already begun were sharply emphasised, to the surprise of many of his closest friends. Some of them saw a rebellious actor who, after a lifetime in experimental fringe theatre, had suddenly taken the leading role in West End drawing-room comedy. Barbara Castle asked herself what had happened to the Robespierre of British politics, the sea-green incorruptible. Yet anyone who had watched the progress of his thinking during the six years of the Wilson government could see what was likely to happen. Someone who believed that the Labour government had been a tremendous disappointment on almost every count, but who felt that a Tory replacement would be even worse, had only one logical position to adopt: to work hard for the return of another Labour government and then attempt to influence it from within.

After twenty-five years away from his party's front bench, Foot decided in 1970 to stand for the Parliamentary Committee, hoping to be one of the twelve elected members of the Shadow Cabinet. He stood in the first election after the House returned and came sixth, with 124 votes, just behind Tony Benn who took 133. This was quite an achievement, since after a Labour defeat the places tend to go to ex-ministers as a reward for loyalty and diligence. In spite of this, Foot managed to get the votes of nearly half the PLP, and under an electoral system which sometimes excludes the left altogether. In 1971 he stood against Roy Jenkins for the deputy leadership, again with no hope of success, but to demonstrate his willingness to swim in the political mainstream. He scored ninety-six votes, forty-four fewer than Jenkins, but fifty more than Tony Benn. Then in 1972 he stood for the National Executive, the first time since 1949, and came top of the poll. The Conference erupted in a great cheer when this was announced.

Most people missed the emergence of the new, born-again, Foot. In 1970 the Crossbencher column in the *Sunday Express* pondered his decision to stand for the Shadow Cabinet and decided:

> In the past Mr. Foot has been able to register angry protest only by stumping through the voting lobby. He has not had a job to give up. Although he has not much of a job now, it still affords him an unaccustomed luxury. Resignation. When he and his colleagues diverge, he can pack his bags and stalk dramatically out of the Shadow Cabinet. He will have the warmest glow of conscience he has ever known.

This misconception was probably shared by most Labour MPs at the time. Some politicians are resigners by nature; Bevan, for instance, and Enoch Powell. But Foot has always been a stayer, grimly sticking out whatever job he has set himself. That has on occasion been supporting a Labour government with all his might, and on others tearing it to shreds. But having started, he tends to finish.

Wilson gave Foot the less than politically exciting job of spokesman on Fuel and Power. He made his first speech from the front bench in October 1970 in a debate on coal, though the speech carried only a few passing mentions of this topic, being concerned more with a generalised and amusing assault on the new government. He crouched behind the despatch box, as if lashed to it in the middle of some terrible maritime storm, occasionally lurching forward with the swell to pound the box.

In January 1972, Wilson promoted him to Shadow Leader of the House, with the special job of fighting the government over the Common Market. At this stage in events many on the left were pressing for a full-scale examination of the failures of the Wilson years. Foot opposed the idea. "The left within the Labour Party," he wrote, "could have demanded a grand inquest on all the delinquencies of 1964-70, could have mounted a furious attack on the leadership," but the result, he thought, would have been the fragmentation of the Labour government in the "face of the most hard-faced Conservative government since Neville Chamberlain". It is a sign of how much Foot had changed that these arguments could have applied at any time during the bitter factional fights of the 'Fifties.

Later that year his reputation was boosted by his performance both in the House and behind the scenes over Europe. In public he angrily attacked the Labour right, whose votes, he said, had prevented some famous victories against the EEC, though why the pro-Market right should have been obliged to vote against the Market he did not explain. The pro-EEC rebels had invoked their right to follow the conscience clause in Labour's standing orders: "Quite right too, I've used it myself," he said in Aberystwyth. "But I can't ever recall that I went into the lobbies to help a Tory government." In the House, however, he was careful to spare the feelings of the pro-Marketeers. While the left demanded three-line Whips for each dot and comma of the Bill, he looked for a compromise to accommodate the Europeans. Crossbencher, which had by now cottoned on to the new Foot, observed that as some men in middle age "get religion", so Foot had "got responsibility". The column wondered whether one day the "top prize" of the Labour leadership might be within his grasp, a reflection which at the time seemed a bizarre flight of fantasy.

His performances in the House had suffered and had, many friends thought, become duller and more predictable. But sometimes a workaday speech would be suddenly enlivened. In May 1972, tackling the guillotine motion on the EEC debate, he had the house roaring with laughter. Attacking Sir Geoffrey Howe, the author of the Bill, he said, "To point out the least defect in his masterpiece is like telling Leonardo that the Mona Lisa had a built-in squint." In November of that year he came fourth in the Shadow Cabinet elections, and the man who had been at odds with most sections of the party for most of his career had now been warmly endorsed by Conference, the unions, the parliamentary party and the Shadow Cabinet. The supply of fatted calves seemed endless.

Perhaps the most telling incident came in May 1973, when the NEC met to discuss the controversial plan for a future Labour government to nationalise "some twenty-five of our largest manufacturers". This proposal, seen by the right and centre as a sure election loser, was supported in the crucial vote by all the left. Against the left, with Callaghan, Healey and Shirley Williams, was Foot. His reasoning was simple enough: the most urgent task facing Parliament was to get Britain out of the EEC and the only way to obtain this was through a Labour government. Ergo, nothing must be done which might interfere with that happy eventuality. Foot's decision was symbolic of his entire change of attitude to the complex problems of power, and it made it almost certain that he would belong to the Labour government he helped to get elected.

11

HAROLD WILSON'S HANDYMAN

Heath called a general election in February 1974, the day before the striking miners closed every pit in Britain. To save fuel industry had been obliged to work a three-day week. Heath toured the country on a platform of reconciliation with everybody except the miners. He praised the efforts of the nation during the emergency, but asked, "Why, oh why, oh why must the people of Britain always have to have a crisis before they can work together like this?" Foot toured the country on a platform of attacking Heath. He had already set the tone at a meeting in Taunton. Considering, he said, how much the well-being of British industry depended on coal, the Heath method of solving the problem amounted to "obstinacy carried to the point of paranoia". He went on: "We must have miners. They will only come from mining communities. People in Bexley and Broadstairs who may imagine that coal drops like manna from heaven may not be able to understand that, but someone should have drilled it into Heath's thick skull by now." A fortnight before the poll he promised that Labour would settle the strike on "honourable terms" within a few days of returning to power.

Foot had also written the party manifesto, a gentle canter round the field of policy notable for its moderate tone on all subjects including nationalisation. It had originally been drafted by the Labour head of research, Terry Pitt, but his work had been deemed inadequate. Wilson found Foot's redrafting "brilliant" and was especially pleased because he saw it as the first such document which Foot had drawn up to appeal to the entire party rather than to reflect the views of one particular wing.

The election result gave Labour 301 seats to the Tories' 297, though Labour took 230,000 fewer votes than the

Conservatives. Heath, who had hoped that it might be possible to patch together an agreement with Jeremy Thorpe and the Liberals, did not immediately resign. The Shadow Cabinet met on Friday, the day after the election, and wisely decided to keep quiet for the time being. The following Monday, after there had been still no sign from Heath, Foot and Shirley Williams were sent by their colleagues to draft a statement asking him to make his intentions clear; while they were drafting it, the Shadow Cabinet heard that Conservative ministers were clearing out their desks and filing cabinets.

There was never any question about Foot having a place in the Cabinet, and the job of Employment Secretary followed naturally. The so-called "three great offices of State", Foreign Secretary, Home Secretary and Chancellor, were already earmarked for Labour's three senior men of the right, Callaghan, Jenkins and Healey. Nevertheless Employment was a senior post, it would cash in on Foot's increasingly warm relationship with the trade unions, and it was conveniently vacant. The MP who had held the "shadow" job was Reg Prentice, who had already begun his move rightwards towards the Conservative party, and who had contrived to antagonise many union leaders. His appointment would have been taken by the unions as a sign that Wilson was not interested in their co-operation. Wilson saw the TUC General Council on the day he appointed Foot, and records their "considerable satisfaction" when they heard the news. Foot's first job was to let the National Union of Mineworkers and the Coal Board reach agreement on miners' pay, and this they did at a figure roughly half way between the miners' demand and Heath's offer.

Both Callaghan and Wilson are now eager to say what an excellent Cabinet minister they discovered Foot to be, and Wilson particularly stresses his skills as an administrator. They found him undogmatic at Cabinet meetings, prepared to make his own case but not to trample over others' views. Both Prime Ministers were impressed by his loyalty, his refusal to attack Cabinet decisions in public and his dislike of leaking. They also recognise the extraordinary strains he suffered, in particular the demoralising effect of the chorus of attacks on him from the left.

His continuing membership of the Cabinet had an importance that went beyond his ministerial skills. He had taken on a
symbolic significance. Since 1972, when he had stood for the
NEC and come top of the poll in the important constituency
section, it was clear that he had come to embody the party's
left-wing conscience. He was the single most revered figure
among the leftish activists and party workers who make up
Labour's grass roots. At the same time, his ability to inspire
affection, his loyalty and his evident lack of personal ambition
had made him remarkably well trusted by the right in Parliament, unlike Tony Benn, his successor as favourite son of the
constituencies.

For all these reasons, Foot came to resemble the ravens in
the Tower of London, or the apes of Gibraltar; as long as he
remained, the government would, in some magical way,
survive. While Foot, sometimes wincing and gritting his teeth,
acquiesced in the unpleasant policy decisions which had to be
made, then the party could be expected to tolerate them too.
Friends say that his inner stresses often showed. He would
become uncharacteristically bad-tempered when defending the
government, possibly because onslaughts from the left always
carry a powerful undertone of disloyalty.

His loyalty to Wilson did not prevent him from frequently
attending a left-wing cabal of ministers, named the "Husbands
and Wives" dinner. This consisted largely of Cabinet ministers
and their spouses, and the presence of helpmeets was designed
principally to give the occasion a spurious social air. This
would, it was hoped, prevent the Whitehall grapevine from
learning that ministers were conniving to discuss policy behind
the backs of their colleagues and civil servants. The dinners,
sometimes in expensive restaurants and sometimes at each
other's homes, were certainly greatly entertaining, and the
husbands and wives saw no reason to keep quiet while the
ministers debated; people such as Caroline Benn, Elizabeth
Shore, Jill Foot and Lord (Ted) Castle are in many ways as
politically astute as the people they married. What the meetings failed to do was to evolve a left-wing front in the Cabinet,
which was probably just as well; the arrival of a highly
organised group would have been perfectly obvious to other
ministers and thus counter-productive.

One aspect of Foot's thinking, or rather his manner of tackling problems, which emerged around this time was his close identification of socialism with whatever happened to be practical at the time. One searches his speeches in vain for what might be called a coherent set of specifically socialist beliefs which might then be applied to whatever problem or issue was in hand. Instead, Foot works the other way round. Faced with a difficulty — a threatened strike, or a Bill which risked failure in the Commons — his first response would be to consider how this might be averted. Having fixed on a solution which seemed fair and reasonably workable, he would then try to implement it. If it later became necessary to grace his action with the title of socialism, this would be done on the public platform. This is not to imply that Foot merely uses the word as a handy justification for whatever he wants to do. But there has always been in his mind a close association between what is morally right and what is immediately practical. His claims for the miners were less to do with egalitarian principles than with the more mundane consideration that if they didn't get the money they wouldn't mine the coal. It was Heath, the visionary with the "thick skull", who was making a thunderous moral appeal to the nation while Foot was pointing out that moral imperatives do not fuel power stations.

The gap between his socialist rhetoric and his actual message was vividly demonstrated at the difficult 1975 Labour Conference in Blackpool, the first held since the party had returned to power. The main issue of the Conference was the £6 limit on pay which had been announced that summer, the first of four stages of voluntary incomes policy which the government, with diminishing success, attempted to operate. The policy, though drafted with the enthusiastic co-operation of the leading trade unionists, offended the left which saw it as an assault on the sacred principle of free collective bargaining, and a harbinger of a return to Heath's old statutory incomes policy. Foot, as one of its chief architects, was especially suspect, though he had made it clear that he would not support any use of the law to enforce the new limits.

Foot made the final speech in the debate on unemployment, and used it to defend the £6 policy. He began quietly and to what he politely termed a "mixed" reception. Then he wound

up towards his familiar rhetorical pitch, beginning his peroration with, inevitably, a literary reference, a favourite of his
father's.

We face an economic typhoon of unparalleled ferocity,
the worst the world has seen since the 1930s. Joseph Conrad
wrote a book called *Typhoon* and at the end he told people
how to deal with it. He said, "Always facing it, Captain
McWhirr, that's the way to get through." Always facing it,
that's the way we have got to solve this problem. We do not
want a Labour Movement that tried to dodge it. We do not
want people in a Labour Cabinet to try to dodge it. We want
people who are prepared to show how they are going to face
it, and we need the united support of the Labour Movement
to achieve it. I am asking this Movement to exert itself as it
has never done before, to show the qualities we have, the
socialist imagination which exists in our Movement, the
readiness to reforge the alliance, stronger than ever, between
the government and the trade unions . . . and above all to
show the supreme quality in politics, the red flame of
socialist courage.

This bellowing evocation of all the sentiments held vaguely,
if dearly, by the delegates drew them almost as one man to
their feet, though it was noticed that among those on the
platform who did not rise were Foot's old comrades from the
left, Tony Benn, Ian Mikardo and Judith Hart.

This is perhaps not surprising, since the actual content of the
speech included little that had much to do directly with either
red flames or socialism. What he spoke of with most pride was
not any fundamental change, past or promised, in British
society, but of the avoidance of a number of tricky industrial
conflicts: an engineering stoppage, trouble on the railways,
and a potentially damaging steel strike. "We have avoided
these perils. I know that the daily newspapers would say that
we avoided them by giving in. We did not. It was intelligent co-
operation with the trade union movement." The end of this co-
operation would not merely mean that we would all be the
worse off financially: "I shudder to think what would be the
consequences for our people, for our young people and our old

alike. I shudder to think also what would be the consequences for our democratic institutions themselves." Stripped of this emotionally charged language, the speech was a call for the nation to work together; the style was different, and the stress on the absolute need for a voluntary incomes policy would not have pleased the former Tory leader, but the spirit of the speech could have come straight from one of Heath's election meetings. The red flame he sought to ignite was not of socialism, so much as the traditional, reasonable, amiable British ability to rub along together.

This classic example of Foot in government cut little ice with the left. *The Times* reported that at the annual festive Association of Scientific, Technical and Managerial Staffs cocktail party, Foot looked "lost and alone, being fawned over by his former critics and shunned by his old friends". He looked so sad that Norman Buchan, the Tribune MP for East Renfrewshire and one of the kindest souls in the Commons, sought him out and said, "We still love you, Michael."

On the Wednesday of Conference came the Tribune rally, traditionally a gala for the left, where delegates can hear the socialist message undiluted by revisionism, backsliding or, sometimes, harsh reality. This time they heard a stinging condemnation of the trade unions for engaging in co-operation with the government to keep down wages. The attack came from Ian Mikardo, Foot's old comrade of the Keep Left and Bevanite groups. He said that the unions had signed away their rights. "They have totally failed — if indeed they ever tried — to hold the government to its manifesto commitment to maintain full employment and to plan the economy." He got little further because, badly goaded, Jack Jones, the general secretary of the Transport and General Workers Union, rushed up to the platform and began shouting at Mikardo while jabbing an accusing finger at him time and time again. Few people could hear the burden of his assault, since he had no microphone, but the words, "I detest these attacks on the trade union movement", could be heard above the uproar. The audience began to argue noisily among themselves, and soon Mikardo sat down to roars of applause from those who took his part.

Foot rose and again repeated his defence of the government,

the need to maintain co-operation between ministers and the unions. Barbara Castle, who was in the audience, wondered where he had managed to dredge up his energy. "It must be from his spirit, because it can't be from that emaciated frame of his." She too noticed the disparity between the words and the passion with which they were uttered: "He even managed to make the pay policy sound like a socialist crusade . . . only a few people remembered, as I did, the contrast between Mike's speech that night and the speeches he had made at Tribune meetings before he became a member of the government." Afterwards Foot returned to the upholstered comforts of the lobby of the Imperial, the main Conference hotel. He was drinking coffee with Jill when Mikardo entered. Suddenly the anger and frustration of the week welled up and Foot rushed forward to intercept his old friend, grabbed him by the lapel, and proceeded to harangue him for some fifteen minutes, shouting and waving his finger under Mikardo's nose. He cooled down, went upstairs to collect his dog, and took her out for a walk, looking, as he passed Mikardo, the other way.

Foot's ministerial career had begun with a triumphal success. The government's narrow majority made defeat on a confidence issue likely at almost any time. In particular, defeat threatened in March 1974 on the first Queen's Speech, the speech which contains the government's programme. Wilson had threatened a general election, warning Heath that he would use his troops to defeat the Queen's Speech "at his peril". But, as Wilson admitted later, this was to an extent mere sabre rattling, since there was no certainty that the Queen would agree to dissolve Parliament and permit another general election so soon. Nobody wanted a crisis; there was general agreement that the Crown should not be drawn into party politics, and the Conservatives judged that they would be unlikely to win an immediate election. At the same time, it goes against every political instinct for an Opposition to fail to defeat a government whenever it sees the chance. Foot, who was to make the main government speech on the final day, had the tricky job of offering the Tories an excuse to duck out of the vote, while not offending his own side. He executed this task masterfully, combining wit, erudition, rumbustiousness and evasiveness in roughly equal proportions. Robert Carr, the Shadow Employment Secretary, had called much of the Queen's Speech "innocuous". Foot declared, "I seem to recall that he was the father of the Industrial Relations Act. The Queen's Speech proposes to repeal that Act. Never was a father so impassive in the face of the prospective slaughter of his pride and joy." He rebuked Heath, who had seemed "strangely tender" in offering his good wishes to the incoming government, and who had then tabled a "gruff and uncharacteristic" amendment to the Queen's Speech. It had been the "shortest and sharpest honeymoon since Lord Byron". This was, instead, a "treaclemoon".

The Tory amendment called for statutory control of wages to continue until a voluntary system was evolved, and this, somewhat muzzily and ambiguously, was what Foot proposed. The statutory control of incomes was, he said, a "cancerous constitutional growth". He went on: "I have consulted the leading surgeon in the country, who tells me that there may well be cases when it is better to deal with such a cancerous growth by X-ray therapy over a period rather than by surgical action, particularly at a moment when somebody wants to jog your elbow." He concluded with another appeal for national unity, this time furnished from his reading of Cromwell: "Let us apply ourselves to the remedy which is most necessary. And I hope we have such true English hearts and jealous affections towards the general weal of our mother country as no members of either House will scruple to deny themselves, and their own private interest, for the public good."

The Shadow Cabinet met, and, grateful for the escape hatch Foot's ambiguity had opened for them, clambered to safety and decided not to vote against the government that night. Some of their own Powellite members were threatening to abstain on the Tory amendment, and this may have nudged them into their decision. But Foot's speech had contained exactly the right degree of confusion and caution and had, incidentally, swept away most of the fears on his own side that he might not be able to cope with the job.

Clearly the general election had been postponed only briefly. Foot pressed Wilson keenly to go to the country as soon as possible to get a majority and implement the Labour manifesto. Wilson said that he wanted to offer some tangible evidence of progress first, and that an early election would imperil the repeal of the Industrial Relations Act. Foot reluctantly agreed.

In this period it was Foot who redrafted the pre-election White Paper on industry. Benn, who was in charge of the Department of Industry, had produced a markedly left-wing document which Wilson found "sloppy and half-baked . . . polemical and indeed menacing in tone". Foot's redraft played up the mixed economy and played down the proposed powers of the National Enterprise Board, another example of his tailoring his views to the immediate needs of an election.

His two years as Employment Secretary were a whirlwind of legislation. In a Parliament where the government swerved giddily between having a minuscule majority and none at all, he persuaded the Cabinet to allow him no fewer than four substantial and highly controversial Bills. He even contrived to get, in effect, a fifth Bill by tacking the abolition of legal pay controls like a pilot fish on to a Bill being steered through by Shirley Williams. No other minister managed to get anything like so much legislative time.

Part of his success and his ability to conserve energy came from the skills he had at delegation. Foot willingly handed work over to his deputies, Albert Booth and Harold Walker, two of the self-educated working-class MPs he admires so much. Walker, for instance, was in charge of the Health and Safety at Work legislation and, invited by the Chancellor to discuss it, Foot simply took Walker along to do it for him.

He delegated to his full-time officials too, sometimes against their will, since civil servants tend to be shy of taking decisions, or at least responsibility, on themselves. Whole sections of the Employment Department's work were farmed out to independent agencies, the Manpower Services Commission, the Health and Safety Executive, and the Advisory Conciliation and Arbitration Service. This body, which Foot now regards as one of his proudest achievements, had been set up at the suggestion of Jack Jones, who saw it as the absolute cornerstone of the Social Contract, the informal agreement with the unions which was, in the brief period before the £6 limit, being proffered optimistically by the government as its guarantee of pay restraint. The Advisory Conciliation and

Arbitration Service solved one very knotty problem. Before the late 'Sixties, the Department of Employment, or Ministry of Labour as it had been known, existed largely as an industrial conciliation service and its civil servants were skilled and experienced in the techniques of arbitration. Under Barbara Castle, and later under Heath, the Department had become something more like an arm of government. The whole point about ACAS was that it had to be entirely independent of government, and could not afford to be seen merely as a tool for enforcing whichever pay policy happened to be in favour at the time. Under Jim Mortimer, a former union official, it managed to persuade management and unions of its independence, and ACAS has so far been untouched by the Conservatives.

Other innovations were received with less enthusiasm by the Opposition. The Trade Union and Labour Relations Bill was published on the eve of May Day, 1974, and began resoundingly enough: "The Industrial Relations Act 1972 is hereby repealed." Other clauses were rather more complicated and even more disputatious: it ended the National Industrial Relations Court, abolished the legal concept of "unfair industrial action", removed the unions' liability to civil action for damages connected with trade disputes, made peaceful picketing legal within certain limits, and restored the closed shop to the position which had obtained before the 1972 Act. Anyone dismissed for refusing to belong to a union in a closed shop could not seek compensation unless he had refused on religious grounds. This section of the Bill, and refusal to build in legal safeguards to protect people who were either thrown out of their union or not permitted to join, was and remains one of the most controversial issues of Foot's career. It stayed so even after he had agreed to a suggestion from the TUC that there should be an independent review committee for people in closed shops disputes.

This debate was marked by a luridly heightened tone, typical of so many in Foot's career. No political point could be argued, it seemed, without both sides finding fresh extremes of abuse. Foot had concerned himself in 1975 with the case of the "Ferrybridge Six", members of a small electrical union which was not recognised in the closed shop agreed with the

Electricity Council. They refused to join recognised unions, their case was adopted by the Conservative press, and they then discovered that they were refused unemployment pay. Foot wrote in a letter that when a man declined to fall in with the new conditions of employment which resulted from collective [closed shop] agreements, then he "may well be considered to have brought about his own dismissal". The gist was that if you didn't join the union and so got sacked, then legally it was your own fault.

The Times aimed its attack in a manner skilfully designed to create maximum distress in its victim. Was Mr. Foot, it asked its readers, a fascist? Fascists believed that the state should be organised on a corporate and not an individualist basis, and so, they argued, the term was being employed in a legitimate descriptive sense. "The question is not therefore 'is Mr. Foot a fascist?' but 'does Mr. Foot know he is a fascist?'" A letter steamed from the Foot pen that very day; it complained of "gross misrepresentation" and pointed out that he had no control over who received unemployment pay. On the basis of a single quotation, The Times had called him a fascist. "I can only return the compliment by saying that shows the discrimination and taste of Dr. Goebbels." The Times continued the skirmish and Foot described the paper's editor, William Rees-Mogg, as "the lamest duck ever to waddle down Fleet Street". The point at issue remained, however, whatever Foot's degree of responsibility for the Ferrybridge Six. Even some of his friends were uneasy about the suggestion that a worker might lose his job simply because he did not wish to belong to a particular trade union, a principle which they thought went directly against his earlier libertarian instincts. They pointed to his championship of the small and weak Blue Union against the might of the TGWU. Foot, however, did not change his mind. He pointed out that the closed shop situation had returned to that which had applied before the Industrial Relations Act; that it had always proved impossible to ban closed shops by law, or even to reduce their effect; that to allow large numbers of employees to remain outside the closed shop would inevitably lead to damaging strikes. In any case, the TUC itself had suggested the independent tribunal.

Later Callaghan was to ruminate that the unions had done

better than they might have expected in their dealings with Foot. He had never belonged to any real industrial union, except in an honorary way, and had never before been a minister. Consequently he did not appreciate that the unions' negotiating technique was to pitch their demands as high as possible — even when dealing informally with friends. For his part Foot believed that he was merely giving the unions the honoured place their co-operation merited and that all his legislation had the primary aim of reducing strikes and disputes. The moral issues, such as they were, came second to the practical ones.

One simmering problem which was waiting for his arrival at the Employment Department was the £47,000 owed by the AUEW, the huge engineering union, in payment of various claims against it under the outgoing Industrial Relations Act. The union faced the seizure of its assets unless it paid the money. Foot pleaded with the union to appear before the National Industrial Relations Court, which it promptly refused to do. Next month the Court announced the sequestration of all the union's cash, some £300,000, until the claims were met. The strike was called "forthwith", and Foot used a debate in the Commons as an opportunity to tear into the Court and its president, Sir John Donaldson, whom he described as "trigger-happy". He said, "Nobody could be better pleased than I if I could have been shown a practical, proper and constitutional way of wringing the neck of the Court before it caused more commotion and disaster." Like so many of Foot's sudden outbursts, it called forth replies in equally overheated language: Lord Carrington, then chairman of the Conservative party, decreed that it was "the most disgraceful episode in our public life for many years". Foot had attacked "not the union leader who had defied the law, but the judge who sought to administer it". We have Barbara Castle's account of a conversation with Foot's second permanent secretary of the time, Conrad Heron, who blamed the attack on Donaldson as a "slip", the result of Foot's habit of going off for long walks to work out a speech in his head and then ad-libbing large parts of it. Heron also complained about Foot's method of taking decisions: "His only policy is to find out what the unions want."

But of course Foot was not simply siding with anarchy against the law; he was merely attacking what he saw as the cause of the disruption. The strike would not have occurred without the Court's decision, therefore the Court itself was at fault. Frequently his decisions appeared to imply that unions and their members were incapable of, or at least not obliged to make, their own moral decisions. If they were driven to strike, then this had to be the result of some monstrous injustice or block-headed administrative decision, which must be removed. That was all there was to it.

The Trade Union and Labour Relations Bill was heavily amended by the House of Lords and their changes were largely upheld by the Commons. Foot decided, after the October 1974 election, to put through an amending Bill, and this led to a dispute with newspaper editors which lasted on and off for most of the Parliament. Considering the acres of newsprint devoted to the problem and to Foot's alleged intransigence, it is surprising how ill-founded the forebodings of the editors have been so far. They feared that the closed shop, applied to newspapers, would oblige them to join the union and so limit their editorial independence. They also feared that it might be used to prevent them from printing contributions from people who did not happen to belong to the union, which would indeed have been a serious interference with the freedom of the press. Foot thought it inconceivable that journalists would attack press freedom in this way, and feared the disruption which might result if journalists were not allowed to negotiate closed shops like any other workers. He flatly refused to compromise on this central issue, and finally got the whole Bill through both the Commons and Lords, at a cost of much delay.

In the meantime the unions were able to savour their success in winning the Employment Protection Act, another bitterly opposed piece of legislation which made it substantially more difficult for workers to be sacked. They won the Health and Safety at Work Act, and the Dock Work Regulation Act — the last a special request for Jack Jones, although the core of the Bill, which gave dockers a lien on all loading and unloading work within a five-mile "corridor" around the ports, was defeated by a rebellion from two right-wing Labour MPs.

During the same period, however, the unions' persistent demands for import controls and other protectionist measures to shelter manufacturing industry were voted down in Cabinet. Unemployment continued to rise steadily, and though the Employment Secretary traditionally takes the responsibility for this, it is generally the Chancellor's policies which are to blame. The party took its revenge by voting Denis Healey — who had said that one million out of work was the barrier he would not pass — off the NEC in 1975. Unemployment peaked at 1,636,000 in August 1977.

It was Jack Jones who was the principal midwife in the first incomes policy to be agreed between the new government and the unions. When the Cabinet debated it in the summer of 1975, Healey insisted that the voluntary pact had to be supported by legislation which would give the government powers to act against employers who broke the policy. Foot led the fight against these powers, arguing that they would so alienate the TUC that the government would, in the long run, be destroyed. Somewhat to his own surprise, the Cabinet agreed, and a compromise was reached by which a Bill containing the powers would be prepared, but presented to Parliament only if it became necessary. In the event a "heads of bill" — a skeleton draft — was prepared, and Foot hinted in the speech he made in the Commons that he would resign if it were ever introduced. At this time Jones was pressing him to stay inside the government whatever transpired. Foot's judgment at this time appears to have been correct. The £6 limit and the agreement which followed it in 1976, a five per cent rise up to a maximum of £4, produced two of the most successful years in the sorry history of British incomes policies.

Foot was one of the seven ministers who, in 1975, voted in Cabinet against Britain's continued membership of the EEC on the new terms negotiated by Wilson and his Foreign Secretary, James Callaghan. Wilson agreed to the suspension of the "collective responsibility" doctrine for the period of the Referendum campaign, and was appalled to see that Foot and his friends took this as a licence to stump the country speaking against the new terms. Foot tried to soothe Wilson, saying, "If you say to me, Harold, that you feel very strongly about it, of course I take that into account and concede that I may have been wrong about it." Barbara Castle, who overheard this exchange, wrote in her Diary: "As I listen to Mike these days, the more conscious I am that as they grow older, these Foot brothers all merge into one collective Foot type — rational, radical, and eminently reasonable. They even speak in the same voice and in the same terms; they are natural Liberals. No wonder Paul Foot has rebelled against his elders!"

Foot's own campaign against the EEC was muted by the fact that he had to go into hospital in the period leading up to the Referendum, in order to have a benign growth on his scrotum removed. Jill wrote angry letters to the newspapers complaining about allegations that he had jumped the NHS queue and been given a private ward. Foot, one of the most unlitigious of politicians, finally sued the *Daily Mail* and received £500.

Having recovered, he toured around the country as part of an anti-EEC team which was distinctly short on popular appeal. With every party leader backing the EEC, even the comparatively luke-warm Margaret Thatcher, and familiar figures such as Edward Heath and James Callaghan adding their support, the Labour left, working in improbable partnership with right-wingers such as Enoch Powell (on whose platforms they actually refused to appear), had an almost impossible struggle. Foot argued on economic as well as constitutional grounds; at a rally in April he said scornfully that there was no common sense in cutting ourselves off from the food markets of the world. We were told that outside the EEC Leyland would not be able to sell its cars. "If that is so, how are the people of Europe to sell their VWs, Fiats and Renaults in Britain?" In May he debated on television with Heath, and got back some of the fire of his old "In The News" days. Heath said he was astonished at people like Foot, "who always say they believe in the brotherhood of man, though it doesn't extend beyond Margate". Foot leaned forward, glowering. "Don't talk rubbish! We'd been fighting for internationalism long before you ever . . ." and Heath, so often tormented by Foot's tongue, leaned forward to tell him not to lose his temper.

It was the effect on his beloved Parliament which he most feared, however. In an article published shortly before the poll he said that the EEC had reduced several debates to a shambles, indeed made the whole system in part "farcical and unworkable". Ministers were no longer responsible to MPs, but to decisions reached in Europe. "Instead of being responsible [a Minister] is constitutionally irresponsible; instead of being required to answer, he is specifically required not to do so; his business is to circumvent any immediate challenge, to sidestep any vote; in short to blur by every available means the issue presented to the Commons by meddlesome MPs."

The fight was, however, lost from the beginning. Fully sixty-seven per cent of those who voted agreed to the new terms. Gwent, the county which includes Ebbw Vale and the rest of the heartland of socialist Wales, was humiliatingly close to the same figure: sixty-two per cent said "yes".

Wilson took a modest revenge on the left by a small reshuffle, of which the centrepiece was the shifting of Tony Benn from the Industry Department to Energy. Foot, who was thought irreplaceable, and whose presence in the Cabinet was essential to secure the left's acquiescence, pleaded with Wilson to keep Benn in his old position, but was not prepared to resign on the point. But he was prepared to do just that if Wilson went ahead with his plan to demote Judith Hart who, as Minister for Overseas Development, was a member of the Cabinet. Foot behaved, according to Mrs. Castle, "in his inimitably gentle way", but insisted to Wilson that the left-wing ministers would resign. "We're not trying to blackmail or threaten you, Harold. You have the right to make what appointments you choose, but then other people have the right to decide their position." Wilson complained that he was already over the limit of Cabinet posts. Foot said tenaciously, "You can do it if you want to." Judith Hart finally pulled the carpet from under them by resigning. Foot told Barbara Castle angrily the next day, "It's a bloody nuisance . . . we would have won."

When Wilson resigned in March 1976, he claimed that he had planned this decision from before 1974, and there is now absolutely no reason to doubt this. Again Foot had to be pushed into standing for election by his friends, though the problem was fairly academic. Neither he nor his supporters thought he had more than the remotest chance of winning, though as the favoured candidate of the left he survived into the third ballot as the last challenger to the winner. So it was that in April 1976, he entered into government under the man he had scornfully called "P.C. Callaghan" and who, in 1961, had willingly voted to expel him from the Parliamentary Labour Party. It did not seem a propitious partnership, but then over the years both men had changed greatly.

"Don't worry, Denis, Michael isn't even in sight."

12

A STUDY IN LOYALTY

The leadership election left Foot unquestioned as the second most influential figure in the government. Not only had he been far and away the strongest challenger to Callaghan but he had managed to win the votes of nearly twice the number of MPs in the Tribune group. It was a remarkable personal success, it added greatly to his own standing, it gave impetus and encouragement to the left, and it drove home to Callaghan the message that he would be obliged to run the party through conciliation and compromise. This was an important point, since some MPs, recalling the 'Fifties, suspected that the new Prime Minister might be tempted to employ the same heavy-weight tactics the right had used then. Benn and Foot himself felt before the election that they would have preferred Healey to their old sparring partner Callaghan.

Foot decided to act swiftly to influence his new leader, to the extent of visiting him for a talk about Cabinet placings a few hours before the final ballot was counted. He had four main items on his shopping list. Though Callaghan hoped he would stay as Employment Secretary and keep up the good relations with the unions he had developed, Foot wished to cash in on his success in the vote. The job he wanted, to the surprise of many of his friends, was Leader of the House of Commons. Since Callaghan proposed to sack the existing leader, Edward Short, this was easily granted. Secondly, Foot wanted to confirm that the dedicated pro-Marketeer Roy Jenkins, who had done poorly in the leadership contest, should not be made Foreign Secretary. He wanted his own deputy, Albert Booth, to step up as Employment Secretary and, rather less willingly, Callaghan agreed to this. Finally Foot made strenuous efforts to keep Barbara Castle, his old intimate, inside the Cabinet. Mrs. Castle, who was in the midst of some difficult legislation, clearly feels that Foot could have done rather more to help her. In her Diaries, she records that Foot was "sorry but not desolate" about Callaghan's decision to sack her, adding that he had told her there was nothing more he could have done short of threatening resignation. "Perhaps I should have done that," he had said. Mrs. Castle leaves little room for doubt that she felt that was precisely what he should have done, saying, "We wouldn't have let Harold get away with this!" In fact, not only did Foot hold several meetings with Callaghan to press Mrs. Castle's claim, but he also wrote more than one lengthy letter to the new Prime Minister. But Callaghan wanted the place for a younger MP, and realised that Mrs. Castle was not so popular that her dismissal would lead to an unmanageable outcry. The issue is important, since the myth that Foot abandoned his old friend to her fate took root with some MPs, though the soil proved shallow. He is on good terms with Mrs. Castle now, though she cannot forgive lightly his intense regard for Callaghan. In November 1980 she sent him a brief congratulatory note after his election, and he replied with a letter full of warmth and friendship.

The job of Leader of the House meant that Foot had to pilot government legislation through the Commons. It also carried the title of Lord President of the Council or, in effect, the chairmanship of Her Majesty's Privy Council. The Lord President meets the Queen weekly and on other formal occasions — to hear, for example, of her approval of the marriage of her children — and sometimes busy Cabinet ministers, all of whom are Privy Councillors, are whisked north as far as Balmoral to attend on the Queen. Her unfailing politeness is well known, and this, combined with Foot's own natural diffidence, must have created meetings of unparalleled courtesy between the Queen and the old-fashioned republican. Foot liked the Queen, and told friends he found her "highly intelligent".

The job also presumes that the holder will occasionally wear formal dress. The Lord President's traditional garb at the state opening of Parliament consists of a dark blue cloth single-breasted coatee with stand collar and nine gilt buttons, with white Kerseymere breeches, white silk hose and a sword. Foot wore a lounge suit instead. One Tory MP, Nicholas Fairbairn, demanded angrily, "Why should the Lord President of Her Majesty's Privy Council imagine it is clever to turn up like a demobbed soldier?" Fairbairn himself attended the same ceremony in a grey frock coat, wing collar, cravat with diamond pin, and carrying an ivory-topped cane. It was another example of Foot's extraordinary ability to excite Conservatives to heights of wrath on issues of stupendous triviality. For instance, the Cromwellian beliefs inculcated in him since childhood frequently led him to make brief and unimportant nods in the direction of republicanism. In April 1977, speaking at the Ashfield by-election, he said that the constituency would be certain to return a socialist candidate, adding, "and this will help gain a socialist majority in the Commons and help Britain on the way to becoming a socialist republic." The Conservatives attacked him fiercely in the Commons on the grounds that as Lord President he spent much of his time dealing with the Queen. Mrs. Thatcher returned to the subject more than a fortnight after the remarks had been made. Foot, who clearly had not the slightest recollection of what he had said in the course of an unscripted speech, replied that he thought nobody took it very seriously. A year later, in July 1978, he made another error of judgment, when he said in the House that he might prefer a "Republican Commission" to a Royal Commission for the purpose of examining British management. Tories jeered and bellowed; Mr. Patrick Cormack hauled himself to his feet to demand whether it was in order for the Lord President to voice republican sentiments in the House. Foot rapidly said if the Queen were to ask for an apology he would eagerly and immediately give one. "When I see her next week I will ask her and will set the matter right as courtesy and common decency allow."

These silly rows had a slightly greater significance than might appear; they marked a period when the casual, all-party amiable liking for Foot was beginning to disappear among the Tories. The general view that Michael Foot was a lovable old buffer, a fine traditional parliamentarian whose quaint opinions merely added to his eccentric charm, was being dissipated by Foot's effective, unconventional and occasionally ruthless manipulation of the House. Foot was absolutely determined to ram government business through, and the trifling fact that the government lacked a majority was not going to prevent him. This attitude inevitably stirred deep antagonisms, and it was possible for the first time to hear Conservatives express personal hostility. MPs of a more apocalyptic turn of mind began to see him as a sinister figure, a remorseless zealot who would hide behind his reputation as a constitutionalist in order to destroy the nation's democratic freedoms. The absurd affair of the attack on the judges added to this mood.

In 1977, the Union of Postal Workers proposed a ban on handling mail destined for South Africa as a protest against apartheid. Three judges then ruled that such a ban would be unlawful under the terms of the Post Office and Telegraphs Act. In May of that year Foot told the Union of Postal Workers' conference in Bournemouth that the government intended to amend the act so as to restore the postal workers' right to strike. He went on to make some more general remarks about judges. If the freedom of the people and the rights of trade unionists had been left to judges, "we would have precious few freedoms left in this country . . . time and again Parliament has had to be invoked in order to establish trade union rights which others thought had been established years before."

The remarks now seem unexceptional enough, consisting, as Foot said the following day, largely of a history lesson which would have been familiar enough to anyone with the faintest schoolboy knowledge of trade unions and the law. This was not enough to prevent the storm bursting over his head. No doubt some of his accusers remembered his attack in May 1974 on Sir John Donaldson, the president of the National Industrial Relations Court. Some scented an opportunity to present Foot as a wild anarchist, a man whose assault upon the whole judicial system made him as guilty of fostering crime as any mugger or football hooligan. Others discerned a more sinister motive, seeing the attack as necessary to Foot's plan to impose a Marxist republic, requiring first the destruction of the independent judiciary. Lord Hailsham's attack the following day was perhaps the most skilled; as a considerable platform ranter himself, he knew his victim's weaker points:

The shrill hysterical scream in which his utterances are delivered is perhaps the best guarantee against taking Michael Foot's extravagances wholly seriously, since, when he gets on a platform he is clearly not wholly responsible for what he says . . . he was, he says, merely indulging in a little historical reminiscence of past judicial decisions beginning with the Tolpuddle martyrs. Mr. Foot is too old a hand at this game for this explanation to be acceptable . . . his speech was both intended and understood to be a deliberate attack on the judiciary as a whole.

Hailsham demanded that the Lord Chancellor, Elwyn Jones, should insist on Foot's resignation or else himself resign.

This extraordinary suggestion was only the harbinger of a row which became quite as shrill as any Foot speech. Mrs Thatcher raised the subject repeatedly at Question Time, and while Callaghan defended him by artfully quoting a passage from Sir Winston Churchill, the latter-day Conservative leader demanded that he wholly repudiate Foot's words: "It was a totally disgraceful remark." Lord Shawcross, the former Labour Attorney-General, mused, "Most of you are too young to have heard Hitler. But that ranting, rising, sometimes almost screaming voice that I listened to reminded me more than a little of Hitler. Mr. Foot, once thought of as such a good parliamentarian, seems to be developing some of the instincts of a dictator. Fortunately, he's too old to be one; he's almost as geriatric as I am." This passage may perhaps be attributed to the curious belief among lawyers that they, unique among the professions, may not be criticised. However, the Conservatives, recognising an arsenal which could be raided whenever fresh ammunition was needed, returned repeatedly to the attack. A year later, for example, Airey Neave, Mrs. Thatcher's spokesman on Northern Ireland, alleged that the left believed the courts should be subject to political pressure or even control. "When Michael Foot attacked the judges, he reminded me of Hans Frank, Hitler's legal expert, who informed German judges in 1936: 'The judge has no right of review over the decisions of the Führer as embodied in a law or decree.' " The grotesque exaggeration of these claims is typical of much of the rhetorical brawling which has marked Foot's career. The pattern was usually the same. Foot would have a few modest thoughts. He would then express them with a degree of excusable, if unnecessary, hyperbole. His opponents, enraged by his tone, replied in the same terms, partly from political expediency, partly because Foot had actually misled them through the force of his language. The whole process, which appeared merely amusing when Foot was the back-bench pamphleteer and orator, seemed much graver when he was — as the Conservatives never failed to point out — Lord President of Her Majesty's Privy Council. Foot also ran into fire from the left when, in October 1976, he went to India. Mrs. Gandhi, the premier, had suspended constitutional liberties. Foot would not publicly denounce her. He privately told her she was creating a bad impression by gaoling a former delegate to the Socialist International, interfering with BBC coverage, and not holding an election. She eventually softened on all three issues: Foot, his image badly bruised, must have felt inwardly vindicated.

As a Cabinet Minister he set himself doggedly to ensure the government's survival. He was totally loyal to the government, a commitment made easier by his growing respect for Callaghan. A man he had seen for years as one of the most shameless right-wing operators turned out not only to like and respect him, but even to an extent revere him. Callaghan says that he had always found Foot a sympathetic colleague, and had been highly flattered by one or two friendly references to himself in Foot's old *Daily Herald* column. Foot's good opinion was one of the more valuable things life had come to offer him: "It arrived late, unworthily perhaps, but it did come," he says.

In Cabinet Callaghan found him often shy and self-effacing, anxious not to push himself into discussions. Callaghan learned to sense when he had a contribution and would tap him on the knee to bring him into the debate. The Prime Minister felt a shade protective to his deputy, sensing that he lacked the hard edge which most politicians find they need. He saw Foot as a male Shirley Williams, warm, sincere, invariably eager to see the best in everybody, but in the end lacking in ruthlessness.

In the autumn of 1976, when Callaghan was about to face his first party Conference as leader, the sudden fall of sterling forced Denis Healey, the Chancellor, to turn back at London airport. He had been on his way to Manila to an International Monetary Fund conference where Britain was to ask for a loan of 3.9 billion dollars. Inevitably, the eventual loan was hedged about with strict conditions, among them a £1.5 billion cut in the public sector borrowing requirement. The left in the Cabinet were already under heavy pressure from activists in the constituencies and left-wing back-bench MPs, who were accusing them of accepting in docile fashion the age-old capitalist remedy for getting the system out of trouble. Even those, like Peter Shore, who were not left-wing by inclination, felt that any cure which actually increased unemployment was a most improbable panacea. In July 1976, after the Cabinet had agreed a mere £1,012 million of cuts in spending plans, coupled with a two per cent increase in employers' national insurance contributions, several MPs had demanded to know why Foot had not threatened to resign if the cuts went through. He faced a special meeting of the Tribune group on his sixty-third birhday, and told them they could not expect left-wing policies from a right-wing Cabinet. It was unreasonable for them to behave as if there were a massive left-inclined majority in Parliament, the PLP and the Cabinet. He asked them not to vote against the Labour government.

But when the IMF loan was negotiated, the left felt that the time had come to dig in their heels. Foot and five others — Peter Shore, Benn, John Silkin, Stan Orme and Albert Booth — decided they wanted a debate in Cabinet, a general *tour d'horizon* of the economy which would permit ministers to look at the situation broadly without being faced with a list of cuts, to be rubber-stamped or else tossed out. Foot asked Callaghan for permission for the six to meet in order to discuss their strategy and tactics. It is a fine point whether such permission was actually required, though it would have been fairly obvious to all if the left had been secretly acting to concert their opposition. Callaghan, somewhat reluctantly, agreed, and they met at Lockets restaurant, the venue of the old Husbands and Wives group, on the night before the Cabinet debate opened. In the event, the left came nearer to victory than its numbers might have suggested. Their policy for a Britain as a castle defended against an aggressive world by fortifications of import controls, did win some limited support from a number of "centrist" ministers within the Cabinet who, while fearing foreign retaliation and the immediate effect on the standard of living, were equally opposed to the greater unemployment which deflation would create. The most effective contribution came, by all accounts, from Anthony Crosland who was then Foreign Secretary; although he attacked Tony Benn's arguments on the left, he also set himself to wreck those of the Chancellor who supported the IMF demands. The left was defeated in the end only by Callaghan's decision to join the hard-liners. Crosland, realising that he could not expect to take on both a Chancellor and a Prime Minister, withdrew his opposition, and the six were left isolated again.

Foot accepted the situation without demur. One of the aspects of his behaviour at this time which most annoyed his erstwhile companions on the left was his refusal to play the game of publicly backing Cabinet decisions, while covertly making plain his opposition. There were no winks and nods in his speeches, no little messages to the troops saying, in effect, "Don't blame me, I voted against it." Even in private conversation he remained scrupulously, and some thought obsessively, discreet. Foot would demand, "What's the point of having a leader and undermining his morale all the time?" Many of his friends felt betrayed, not by any lust for power on Foot's part, but by what they saw as misguided loyalty to a misguided government.

Though the Leader of the House is a committed supporter of the government, he is also to an extent the representative or tribune of the House as a whole and is thus supposed to have a dual loyalty. For this reason most governments give the job to some centrist figure popular on both sides, and Rab Butler, Jim Prior and Fred Peart were all recent successes. Faced with continuous pressure to make way for this or that debate, to provide time for one private member's Bill or another, the Leader tends to develop a number of stonewalling tactics: "I shall keep the honourable gentleman's remarks at the front of my mind," and so forth. Foot never did, and occasionally picked up the scent of debate when he would have been better advised to damp down controversy and proceed to the next business. For this reason Tories came to view him, to an extent, as an enemy of the House's traditions and safeguards.

Added to these difficulties was the fact that his team was almost entirely new. The Chief Whip, Michael Cocks, with whom the Leader must act closely, had been appointed at the same time as Foot, and between them they made a number of misjudgments. In the summer of 1976 back-bench MPs began referring to them, not altogether fairly, as "Foot-in-it" and "Cock-up". Two such inexperienced navigators of government business must inevitably rely heavily on the pilot, in this case Sir Freddie Warren, private secretary to the Chief Whip, a civil servant of long experience, utter self-confidence, and frequent truculence. The relationship between Foot and Warren is one of the stranger aspects of the 1974–79 government; frequently affectionate, just as often intransigent and abusive. Sometimes the convivial Warren would sit and abuse Foot for minutes on end, to the fury of Foot's staff and colleagues. At other times Warren, whose knowledge of Commons procedure was encyclopaedic and whose contacts with the Conservative Opposition made him invaluable, would simply refuse his co-operation. Foot would get as near to losing his temper as he does with anybody, and would say threateningly, "So you don't want to help me. I see. Nothing more to be said." In the end the quarrel would always be patched up. Warren, ebullient and thick-skinned as ever, would tell people that Michael was "an absolute darling".

In the light of all these difficulties it is extraordinary how much legislation Foot and his team managed to push through a grudging House. There were a number of bitter rows. In July 1976 he drove the Conservatives into a rich lather of indignation when he announced that no fewer than five major Bills were to be guillotined: Education, Aircraft and Shipbuilding, Dock work, the phasing out of paybeds in hospitals and the abolition of tied cottages. Guillotines, or "timetable motions" as they are officially termed, are the last resort a government employs when the Opposition is speaking at such length that a Bill's chances of completion are threatened. The Opposition traditionally greets them as a monstrous attempt to destroy free speech and parliamentary democracy, and indeed on this occasion Mrs Thatcher called the mass execution "a contempt of Parliament unprecedented in our history". The Tory attack was helped by the words of one particularly fiery Labour

speaker in 1972: "No one can say that he has the full-hearted
consent of Parliament and at the same time introduce a guillotine. No one can say that, unless he emasculates the English
language, just as the government propose to emasculate the
British constitution." Michael Foot's remarks had been
heartily cheered by Labour MPs then, and the House was
roughly divided between those who regretted the disappear-
ance of the old crusader for parliamentary freedoms and those
who welcomed the born-again wheeler-dealer.

The complicated affair of the hybrid Bill caused even greater
ill-feeling. A Tory MP had discovered that the Bill to nationalise the aircraft and shipbuilding industries was "hybrid", that
is to say was a cross between a public Bill — which affects the
whole country and everyone in it — and a private Bill, which
applies only to certain individuals or institutions. The procedure for dealing with hybrid Bills is complicated, and would
have created an intolerable delay. Foot cut the Gordian knot
by the simple process of introducing a motion in the Commons
declaring that although the Bill was a hybrid, it should be
treated as if it wasn't, that is to say with great speed and
without the safeguards built into the hybridity procedure. The
Conservatives erupted; Foot again found himself called a
"fascist"; Nigel Lawson, who became a Treasury Minister
under Mrs. Thatcher, shouted "Leader of the Reichstag!" and
there were a few shouts of *"Sieg Heil!"*

Later that night the motion was debated and the government managed to win the crucial division by 304 votes to 303,
by the straightforward expedient of sending an MP who had
been paired through the Aye lobby. This device caused fresh
anger among the Conservatives, who immediately broke off all
pairing arrangements with the government in protest, so
adding greatly to Foot's difficulties. The rights and wrongs of
the original decision to table the motion are more evenly
balanced than either side would like to admit. The hybridity
was on a technicality and so in reality no real threat to
anyone's freedom was involved, and in any case the House can
vote at any time to decide how to conduct its business. On the
other hand, it is the easiest thing in the world for a determined
government, capable of scraping together a parliamentary
majority, to ignore the unwritten British constitution whenever

it pleases. Foot's passion for Parliament does not extend as far as reverence for its time-hallowed procedures and safeguards.

These attempts to rewrite inconvenient chunks of parliamentary practice combined occasionally with the more mischievous antics of the Whips, in particular the deputy Chief Whip, Mr. Walter Harrison. Mr. Harrison, a short and pugnacious Yorkshireman, specialised in devices of inventive

"I am in blood stepped in so far that, should I wade no more,
returning were as tedious as go o'er"   (Macbeth)

and ruthless cunning. His energies quite possibly did as much to keep the Labour government in office for two years longer than its parliamentary support might indicate, though it is unlikely that historians will ever give him the full credit. On one occasion Harrison sent several Labour MPs through both the Aye and No lobbies in the hopes of getting the necessary quorum to pass a Bill. In January 1978, faced with the near certainty of losing an important vote on the Scottish devolution Bill, Harrison attempted to prolong the previous vote until the guillotine had fallen and the next division would have to be cancelled. He did this by occupying the division lobby together with two other Labour Whips and two Scottish nationalists, holding a prolonged discussion and so preventing the vote from, technically, ending. A Tory MP realised this and the Serjeant-at-Arms was despatched to settle the matter. Foot, who had had no idea of what was occurring, was obliged to apologise to the House the following day, but the general impression remained of a government ready to employ sharp practice whenever it thought it could get away with it.

Perhaps the most wearing part of Foot's job as Leader of the House was his responsibility for devolution, the attempt to give a measure of Home Rule to Scotland and Wales. This had long been a commitment by the Labour party. It had become increasingly worried by the success of the Scottish National party which had eleven MPs in the new Parliament, and it had convinced itself that without devolution not only the Labour party, but the whole structure of the Union of Great Britain and Northern Ireland would be threatened. The proposals, which were finally embodied in the Scotland and Wales Bill, were modest enough. Scotland would have an assembly with legislative powers over several fields, while Wales would have an assembly with basically administrative authority. The Bill got its second reading in December 1976, and the measure of the importance the government attached to it can be seen by a television interview Foot gave at the same time. In this he drew a comparison with the failure to grant independence to Ireland in the nineteenth century and implied that a failure to grant devolution could meet a similar conclusion: "I don't want them to turn to violence, of course, but I think it's quite likely."

Given the apparent strength of Foot's feelings on the subject, it is surprising that he did not take further steps to guarantee the success of the Bill, which was being ferociously attacked by several Labour back-benchers. Many had made it plain that they would vote to obstruct and preferably kill the Bill under any circumstances, and it must have been already obvious that it could succeed only with the support of the thirteen Liberal MPs. Foot managed one concession to dissatisfied members of his own party — there would be referendums in both Scotland and Wales before either assembly was established — but he had done nothing to placate the Liberals who found the Bill confused and inadequate. Like most members of the Cabinet, Foot assumed that the Liberals would never act to kill the Bill and concentrated his efforts on mollifying those who were opposed to the entire principle. Some of Callaghan's closest advisers began to warn the Prime Minister of the dangers of Foot's apparently high-handed attitude, and at least one right-wing Cabinet Minister later alleged that there had been "gross incompetence from start to finish" in the handling of the Bill. Foot certainly troubled himself hardly at all with the fine print of devolution; this was left to his capable deputy, John Smith.

By February 2nd, 1977, after the Bill had been debated for four weeks in the House, Clause 3 had been reached, leaving fully 112 clauses to go. It was clear that the Bill could not survive without a guillotine, and against a background of almost certain defeat, the Cabinet attempted to persuade the House to impose one. Forty-three Labour MPs abstained, all but two Liberals voted against, and the Bill's chances were destroyed. At this point Foot was one of the very few MPs at Westminster who thought there remained the remotest chance of devolution going through.

It would be hard to exaggerate the weakness of the government's position on February 23rd, 1977, the day after the devolution guillotine failed. It had a total of 310 voting members in the House, against 319 who belonged to other parties. For more than a year it had survived because the fourteen nationalist MPs had been anxious to see the devolution legislation reach the statute book. Now they had no reason whatever for continuing to prop up the government. Indeed they had every reason to bring it crashing down, since they felt certain that in a general election their disgruntled countrymen would reward them with a rich haul of seats. Even with the support of the handful of MPs from minor parties — the two-man Scottish Labour party, the Catholic Ulster MPs — Labour was still in a minority and could in theory be brought down at any time. On top of this, its own left-wing was increasingly angered by the failure of its economic policy. In March 1976, thirty-seven Tribunites had abstained on a vote backing public spending cuts, causing Harold Wilson to postpone his resignation and to hold a confidence debate. Now they were being asked to give their assent to further, greater cuts. In spite of this, a strange calm prevailed at Westminster.

The government had managed to juggle the figures so often, the Tory Opposition had so invariably failed to press home its advantages, that the mere figures were not enough to convince Labour MPs of the mortal peril their government was in.

This was not borne in on them until March that year, when the government attempted to get parliamentary approval for the latest spending cuts. Knowing that left-wing MPs would not stomach "approving" the White Paper which outlined the cuts, knowing that they would not even vote for the parliamentary formula of "taking note" of the White Paper, Foot and the Whips hit upon the wheeze of holding the debate on the technical topic of whether the House should adjourn, the most anodyne of all Commons formulations. Defeat on such a meaningless motion would matter little and the government could argue that the House had not actually thrown the cuts out.

When the vote came, the government decided to call upon all Labour members to abstain. This dramatic, if constitutionally meaningless move had been graced with the title of "the rug technique", on the grounds that it pulled the rug from under Mrs. Thatcher. After a brief discussion with her Shadow Ministers, the Tory leader came to the House the following morning and announced a motion of no confidence in the government. Foot, standing in for Callaghan, announced that the debate would take place the following Wednesday. This time gap was essential; it furnished Foot and Callaghan with three working days in which to cobble together an agreement with another party so as to keep the government in office longer.

Foot sprang into action. On the very morning that he had announced the confidence debate, he saw James Molyneaux, the leader of the Ulster Unionists, and enquired what terms he and his seven colleagues in the official Ulster Unionist party would need to support the government the following Wednesday. Not many years before, Foot had been one of the keenest opponents of Unionism and one of the most vocal supporters of the Ulster civil rights movement. Now he found himself acting as a supplicant to the Unionists. Molyneaux, as diffident and courteous in his own way as Foot, said politely that the government had come a trifle late, but listed their requests for a devolved government for Northern Ireland, a new upper tier of local government and an increase in Ulster's representation at Westminster, bringing it up from twelve to the seventeen or eighteen seats which its population would justify. Foot took these suggestions back to Callaghan, and while both sides agreed that there was only the most slender chance of an agreement with the eight Unionists, Foot did not give up trying until the very eve of the confidence vote.

Long after the pact between the government and the Liberals had been agreed, it became an article of faith among many back-bench MPs at Westminster that a secret, formal agreement had been signed between the government and Unionists by which the Unionists would give covert support to the government in exchange for certain unnamed promises. This is a garbled version of what had happened; in fact, at a meeting in Number 10 Downing Street on the Monday before the confidence vote, attended by Callaghan, Foot, Molyneaux and Enoch Powell, by then the Unionist MP for South Down, Callaghan offered the Unionists the extra seats, irrespective of how they voted two days later. He also promised, without much optimism, to look into the question of a devolved government for Ulster. These two promises were later cast in the form of a letter, but Foot and Callaghan were careful to make it clear that their one commitment to action did not depend on Unionist votes; any suggestion of a formal deal would have caused the deepest reaction among many of their back-benchers, and not left-wingers alone.

Even on the Tuesday night Foot was seeking out Molyneaux and hoping that he might persuade his colleagues to support the government; at that stage, the deal with the Liberals which was, for the most part, being handled by Callaghan, was not quite settled. The industrious Foot was anxious not to sacrifice the possibility of a single vote.

The chief stumbling block with the Liberals had proved to be the question of direct elections to the European Parliament, and the Liberal demand for these to be held under a system of proportional representation. The Cabinet held a difficult meeting shortly before the crisis; it had emerged that there were a few members who were so deeply opposed to these elections — especially elections under proportional representation — that they might resign rather than agree. It was equally clear that the Liberals would not accept a pact unless the government committed itself to direct elections — and indicated a strong preference for proportional representation. It is a measure of Foot's desire to prop up the government at any cost at all that he agreed to these two demands, both of which were anathema to him. Those who knew him at this stage say that the wish to support the government overrode everything else.

The pact with the Liberals was finally agreed and set up as a formal arrangement. Foot was made chairman of the joint committee which was supposed to iron out differences between the two parties and, where necessary, to agree policy in advance.

The Liberals found him helpful, courteous, and above all else absorbed in the problem of keeping the Conservatives out of office. On the question of proportional representation, for example, he never bothered to argue the merits of the case; if it was necessary to vote with the Liberals on this issue to maintain the government, then vote with the Liberals he would.

People who had expected to find Callaghan the artful fudger and seeker of compromises discovered that it was, in fact, his deputy who filled this role. Foot's style of negotiation was curious; he would never say anything as direct as "you give us this and we will concede that"; instead he would pause, bark, "well", pause again, then go away to think about things. In spite of his warnings about violence in Scotland, the Liberals never got the impression that he cared very deeply either way about devolution. It, too, was necessary to keep the government in office. The small group of ministers and Liberal spokesmen who met to discuss the form of the devolution Bills frequently reached deadlock, and on one occasion Steel found himself summoned by Foot. Foot had nothing to say, but merely wished to communicate a general sense of goodwill and a promise that the matter was not closed. Steel left slightly puzzled, wondering why he had been invited to listen to the Lord President flannelling to such slight apparent purpose. Foot never communicated any sense of crisis; instead those who dealt with him were left permanently with the feeling that something would crop up to save the day in the long run. He was usually right.

James Molyneaux, the leader of the Ulster Unionists, remembers him as the best Leader of the House he ever worked with. Direct rule in Northern Ireland meant that the province was governed from Westminster, and the quantity of frequently trivial subjects before Parliament was just another of Foot's headaches.

Foot managed the problem by a host of small compromises, agreeing to long debates on some issues in exchange for getting other legislation through "on the nod". The Unionists were able to block two items they wanted to stop: a proposal to use the province as a guinea pig for the compulsory wearing of seat belts in 1977, and the extension of homosexual law reform to Northern Ireland in 1978. The plight of Ulster's homosexuals is one which the earlier Foot might have adopted with all his crusading energy. This time they were brushed aside because of the overwhelming need not to risk the government's artificial majority.

The pact ended in May 1978. In March the next year Wales voted on the devolution plan and rejected it. Scotland voted for its assembly, but by a margin which Parliament had decreed was too small for the Act to be put into force. At that moment there remained no reason for any of the smaller parties to continue to prop up the government, and on March 28th Labour lost a motion of confidence in the Commons by a single vote: 311 to 310. Foot had been desperately trying to find a way of carrying on. There had been further soundings of the Ulster Unionists, and the three Welsh Nationalists were offered compensation for slate quarrymen suffering from pneumoconiosis, a minor issue which had assumed great importance with the Plaid Cymru MPs. However tireless Foot was, it seems fairly clear that by this time Callaghan was resigned to inevitable defeat; the "winter of discontent" with its industrial disputes and the piles of rubbish he had seen lining the roadways had convinced him that Labour had only a faint chance of winning an election whenever it was held.

Yet he could have gone to the country earlier, in the autumn of 1978. Foot was one of the main influences on him, encouraging him to hold on. The two men discussed the election date in June and July of 1978, and managed to convince themselves that an early poll would be a mistake.

Callaghan had spoken to MPs, regional organisers, party officials at grass roots level, and the reports which they sent him were pessimistic. Callaghan decided that Labour would in all probability lose an autumn election, or win by such a narrow margin as to inflict on the country another few years of difficult, uncertain minority government. Either way Mrs. Thatcher would be able to decree the date of the next election. The Prime Minister was irresistibly reminded of the situation in 1950, when the Conservatives harried a tired Labour government with a narrow majority into an election. Meanwhile, the economic indicators were getting better, inflation had fallen to single figures, unemployment was dropping. Lower tax rates and higher child benefits would come into force in November; devolution would, it was assumed, have brought delight and gratitude to the bosom of the Scots, and the first effects of the economic recovery would be felt. There was, of course, the problem of the five per cent figure for wage rises which the government had laid down and the unions had rejected, but no doubt things would not be too bad; they hadn't been until then.

It is an indication of the way in which Foot and Callaghan had allowed themselves to become isolated from the real world that they failed to foresee the failure of the five per cent policy. They were, by this stage, extremely close. Callaghan regarded Foot as his closest political confidant. While he would discuss important issues with Healey, it was Foot to whom he unburdened the deeper issues preying on his mind. Their relations with the trade unions remained good, and Foot attended the monthly dinners held at Number Ten with the "Neddy Six" — the six leading trade union general secretaries. Yet, says a close colleague of Foot's, he always believed that the unions would accept five per cent merely because it had the force of logic behind it. "Michael thought that all he had to do was to go to the unions and say, 'Look, our chaps have worked it all out and have come up with this five per cent figure', and the unions would accept it." When the news came in of the rejection, those around him at the time say Foot was thunderstruck.

Thanks in part to Foot's urgings, Callaghan had decided during the summer not to hold the election in the autumn of

1978. His deliberately ambiguous speeches and his refusal to attend "farewell parties" being thrown that July by retiring MPs were regarded as amusing teases; he now regrets not having made his views plain earlier. On Setember 7th he appeared on television, and dramatically announced — nothing.

At the Labour Conference four weeks later, Foot summed up the debate on pay. He said that the absence of any plan for wages was "a policy for hermits" which could lead to the destruction not only of this Labour government but of any Labour government. The message should go out to workers throughout the country, "We will work within the Movement to get what we suggest, but we will work ten times harder to see that Margaret Thatcher will never become Prime Minister of this country." But appeals to the terror of the bogey-woman were, by now, not sufficient; three years of a stringent pay policy meant that the workers now believed they had suffered enough. The fact that real disposable income rose by a remarkable nine and a half per cent in the course of 1978 was not, at that stage, apparent. The Conference defeated the five per cent policy in spite of Foot's pleading. At the *Tribune* rally Foot offered a new reason to explain the postponement of the election. He said that the situation in Southern Africa, both in South Africa and Rhodesia, was coming to a head: "It is a matter of paramount importance for the future peace of the world that we should keep a Labour government in office to deal with that problem." Ironically its handling of the Zimbabwe–Rhodesia situation was one of the few un-challenged successes of the Thatcher government's first two years.

In January 1979 the lorry drivers began a strike which their union made official on January 11th, the day after Callaghan had returned from the Guadeloupe summit of world leaders and declared at the airport, "I see no evidence of mounting crisis", an unfortunate remark made as he landed in a freezing and anxious country having spent the previous few days on a delightful tropical island. His comment was condensed by one newspaper to "Crisis, what crisis?", another of the many remarks, like Edward Heath's "Cut prices at a stroke", wrongly attributed to political leaders. The public service strikes, which lasted on and off for six weeks, began on January 22nd. As well as causing a massive accumulation of rubbish in the streets, in parts of the country there was no labour available to bury the dead, a fact which appeared to make a considerable impact on the public mood. When the general election was forced on May 3rd, almost all hope of a Labour victory had been abandoned.

Foot toured the country using his rhetorical skills to defend the government's record and to warn of the horrors of a Thatcher administration. At the end of April he attacked the Conservatives' incomes policy, saying that you could only get one through voluntary agreement. "You cannot do it by force. You cannot do it by shooting people." It was a sudden flash of the old Foot, a burst of manic hyperbole, and the Conservatives were quick to cash in. Foot also made his, by now traditional, attack on the judges. Lord Denning, the Master of the Rolls, had said during a visit to Canada that the power of the trade unions in Britain was a challenge to the rule of law. Foot called this suggestion "grotesque" and said that Denning had made "very shoddy use of the English language". "He really must learn that it is Parliament which makes the laws in this democratic country." Mrs. Thatcher replied that one of the most incredible events of the past five years was the manner in which judges had been criticised.

When he could spare the time Foot and Jill returned to Ebbw Vale to meet a few of his own electorate and to bolster party workers. It was hardly necessary. His majority fell by 2,000, leaving it at a scarcely dangerous 16,000.

But the Labour government he had supported so tenaciously was now beyond recall. However, Foot, as much through good luck as good judgment, had left himself in an extraordinarily powerful position. His willingness to meet the needs of the moment, his unremitting hard work, and his total loyalty to the Callaghan government had won him the trust and affection of the party's right-wing. But it had not lost him the friendship and even the love of a good many left-wingers. It was undoubtedly this combination which enabled him to win the leadership election in November 1980, and which brought genuine pleasure in his victory even to those who did not vote for him.

BIBLIOGRAPHY

One of the most prolific sources for any study of Michael Foot's life and times is his own writing. Most direct quotations in this book that do not derive from personal interviews come from Foot's own works, listed here in chronological order:

Young Oxford and War (with R.G. Freeman, Frank Hardie and Keith Steel-Maitland; ed. Krishna Menon), Selwyn and Blount, 1934

The Struggle for Peace (main text by Stafford Cripps), Left Book Club, Gollancz, 1936

Armistice 1918–1939, Harrap, 1940

Guilty Men, by Cato (Foot, Peter Howard and Frank Owen), Gollancz, 1940

The Trial of Mussolini, by Cassius (Foot alone), Gollancz, 1943

Brendan and Beverley, by Cassius, Gollancz, 1944

Who Are The Patriots? (with Donald Bruce), Gollancz, 1948

Still at Large, *Tribune* pamphlet, 1950

Full Speed Ahead, *Tribune* pamphlet, 1950

The Pen and The Sword, Macgibbon and Kee, 1957

Parliament in Danger, Pall Mall Press, 1959

Aneurin Bevan 1897–1945, Macgibbon and Kee, 1962

Harold Wilson – A Pictorial Biography (compiled & ed., John Parker and Eugene Prager), Pergamon, 1964

Aneurin Bevan, 1945–60, Davis-Poynter, 1973

Debts of Honour, Davis-Poynter, 1980

As well as books and pamphlets, Foot wrote a great deal in newspapers and magazines. His main vehicles included:

Tribune: between 1937 and 1938, he was on the staff as a writer. After 1945 he wrote regularly for it, and became co-editor in 1948. He was thereafter co-editor, editor, or editorial director until 1961, after he had re-entered Parliament. His contributions appear as signed articles, unsigned editorials, and sometimes as pamphlets under the name "John Marullus".

The Daily Herald. Between 1944 and 1963, he wrote a weekly and sometimes twice-weekly political column.

The Evening Standard. From 1938 to 1943, Foot wrote signed articles and editorials as a staff writer, and ultimately as acting editor. He also wrote a number of signed articles for its Beaverbrook stablemate the *Daily Express*, and was transferred there full-time for a brief period in 1943, shortly before his resignation. In 1964, Foot began a new job as chief book-reviewer on the *Standard*. His weekly articles continued until 1974, when he joined the Government, and subsequently at irregular intervals.

Among other books on which the authors have drawn, the following contain significant material about Foot's career:

Crossman, R.H.S., *The Backbench Diaries* (ed. Janet Morgan), Hamish Hamilton and Cape, 1981
Crossman, R.H.S., *The Diaries of a Cabinet Minister* (ed. Janet Morgan), Hamish Hamilton and Cape, Vol. I, 1975; Vol. II, 1976; Vol. III, 1977
Castle, Barbara, *The Castle Diaries 1974–6*, Weidenfeld and Nicholson, 1980
Williams, Phillip, *Hugh Gaitskell*, Cape, 1979
Duff, Peggy, *Left Left Left*, Allison and Busby, 1971
Lee, Jennie, *My Life With Nye*, Cape, 1980
Taylor, A.J.P., *Beaverbrook*, Hamish Hamilton, 1972

The following books, listed alphabetically, also contain relevant material:

Addison, Paul, *The Road to 1945*, Cape, 1975
Boyle, Andrew, *The Climate of Treason*, Hutchinson, 1979
Brockway, Fenner, *Towards Tomorrow*, Hart-Davis, Macgibbon, 1977
Butler, David, and others, *The British General Election of 64, 66, 70, February 1974 and October 1974*, Macmillan, various dates
Butler, David and Sloman, Anne, *British Political Facts, 1900–1975*, Macmillan, 1975
Cameron, James, *Point of Departure*, Arthur Barker, 1967

Driberg, Tom, *Ruling Passions*, (postscript by Michael Foot), Quartet, 1978

Foot, Hugh (now Lord Caradon), *A start in Freedom*, Hodder and Stoughton, 1964

Foot, Sarah, *Isaac Foot My Grandfather*, Bossiney Books, 1980

Goldie, Grace Wyndham, *Facing the Nation*, Bodley Head, 1977

Goodman, Geoffrey, *The Awkward Warrior – Frank Cousins*, Davis-Poynter, 1979

Gordon, Anne Wolrige, *Peter Howard – Life and Letters*, Hodder and Stoughton, 1969

Haseler, Stephen, *The Tragedy of Labour*, Blackwell, 1980

Hatfield, Michael, *The House the Left Built*, Gollancz, 1978

Hoggart, Simon and Michie, Alistair, *The Pact*, Quartet, 1978

Hollis, Christopher, *The Oxford Union*, Evans, 1965

Hughes, Emrys, *Sydney Silverman – Rebel in Parliament*, Skilton, 1979

Lansbury, Edgar, *George Lansbury My Father*, Sampson Low, Marston, 1934

Lockhart, Sir Robert Bruce, *Diaries Vol. I, 1915–38* (ed. Kenneth Young) Macmillan, 1973

Pelling, Henry, *A Short History of the Labour Party*, Macmillan, 1965

Pimlott, Ben, *Labour and the Left in the 1930's*, C.U.P., 1977

Rolph, C.H., *Kingsley – Life and Letters*, Gollancz, 1973

Steel, David, *A House Divided*, Weidenfeld and Nicholson, 1980

Wigg, George, *George Wigg*, Michael Joseph, 1972

Wilson, Sir Harold, *The Labour Government, 1964–70*, Weidenfeld and Nicholson, 1971

Wilson, Sir Harold, *Final Term*, Weidenfeld and Nicholson, 1977

INDEX